How Nordic are
the Nordic Medieval Laws

Cover illustration: Fragment of a glossed manuscript from the Digesta (excerpt of Sextus Caecilius Africanus' Questiones) ca. 1300. The manuscript was re-used as a cover for accounts from Hatzburg County, Holstein, 1653/54, The Danish National Archives, Copenhagen, Fragmentsamlingen, Aftagne fragmenter nr. 293.

Per Andersen, Ditlev Tamm
& Helle Vogt (eds.)

How Nordic are the Nordic Medieval Laws

Proceedings from
the first Carlsberg Conference on
Medieval Legal History

Second edition

DJØF Publishing
2011

Per Andersen, Ditlev Tamm & Helle Vogt (eds.)
How Nordic are the Nordic Medieval Laws
Proceedings from the first Carlsberg Conference
on Medieval Legal History

Second edition

© 2011 DJØF Publishing Copenhagen
Jurist- og Økonomforbundets Forlag
DJØF Publishing is a company of the
Association of Danish Lawyers and Economists

All rights reserved.
No part of this publication may be reproduced, stored in a retrieval system,
or transmitted in any form or by any means – electronic, mechanical, photocopying,
recording or otherwise – without the prior written permission of the Publisher.

Cover: Bo Helsted
Photo: Mia Münster-Swendsen
Printing: Toptryk Grafisk, Gråsten

Printed in Denmark 2011
ISBN 978-87-574-2606-9

The publication of this volume is funded by
The Ernst Andersen and Tove Dobel Andersen Foundation

Sold and distributed in North America by
International Specialized Book Services (ISBS)
Portland, OR 97213, USA
www.isbs.com

Sold in Scandinavia by
DJØF Publishing
Copenhagen Denmark
www.djoef-forlag.dk

Sold in all other countries by
The Oxford Publicity Partnership Ltd
Towcester NN12 6BT, UK
www.oppuk.co.uk

Contents

Introduction 1
Per Andersen, Ditlev Tamm and Helle Vogt

How Nordic are the Old Nordic Laws? 5
Ditlev Tamm

*The Importance of Classical Canon Law
in Scandinavia in the 12th and 13th Centuries* 23
Peter Landau

*The Germanic Character of the Oldest Laws
of the Low Countries* 41
Dirk Heirbaut

Some Dark Aspects of Ius Commune 63
Mario Ascheri

*The Nordic Medieval Laws in the Legal History
of the 17th and the 18th Centuries* 75
Lars Björne

Pope Alexander III and the Danish Laws of Inheritance 85
Michael H. Gelting

*Three Kingdoms, Three Laws, One Ideology
– A Starting Point Revisited* 115
Per Andersen

*Property and Land Tenancy in Norwegian Medieval Laws
and the European Learned Law*   135
Tore Iversen

*The Concept of Kinship
According to the West Nordic Medieval Laws*   177
Lars Ivar Hansen

*On Ecclesiastical Jurisdiction and the Reception of Canon Law
in the Swedish Provincial Laws*   207
Mia Korpiola

Nordic Medieval Laws Revisited   235
Kjell Å. Modéer

Contributors   241

INTRODUCTION

Per Andersen, Ditlev Tamm and Helle Vogt

The articles in this volume are the second edition of *How Nordic are the Nordic Laws?* of which the first edition was published in 2005. The articles are based on papers given at the conference "How Nordic are the Nordic Medieval Laws?" which was held at the Carlsberg Academy 22nd to 24th May 2003. The conference was the first in the line of conferences later to be known as *The Carlsberg Academy Conferences on Medieval Legal History*.

In the second edition the articles by Tore Iversen, Per Andersen, Michael H. Gelting, Lars Ivar Hansen and Ditlev Tamm have been edited. The rest are the same versions as were published in the 2005 edition.

The main theme of the conference was the Nordic medieval laws seen in a European context which again raised the question about just how Nordic these laws were. The problem was presented both through studies in the Nordic laws as well as parallel studies. In the following the articles will be introduced briefly after passing on a little information about the Nordic Middle Ages to those readers who may not be familiar with this period in history. In most of Europe the high Middle Ages are seen to have started about the year 1000. In the Nordic countries, however, historians still consider the Viking Age as something that came before the Middle Ages and hence the high Middle Ages are seen to begin around 1200.

The first article by *Ditlev Tamm* is an introduction to the medieval legal landscape in the Nordic kingdoms. In the article he also discusses the question "how Nordic are the Nordic laws?" and wonders if it is possible for legal historians to obtain more information about medieval legislation or if legal science just moves in circles while asking the exact same questions as our predecessors did a hundred years ago.

In the second contribution *Peter Landau* argues that canon law played an important role in the Nordic countries already in the twelfth century. He exemplifies this through a presentation of the manuscripts that were supposedly found in Scandinavia in the period as well as by showing how a political event in Norway from the mid-twelfth century and onward influenced the reception of canon law in Norway.

In his article about the medieval laws of the Low Countries *Dirk Heirbaut* was inspired by the question about the nature of the Nordic laws and thus asked the same question about the laws from the Low Countries. After revealing the great impact the historical development had and still has on legal historians Heirbaut moves on to give an introduction to the great corpus of medieval laws from the Low Countries. Heirbaut comes to the conclusion that the laws neither were old Germanic laws nor inspired by the learned law, but merely local medieval law.

In his article the Italian legal historian *Mario Ascheri* abandons the question about the character of the Nordic laws and raises a greater question about how the ius commune functioned in the later Middle Ages and in early Modern Time. The main focus of the article is how Italian jurisprudence influenced the development of the ius commune.

The Finnish legal historian *Lars Björne* gives an introduction to how the Nordic laws were used by the legal historians in the Nordic countries in the formative phase of the study of legal history in the seventeenth and eighteenth centuries. Björne in particular points out the importance of the Danish lawyer Peder Kofod Ancher (1701-1787) and the Swede Johan Stiernhöök (1596-1675).

In his contribution the Danish historian *Michael H. Gelting* gives a profound introduction the writing, dating and contents of the Danish medieval laws while focussing on the inheritance laws in the legislation. Gelting claims that the creation of inheritance law in Denmark was closely linked to the Augustinian doctrine about post mortem giving a son's share of his inheritance to the church.

In his article about the legislation of the realms in Denmark, Aragon, Sicily and Norway in the thirteenth century the Danish legal historian *Per Andersen* shows that in these corners of Catholic Europe similar ideas about the king's role as legislator – *rex imperator in regno suo* – can be found. Andersen thus concludes that the legislation in the Nordic kingdoms followed the learned ideas of the legal elite in the high Middle Ages.

In his article about property and land tenancy in the Norwegian laws the Norwegian historian *Tore Iversen* shows how big an influence both Roman and canon law had in Norway already in the second half of the twelfth century. Iversen exemplifies this by showing how the meaning of land tenancy and property changes from the older to the younger laws and how it followed the learning of the legalist from Bologna.

The *wergeld* system in the Norwegian and Icelandic laws is the main theme in the Norwegian historian *Lars Ivar Hansen's* article. Hansen concludes that the *wergeld* system in the laws was created by the Church's concept of kinship which before the Fourth Lateran Council in 1215 was the seventh degree and after the Council, the fourth. With this Hansen illustrates the close connection between canon law and the paying of *wergeld* in North-Western Scandinavia.

The Finnish legal historian *Mia Korpiola* has investigated the function of canon law in Sweden and Finland. In her article she shows how canon law was received in civil legislation, the so-called 'provincial laws'. Her focus is on Sweden but parallels are also drawn to Norwegian and Danish legislation. Korpiola also uses the few remaining sources about ecclesiastical jurisdiction in Sweden to show how it worked in practice.

The final contribution is by *Kjell Åke Modéer* and is different in its form in that it is based on the speech he held at the conference dinner. Modéer spoke rather poetically about how views on the Middle Ages and thereby also the legislation have changed in the Nordic countries.

Thus, we return to the starting point for much of the work done on placing the medieval Nordic laws in an international legal tradition in the last decade. We do it in the hope that it may still be worth knowing more about the tradition of departure.

Copenhagen and Aarhus
April 2011

HOW NORDIC ARE THE OLD NORDIC LAWS?

Ditlev Tamm

Introduction

Medieval legislation plays a peculiar and very important role in Nordic legal history. These laws are important landmarks or "lieux de memoires", which to a high degree have been used for centuries as a symbol of a legal culture different from the European continent. Written in the vernacular and even, if not always, too easy to understand these laws are still quoted as models of how to write legal texts in a short, clear style accessible to everybody. Due to a strange mixture of ingenuity and romanticism these medieval laws still hold a position as testimonies of a legal culture on a high level. They came into being at the same time as thousands of churches were erected, golden altars were forged and Saxo Grammaticus in his elaborate silver age Latin "capolavoro" with the title *Res Gesta Danorum* gave the Danish people a past even if not necessarily a past that could stand for modern critics based as it was on a common European, partly legendary, tradition. Also the medieval churches built all over Denmark in the 12th century were part of a European tradition, and then why not the medieval legislation? How Nordic are the Nordic laws actually?

"Why Nordic medieval laws?" This question must necessarily precede the question posed above. The study of Nordic medieval law once had its heyday. For a time it was more or less neglected by legal historians. The time has come to assess whether new knowledge actually has been produced or whether we are just discussing old and well known tropisms in an apparently new context without really doing progress in our understanding of those legal texts from the past that once were the pride of Nordic legal history. Does a renewed study of old Nordic law really give us any new information or are we just left in a situation where it is not our level of knowledge that is increased but only our level of interpretation? And can we distinguish between these two levels?

The scientific discussion in the Nordic countries when it comes to new knowledge of medieval law differs from the situation in other countries. In the Nordic countries the discussion is basically a discussion about normative texts. It is about legislation as legal texts. The way in which the old legislation was actually interpreted and used in legal practice of the Middle Ages is practically unknown due to the lack of a sufficient amount of sources. We can read the texts but we cannot ascertain to which degree the texts reflect any kind of living legal order. The scientific discussion and also new interpretations therefore to a high degree centre themselves around the situation out of which the medieval laws actually did come into being.

The gaps in our knowledge as to what constituted the reality of medieval legal order probably explain why the legal texts themselves have been in the focus of interest. We even know that ecclesiastical courts existed in all Nordic countries but have nearly no sources to inform us about the practice of these courts or about the interplay between secular and ecclesiastical courts. In Denmark, Norway and Sweden more or less critical editions of the legislation as well as modern translations have been provided.[1] However, recently the study and interpretation based on a reading of the texts seems to have given way to considerations as to the position of Nordic medieval law in a broader European context. This is how the question arises: "How Nordic are the old Nordic laws?"

This discussion is not new either but it was enriched and placed in a new context by the Swedish legal historian and later professor in Munich Sten Gagnér in his book *Studien zur Ideengeschichte der Gesetzgebung* from 1960. Gagnér's studies on the idea of positivism in the Middle Ages and his general European outlook on the sources placed the Nordic legislation in a much broader context than had hitherto been the case. If one of the questions earlier discussed in the Nordic countries had been the possible extent of influence from foreign law the situation was now reversed. The position of Nordic law in a general European pattern was now

---

1. See on Denmark: J. Brøndum-Nielsen and P.J. Jørgensen (eds.): *Danmarks gamle Landskabslove med Kirkelovene I-VIII*, Copenhagen 1932-1961. Kromann and Iuul (eds): *Danmarks gamle Love paa nutidsdansk I-III*, Copenhagen 1945-1948. For Sweden there is an older edition by H.S. Colin and C.J. Schlyter: *Samling af Sveriges gamla lagar 13 vol.* Stockholm 1827-77. Cf. also Åke Holmbäck og Elias Wessén: *Svenska landskapslagar, tolkade för nutidens svenskar*, 5 bd, 1933-1945. For Norway: R. Keyser and P.A. Munch (eds.): *Norges gamle Love 1-2*, Chria. 1846-1848; J.R. Hagland og Jørn Sandnes (eds.): *Frostatingslova*, Oslo 1994; Absalon Taranger (ed.): *Magnus Lagabøters Landslov*, Kristiania 1915; Knut Robberstad (ed.): *Gulatingslovi*, Oslo 1952.

taken as a fact. Nordic medieval legislation was part of a general movement of legislation in the 13th century. A question was now how to define what was particular Nordic in Nordic law once it was stated that these laws do form part of European legal history.

Also modern research into the concept of *ius commune* has been an important source of inspiration. The dichotomy of the universal *ius commune* opposed to the local *iura propria* has been refined in later years. It does not make sense to discuss whether the Nordic countries were countries of *ius commune* or not. Roman law was not part of the law of the land but legal thinking influenced from the centres of learning in Southern Europe definitely had a great impact as had canon law on Nordic medieval legal thinking. It may still be considered a valid observation when Calasso in order to describe the situation in the Nordic countries quotes the 17th century lawyer Besold that the reception of Roman law was not due to authority but to acknowledge the qualities of Roman law, "Corpus iuris numquam receptum instar legis sed loco artis iuris".[2] However, this point of view has been infinitely refined since that time not least in the research of Manlio Bellomo that has added valuable new points of view to the understanding of *ius commune*, but it is important to stress that in Nordic legal history the figure of the learned or scientific lawyer only appears in the Middle Ages in the role of a leading ecclesiastical figure. We do not find a tradition of secular lawyers trained in the aulas of European universities. The opposition of a learned tradition, as opposed to an unlearned legal practice, which is part of what Paolo Grossi calls an "esperienza giuridica"[3], has a completely other and much lesser relevance in the Nordic countries than in the other Western European tradition.

The Germanic Inheritance

For quite some time Nordic law has been neglected by European legal historians. The language is one of the reasons. The gradual softening of the opposition between a Germanistic and a Romanistic branch of legal historians has been another. There was a time when at least certain leading German legal historians showed an interest in Nordic law and dedicated their scientific skills to the study of those old laws. Great names of the 19th century as Konrad von Maurer who possessed an enormous learning of old

---

2. F. Calasso: *Medio evo del diritto I*, Milano 1954, p. 626.
3. Paolo Grossi: *L'ordine giuridica medievale*, Bari 1995, p. 25.

Norwegian and Icelandic law and especially Karl von Amira[4] may here be mentioned as examples of a method in legal history that considered Nordic medieval legislation as a examples of a legislation that might be rather young compared to other "Germanic" laws but which reflected layers of law that could lead to the understanding of the original Germanic law supposed to be an archaeological layer that could be dug out partly through deductions from Nordic legal texts partly through texts like Tacitus' *Germania*. This way of thinking lead to imposing scholarly works like von Amira's two volumes on North Germanic law of obligations, *Nordgermanisches Obligationenrecht*, that today may stand as monuments of great learning but even if they do contain valuable information are hardly consulted by modern researchers. Nobody today seriously believes in the Germanic "Urrecht" any more and it also is common knowledge that the Nordic laws in no way can be considered especially pure examples of old Germanic law. Since at least the 1920s and 1930s it has been acknowledged in Nordic legal history that the medieval laws do reflect a society in brutal change, that the law written down was not necessarily very old, that many changes were brought into the laws in the 12th and 13th centuries, and – not least important – that many institutions thought to be very old, actually were quite new.[5] In later years we have learned to question whether even one of the cornerstones of the old Nordic society, the idea of kinship, was really as the basis of old Nordic society.[6]

In the field of criminal law old Germanic concepts played a significant role. However concepts like "Friede", "Treue" or "Gefolgschaft" or similar words connecting the old law with certain values are hardly found in Nordic law, and when found they can be identified as an influence either form canon law or as a consequence of a structure in which the position of the King was highly strengthened and thus be seen as more recent contributions to medieval legal order. That goes particularly for the use of the death penalty ("die germanische Todesstrafe") and the concept of outlawry ("Friedlosigkeit"). Since the 1920s and 1930s it has been the position in Danish legal history that the ideas of a sacred death penalty as described by von Amira or the idea of outlawry as an old institution linked to a specific

---

4. See on Amira and his Danish connections e.g. Ditlev Tamm: "Kjære Herr Professor – "Geehrter Freund", in: Peter Landau a.o. (eds.): *Karl von Amira zum Gedächtnis*, Bonn 1999, p. 189-195.
5. See for instance Stig Iuul: *Fællig og Hovedlod. Studier over Formueforholdet mellem Ægtefæller i Tiden før Christian V's Danske Lov*, Copenhagen 1940, for household community and for procedural law: Per Andersen: *Lærd ret og verdslig lovgivning. Retlig kommunikation i middelalderens Danmark*, Copenhagen 2006, and *Legal Procedure and Practice in Medieval Denmark*, Leiden 2011 (forthcoming).
6. Helle Vogt: *The Function of Kinship in the Nordic Medieval Laws*, Leiden 2010.

Germanic concept of peace and security in the society was not in conformity with the existing Danish medieval sources. Nordic legal history thus long ago has emancipated itself from ideas of the medieval legislation as a reflection of a particularly old and pure legal order. The connection between Nordic legal history and German legal history was thus severed. It does not make sense to study the medieval laws on a comparative basis aiming at excavating common roots. This position to a certain extent brought the study of the old Nordic laws to stand still.

Today the research in the Nordic medieval legislation must be done by Nordic scholars. Gone with the wind is the idea of "Germanic law" and Nordic law therefore does not really belong in any legal kinship or specific European legal family any more. Nordic law constitutes its own family as is also recognized by modern legal comparativists like the leading manual by Konrad Zweigert and Hein Kötz.[7] Nordic scholars have to dig out their own past. In this sense the Nordic laws are so much more Nordic today that only Nordic historians and legal historians can be supposed to take more than a distant interest in this old legislation. One of the questions to rise therefore is also whether there really exists a common core that can be conceived as specifically Nordic in the old Nordic laws. Is it meaningful to speak of the old Nordic laws or would it rather be more convenient to talk of different Danish, Norwegian and Swedish laws which can only be seen as more distant relatives?

At the same time as Nordic laws was written down in Denmark, Norway and Sweden in the Italian city states we find a legal culture with an amazingly wide-ranging and far-reaching legislation. In Saxony in Northern Germany Eike von Repgow composed his Sachsenspiegel. England already in the seventh century A.D. had laws of a kind similar to the much later Nordic laws and it seems probable that especially the Old Norwegian law was influenced from the West in the same way as Norwegian cathedral architecture may have been inspired from England. This legislation has recently been described by Patrick Wormald.[8] Other imposing legislative monuments from this same period which partly shows influence from the same European sources as we find in the North are the legislation of the Emperor Federico II of Sicily[9] and Alfonso X el Sabio of Castille[10].

---

7. Konrad Zweigert and Hein Kötz: *An Introduction to Comparative Law*, 3. ed. Oxford 1998.
8. Patrick Wormald: *The Making of English Law: King Alfred to the Twelfth Century. Vol I, Legislation and its Limits*, London 1999.
9. See Ditlev Tamm: "La legge dello Jutland del re Valdemar II e la legge dello Uppland - due codici nordici", in: Andrea Romano (ed.):. *Colendo iustitiam et iuram condendo. Federico II legislatore del Regno di Sicilia nell'Europa del Duecento*, Messina 1997, p. 470-484.
10. Ditlev Tamm: "Un paralello nordico a la obra legislativa alfonsina", in: A. Pérez

New ways of looking at the Middle Ages have lead to a rethinking also of the Nordic medieval laws.[11] The general view of the history of legislation made by Sten Gagnér has been mentioned. A new focus on the history of learning and the international community of a learned elite in the Middle Ages is another new trend that can lead to a more positive assessment of the contemporary importance of medieval law. Women's studies also are a focus of enthusiastic approach to Nordic medieval legal texts even if they are not too eloquent. To this should also be added the history of family and kinship that also sheds new light over old legal texts. The ideas of kinship (*Sippe*) as one of the dominant institutions in old Germanic pre-Christian society and early medieval law as already mentioned is also one of those that are contested today. Researchers point to other networks similar to the Roman concepts of *clientela* and *amicitia* as dominant in Nordic medieval history since the 12th century.[12] Still others point to the importance of canon law and the rules on forbidden grades in matrimonial law for the establishment of a coherent system of kinship relations in the Nordic countries.[13] If we accept that the Nordic laws have to be seen as a part of a European project also investigation into medieval legal institutions in France and Italy may shed light on Nordic law.

There has not in the Nordic countries been a revival of the study of medieval law comparable to what happened recently in Italy when several manuals of medieval law were issued almost at the time and thus gave rise to a discussion of methods and means in medieval legal research.[14]

Martín (ed.): *España y Europa - un pasado jurídico común*, Murcia 1986.
11. Lars Hermanson: *Släkt, vänner och makt: En studie af elitens politiska kultur i 1100-talets Danmark*. Avhandlinger från historiska institutionen i Göteborg 24, Göteborg 2000.
12. Birgitte Sawyer: *Viking-Age Rune Stones: Custom and Commemoration in Early Medieval Scandinavia*, Oxford 2000, suggests that the rune stones found in the Nordic countries dating from the 10th and 11th century, in fact are raised by heirs as claims of inheritance and thus reflect the existence of inheritance law. Some inscriptions mention the name of the stone-raiser and the deceased and often mention the family relation between the two. Whether the rather few rune stones that actually mention inheritance can in fact be taken as evidence for the existence of a set of inheritance rules or not seems doubtful but it seems justified to maintain that there is a link between the rune-stones and a set of norms on heritage.
13. Michael H. Gelting: "Peace and the Canonical Incest Prohibitions. Making Sense of an Absurdity?" in Mia Korpiola (ed.): *Nordic Perspectives on Medieval Canon Law* (Publications of Matthias Calonius Society 2, Saarijärvi 1999), p. 93–124. Also Vogt: *The Function of Kinship*.
14. On the Italian discussion of methods in medieval legal history see for a critical summary Emmanuelle Conti: *Droit médiéval - Un débat historiographique italien*, Annales HSS 2002, p. 1593-1613, in which he comments on books by Paolo Grossi: *L'ordine giuridico medievale*, Roma 1997; Mario Ascheri: *Istituzioni*

However from such a revival of interest in the Middle Ages, from German deconstruction of old concepts, from new American and British interpretations of the role of the king as legislator and from a still richer general research in the Middle Ages so many new trends have emerged and can be ascertained. The effect is that the question "How Nordic are the Nordic laws" will be answered quite differently from how it was, when Nordic and particularly Danish legal history, that will be the main theme here, started out in the 18th century as a patriotic science absolutely convinced of the unique national character of its old laws.

The challenge to legal history posed by some of these new ways of looking on history is well known and common to those who look at legal history from a lawyer's point of view. To him or her medieval legislation forms part of a legal development that gradually has lead to a modern legal order. The law, the understanding of legal concepts and the basic idea that change is a fundamental part of a lawyer's understanding of law will necessarily be guiding when the lawyer looks at the law in the Middle Ages. Legislation as a means to create new law is as familiar today as it was in the 18th century. In between there was a romantic period that believed in customary law as the real core of medieval law. The historian will tend to see the law in a historical context as one of the tools that make society function more than he will be interested in the interaction of legal rules as part of an integrated legal system. Both ways of looking at the old law is leading to new interpretations.

The Danish Tradition

Medieval legislation for more than two centuries played not only an important role in a Nordic legal history. Medieval legislation simply was the main field of study. Medieval legislation was considered the core issue of the study of legal history, and even if legal history today is a busy field of study, the question of how to interpret the old laws and how to understand them in a European context remains a challenge to the legal historian. Once medieval legislation could be identified as the heart of the legal history and still in countries like Denmark, Norway and Iceland medieval legislation is linked to national identity. History, language and law come together in the formative years of Danish nation building in the Middle Ages.

---

medievali, Bologna 1994 (2nd ed. 1999), and *I diritti del medioevo italiano, secoli XI-XIV,* Roma 2000; Ennio Cortese: *Il diritto nella storia medievale 1-2,* Roma 1995; A. Padoa Schioppa: *Il diritto nella storia d'Europa. Il medioevo I,* Padova 1995. To be mentioned is also Mario Carnavale: *Ordinamenti giuridici dell'Europa medievale,* Bologna 1994.

11

The historiography of Danish legal history has moved several steps since in 1769-1776 the Danish legal historian Peder Kofod Ancher published his *En Dansk Lov-Historie* (*A History of Danish Law*), a chronological study of Danish legislation since the 10th century that definitely can be considered an advanced study for its time. For Kofod Ancher Danish law was part of Danish identity. He wrote about Danish law, and he was proud of that, and he did not raise the question to what extent Danish law was influenced by foreign law. The front cover of his book symbolically pictured Danish law as it was laid down in the Danish Code of 1683 as a tree that was nurtured from roots all being older Danish statutes from medieval and later times. Kofod Ancher had found this way of depicting the law in the description of the Law of the Franks in Montesquieu's *De L'Esprit des Lois*. The law is like a tree and only by digging up its roots you come to a real understanding of life and spirit of that particular law. So was the attitude of the learned baron of La Brède, which also in Denmark was seen as a modern and stimulating way of explaining the importance of history. History and especially legal history was there to tell what was particular in national law. Legal history did not aim at finding out what the general principles of the law were. The main task of legal history was the opposite. It was to find the roots of a specific national way of conceiving the law. Law and national identity thus became related. "I will restrict myself to Danish legislation", Kofod Ancher wrote in his Introduction and so he did. His method was that of a critical researcher even if he did not live up to modern standards. However he based his study on original documents and even went to Stockholm in order to use a manuscript of The Law of Jutland in the Royal Library there. On the other hand he was highly reluctant to admit any foreign influence on medieval Danish legislation. One of the chapters of his book was dedicated to the complete refusal that the German Sachsenspiegel had had any relevance in Denmark. Danish law was according to him a domestic fruit grown in a well protected garden walled against foreign influence[15].

A second step in the historiography of Danish Law came when in the first decades of the 19th century the study of Danish legal history came under the strong influence of the Germanic branch of the German "Historical School". Especially Karl Friedrich Eichhorn and his "Deutsche Rechtsgeschichte" in several editions since 1808 had a heavy impact on the works of the Danish legal historian J.L.A. Kolderup-Rosenvinge who 1821 published a modern version of Danish legal history based on a systematic view that came close to Eichhorn. In stead of describing as had done Kofod

---

15. See Ditlev Tamm: "Patriotische Rechtsgeschichte und nationale Identität", in: M. Stolleis et al. (eds.): *Die Bedeutung der Wörter. Festschrift für Sten Gagnér zum 70. Gebrurtstag*, München 1991, p. 511-520.

Ancher the old legislation in a chronological order according to the reign of different kings Kolderup-Rosenvinge made a division according to periodical scheme and he acknowledged that law did include not only statutes but also unwritten law.

Kolderup-Rosenvinge's work remained an authority until the end of the 19th century. German legal historians like other German lawyers were taken as models in legal writing and also the new concept of legal history as a field of study the relevance of which did not depend on its importance for the understanding of modern law was readily adopted by Danish legal historians as legitimating a critical study of Danish medieval legislation. The result was the emergence of a small but efficient school of legal historians who soon emancipate themselves from German influence and started out to stress how Danish medieval legislation contrary to what was often claimed by German scholars did not reflect what could be interpreted as an original Germanic law. The law of Denmark and the law of the other Nordic countries were of a much later date and had to be interpreted in quite another context.

Probably the first to understand how deeply influenced Nordic law was by medieval canon law was the Danish legal historian Kolderup-Rosenvinge who already in his manual of Danish legal history from 1822 refers to the Decretum Gratiani as a source for the Prologue of the Law of Jutland. This theme was further and in more detail elaborated later by the legal historian Ludvig Holberg who in 1891 (*Om Dansk og fremmed Ret*) published an article in which he proved how the Prologue of the Danish provincial Law of Jutland almost literally was based on sections of the *Decretum Gratiani* of canon law. Since that time it has been manifest that ecclesiastical influence and canon law is an important source for the understanding of Nordic medieval law. The importance of Holberg's comparative study of canon law and the Law of Jutland was not immediately seen, but it can today be considered as a first important attempt to open up the European dimension of Nordic legal history.

The leading figure of Danish legal history in the first part of the 20th century Poul Johannes Jørgensen in a series of studies especially on homicide and other crimes laid the foundation for a new understanding of the redaction of the old laws. He showed how different layers of law were found when the texts were looked at as an "archaeological" field. However most likely the different layers were not of a very different age. It was thus clear that the laws should be seen as written documents of rather recent origin and that nothing proved that these laws reflected very old legal institutions like an "Urrecht".

Later contributions to the study of Nordic medieval law have been the work of Stig Iuul on the medieval law of family property (*Fællig og Hovedlod*, 1940) arguing against e.g. the thesis that the property community was an institute of great age. Ole Fenger in 1971 published his study (*Fejde og Mandebod*) on medieval criminal law centred around the institution of feud and wergeld in a study which took as its starting point German research on the "Friedensbewegung". Methodologically Fenger based himself in a conception of Danish medieval legislation as royal enactments based on agreements and a certain respect for a tradition of older customary law.[16] He thus later opposed more recent Swedish studies especially brought forward by the historian Elsa Sjöholm who stressed the role of the king and the church as makers of written laws based on a complete new legal culture from which nothing can be deducted as to the earlier unwritten law. In this discussion is reflected some of the old positions taken by Fritz Kern in his today probably completely outdated but sometime famous article on "Recht und Verfassung im Mittelalter" (1919) on the medieval law as "gutes, altes Recht" and of his modern critics[17] from a point of view that stresses the importance of the "voluntas legislatoris".

A somewhat cautious approach to the medieval laws as a reflection of old customary law has been prevailing in Danish legal history. The old law has to be understood as a writing down of contemporary law that does not necessarily base itself on older law. Thus the field is open for the acceptance of a reception of a new legal culture and a complete change of the legal pattern at the time of the redaction of these laws in the late 12th and the first and second halves of the 13th century. Nordic law therefore cannot be categorized as "Germanic" law in any scientific sense of the word. Later scholars of Nordic medieval law have even more stressed that the medieval laws are not of a very old date but have to be seen as testimonies of a legal concern that had to do with the shaping of a new society around 1200. The question is to which degree it makes sense to talk about a "Nordic" law of medieval times. Therefore the question: "How Nordic are the Nordic laws?"

The time has gone when legal historians dedicate themselves only to the investigation of legal questions related to medieval legislation is over. The time therefore has come to consider what has been achieved and to discuss new ways of understanding Nordic law in the Middle Ages. As a Danish historian, Michael H. Gelting puts it: "Our main source for Scandinavian social structures in the high Middle Ages, the twelfth- and thirteenth-century law books, must be interpreted as a part of a common

---

16. An approach which have later been challenged by Vogt: *The Function of Kinship*.
17. Zu Kern: Gerhardt Köbler: "Recht, Gesetz und Ordnung im Mittelalter", in: Kroeschell and Cordes (eds.): *Funktion und Form. Quellen und Methodenproblem der mittelalterlichen Rechtsgeschichte*, Berlin 1996 (Schriften zur Europäischen Rechts- und Verfassungsgeschichte 18); Johannes Lieberecht: *Das gute alte Recht in der Rechtshistorischen Kritik*, l.c. p. 185-204. For a linguistic approach Klaus von See: *Altnordische Rechtswörter. Philologische Studien zur Rechtsauffassung und Rechtsgesinnung der Germanen*, 1964.

European trend to create a new kind of social order and predictability through comprehensive and systematic legislation"[18].

Norwegian and Swedish Medieval Law

Medieval legislation is found in both in Denmark, in Norway and in Sweden. There are of course differences between the Nordic countries. A main difference is that Norway and Sweden achieved legal unity with the edition of national codes by the end of the 13th or the mid 14th century respectively. In Denmark four different medieval regional laws remained in force until the introduction of the Danish Code 1683. This means among other things that a considerably larger amount of old manuscripts of Danish laws are preserved than in the other Nordic countries.

Today it is generally acknowledged that the Old Norwegian laws may be the oldest Nordic laws with parts that may even stem from the late 11th century. Most of the Old Norwegian law however is supposed to have come been made over a period of 150 years from around 1150 till 1300.

From old Norway we know the names of four regional laws. However two of them, the Law of the Borgarting and the Law of the Eidsivating, are only known as fragments containing the so called Kristenrett, the specific law of the church and Christian behaviour.

The Law of the Gulating (the Gulatingslag) may have been redacted around already around 1100 and have been revised in the 1160ies. The Law of the Frostating (the Frostatingslag) probably is another Nordic law with a very old origin. It contains the church law of the Archbishop Øistein from around 1170. The oldest redaction seems to have been supplemented by royal decrees. We know of two laws preserved completely, the Frostatingslag from Northern Norway and the Gulatingslag from the West Coast. The Gulatingslag is preserved in one manuscript from the mid 13th century that probably served the compilers of the Law of Magnus Lagabøter from 1276 by which was introduced legal unity mainly based on the Gulatingslag. The Frostatingslag is only preserved in a copy of an old

---

18. See Michael H. Gelting: "Predatory kinship revisited", in: I. J. Gillingham (ed.): *Anglo-Norman Studies XXV*, Woodbridge 2003, p. 107-118. The author suggests that the oldest part of the so-called Arvebog & Orbodemål (book on inheritance and crime that could not be settled by compensation) stems back form 1170 and that the other redactions of this law and the Law of Scania are in fact draft work for a national codification. This theory even if somewhat attractive does not have any support in existing sources. The theory that the Law of Jutland was meant to be a national code was introduced by Kolderup-Rosenvinge already in 1822, later rejected by others but as can be seen is still discussed today as a relevant hypothesis.

manuscript (the original was destroyed by fire 1728). Also this law is supposed to contain very old parts.[19]

A specific feature peculiar to Norwegian – and perhaps even Swedish law – is the belief that the law was written down in accordance with an oral tradition kept by persons presumed to have known the law by heart and to recite the law when people gathered at the "thing" – the place where the law should be handled. We do not have any vestiges of such an institution in Denmark and even if we find in Danish medieval laws sentences like "This should be noted", the mentioning of an "I" or "we" or "you" or the like there are no convincing proofs of the existence of any significant oral tradition of the law.

There has been some important recent research into the Swedish medieval laws. Especially Sten Gagnér and Elsa Sjöholm should be mentioned. Sten Gagnér has questioned the date of the Upplandslagen, whereas Elsa Sjöholm in a very radical way that shall be mentioned later has maintained that the Swedish laws basically are to be considered as completely new legislation with literally no trace of an older tradition.[20] I think myself that she comes close to the truth even if her arguments are not also too convincing.

Swedish and Norwegian laws are divided into parts called *balkar*. We do not know this kind of system in the Danish laws apart from the tripartite Law of Jutland. There does not seem to have been much direct influence from one Nordic country to another. The Norwegian laws as mentioned may have been inspired from England, but the English connection have been questioned,[21] and also to a higher degree than e.g. the Danish laws have taken Mosaic law as a model. The Danish laws are different from the Norwegian laws and Danish law seems only to have had small if any influence in Sweden on the law of inheritance and procedure. Inside Danish law the Law of Jutland must have been influenced by the Law of Scania, and also the unknown authors of King Valdemar's Law of Zealand much have known the Law of Scania. King Eric's Law of Zealand is a supplement to the Law of Valdemar since it stresses such themes that are not mentioned in the Law of Valdemar.

A Danish legal historian looking at the Norwegian Gulatingslag is

---

19. For the "Stand der Forschung" of Norwegian law see Sverre Bagge: *From Viking Stronghold to Christian Kingdom – State Formation in Norway, c. 900-1350*, Copenhagen 2010, 179-228.
20. Elsa Sjöholm: *Gesetze als Quellen Mittelalterlicher Geschichte des Nordens*, Acta Universitatis Stockholmiensis 21, Stockholm 1977, and *Sveriges medeltidslagar. Europæisk rättstradition i politisk omvandling*, Rättshistsoriskt bibliotek 41, Lund 1988.
21. Torgeir Landro: *Kristenrett og Kyrkjerett – Borgartingskristenrettet i ein komparativt perspektiv*, Bergen 2010.

equally estranged as he is looking at the laws of any other of the "Germanic laws"[22]. He might even feel more at home reading a "Fuero juzgo" supposedly from the time of Alfonso X than looking at the older Norwegian laws. But still there are of course many common points in the laws of the Nordic countries. Family law and heritage, where the Swedish and Norwegian were copied from the Danish, land law, penal law and partly the procedure have similarities. Danish law however does neither know the so called "Christian law" which deals with the law of the church or parts of the laws dedicated to the position of the king which are found in both Norwegian and Swedish law.

The main body of Danish medieval legislation consists of provincial legislation. Two so called Ecclesiastical laws were issued in 1171 as a result of an agreement between the Church of Scania and Zealand and the local assembly. In these laws certain compromises were made between the Church and local people especially relating to dispositions *mortis causa* and criminal law.

A law from Zealand is found in various redactions. This law that in older redactions dates back to the 12th century was later to take the name of the King Valdemar and to be supplemented by a more extensive law called the Law of Eric. From the province of Scania there exists the Law of Scania of unknown origin. The exact date of this law is also unknown, however considering that it contains articles still based on the use of ordeal by fire it is normally dated to a time before the decision of the Fourth Lateran Council 1215 that no clerics could assist at such ordeals was effectively enforced in Denmark. A Royal decree to that effect is known but also in this case the date is unknown. Conjectures of the date of this Royal enactment vary between 1216 and sometime in the 1220ies.[23]

The most important part of Danish medieval legislation stems from the province of Jutland. The Law of Jutland is dated in a Prologue which fixes the time of its promulgation to the month of March in the year of 1241, the last year of the reign of the Danish King Valdemar II later known as "legifer". The Law of Jutland was actually issued at a national assembly in the town of Vordingborg situated in the South of the island of Zealand and thus outside the province of Jutland. It has therefore been discussed whether the Law of Jutland should actually be seen as a step towards a general code for the whole of the Realm of Denmark. Such theories were rejected in the 19th century but recently they have been revived based on new arguments taken from the general situation in contemporary Europe[24]. If in other parts

---

22. Ditlev Tamm: "Gulatingsloven og de andre gamle nordiske landskabslove", *Tidsskrift for Rettvitenskap* 1 / 2 2002, p. 292-308.
23. For the dating of the Danish laws see Andersen: *Lærd ret og verdslig lovgivning*.
24. See above fn. 18.

of Europe the will of the king as legislator managed to manifest itself why should that not have been the case in Denmark? An argument for such an approach to the Law of Jutland is that systematically even if it resembles the older Law of Scania it relies heavily in its systematic concept on new institution in procedure supposed to be royal innovations in the law. The main example is the introduction of the "sandemænd", eight men nominated by the king (or his local representatives) with the task of investigating serious crimes and cases concerning real estate. This institution was only found in the Law of Jutland but was later introduced in other parts of the realm.

However the main interest of the Law of Jutland and its most distinguished feature is the prologue and the introductory words: "The country shall be built on the law", a phrase that stresses the primacy of the law and in its Danish "Wirkungsgeschichte" has traditionally been seen as the foundation of a legal order having its roots in medieval legal thinking. The phrase may be a paraphrase of Roman law and it is found in a Prologue that contains quotations from canon law echoing famous phrases of the "Etymologiae" of Isidor of Sevilla. The Prologue of the Law of Jutland is the most prominent Danish example of the work of a learned canonist in the framing of a *ius proprium*.

Legal historians today who want to study Nordic medieval legislation in action find themselves in a difficult position. There are no new sources to find. All documents have been edited, critical editions of the laws are available and most legal questions arising from the laws have been treated, but we know almost nothing about the way the law was handled until the 16th century. Studies of how the medieval legislation was dealt with in medieval society therefore can only be built on conjectures. The unsolved questions and those that again and again will puzzle the legal historian are those that have to do with the origin of the medieval legislation and the position of this legislation in an international context.

Today the prevailing view is that Nordic medieval legislation must be seen in a European context. Very far from reflecting old legal convictions the Nordic legal sources do reflect a legal order establishing itself in the 12th and 13th century as a result of the influence from the "scientific laboratory" on the legal order. The most provocative approach in this direction was made be the Swedish historian Elsa Sjöholm who nearby shocked a Swedish audience dead when in two studies published in 1977 and 1988 she maintained that old Swedish laws were not old at all but part of a legislative conscious legislative project conceived by the Church. The texts should be seen as the political result of compromises made between existing power groups. Therefore she also preferred to see the Lombardic law and the Bible and especially Mosaic Law as model for this new legislation in Sweden and almost completely rejected the idea that old customary law could be found in the Swedish legal sources. Provocative as it was her theory has been admitted as a new starting point for the understanding of medieval legislation even if her results as to a dominant influence from the church does not seem convincing when it comes to the understanding of a legislative body of a very differentiated character that came into being over a rather extended period.

How Nordic are the Old Nordic Laws?

Another important aspect of the question: "How Nordic are the Nordic laws?" has to do with the actual framing of the law. Are we dealing with local law of local origin or are we actually witnessing a process of internationalizing of the law according to the standard set by leading legislators of the time.

There was a time when it was only reluctantly admitted that Danish law was influenced from Roman law or other foreign laws. In the 18th century it was often denied that Roman law had had any significant impact on the development of what was supposed to be pure Danish Law[25]. Such was the view in the work of Peder Kofod Ancher on the history of Danish law. Kofod Ancher was wrong in denying any influence from Roman law, but he was right in as far the old laws had been a conservative weapon in the hands of those who were against changes in the law. We see that already in a document from 1282 in which references the "Law's of King Valdemar" are used to restrict the king's legislative power. In legal practice as we know it from the 16th century and onwards the old laws are clearly seen as the fundament of the law and as a protection of existing rights that should not be changed without good reason.

It was the great Danish lawyer Anders Sandøe Ørsted who in 1822 - long before the German contest between the defenders of German or Roman law - stated that such a point of view was to be considered as an "exaggerated patriotism". He in a time that did not acknowledge the importance of the concept of ius commune referred himself to certain examples of impact from Roman law, his main argument however was the basic value of Roman law as the foundation of any scientific method in the law. Since that time it has been generally recognized that Danish law was influenced by methods and institutions of Roman law. Denmark was not divided by the schools of Romanists and Germanists. Roman law was taught at the university. The importance of Roman law for the

---

25. Ditlev Tamm: "Why Roman Law? Danish Arguments for the Study of Roman Law", in: *Libellus ad Thomasium. Essay in Roman law, Roman-Dutch Law and Legal History in Honour of Philip J Thomas,* Preatoria 2010, p. 428-434.

understanding of the law of obligations was recognized. In the filed of legal history however Roman law did not play any role. There is no Danish parallel to the discussion of the reception of Roman law, which the Germanist Beseler in his "Volksrecht und Juristenrecht" considered a German "Nationalunglück".

In Danish legal history Roman law still did not play an important role. However gradually canon law was understood as a system that played an important role in the Middle Ages. The interplay between Church and Society led to a great influence that was especially seen in matrimonial law. However in a protestant country it seemed difficult to admit the general civilizing force of the Church and of canon law. Several papal Decretals addressed to Nordic archbishops were known, but it was only in 1890ies that canon law was understood as a coherent system of law worthy of its own study that could lead to important conclusions about Danish law.

Legal history in the Nordic country has not been in the need to invent a legal past in order to find a national law. The medieval laws were such a past. And at least since the time of Kofod Ancher it has also been recognized by legal historians that there are such similarities between the medieval laws of the Nordic countries that the study of the laws of one of the other countries must be considered as useful for the understanding of medieval Nordic law. However, it was only later that the idea of a community of legal ideas found in the Nordic countries was given a high priority. It happened when in 1872 a first meeting between Nordic lawyers was convoked in order to discuss legislative questions of common interest. The inspiration to convoke such meeting came from Germany. However one of the aims of making such meetings was to find a common legal path that could lead to other solutions than those found in German law. The year 1872 may be seen as the year of the birth not only of Nordic legal cooperation in the field of law but also as the year in which the idea of a legal unity the Nordic countries was born independently of historical differences.

The medieval Nordic laws used to be the pride of legal historians. Legal history at least in Denmark to a great part was based on medieval law, scholarship was dedicated to their proper study and the introduction of the Danish Code was enacted 1683 was also for a long time seen as the end of legal history and the start of modern law. All this has changed. Medieval law is not any more the most important field of legal historians. However many historians have given important contributions to medieval law, especially perhaps in Norway, whereas medieval law seems to have been somewhat neglected in Sweden since the days of Elias Wessén. Elsa Sjöholm has challenged the establishment and new studies would be a desideratum. That goes for Denmark too but as will have appeared from this article we do see in these years how young scholars find new ways of approaching the old law. One way is to look more at the social context. Another way is to look outside the Nordic countries for inspiration and for comparison. I do think that the Nordic laws are very Nordic but they also form part of a common European heritage of law from the 12th to the 14th century. New inspiration has come to continue the study of medieval law along the many new roads that have been opened in later years by scholars all over Europe. The Nordic laws belong in a European context. They can still be seen as the most important Nordic contribution to the making of European legal History.

THE IMPORTANCE OF CLASSICAL CANON LAW IN SCANDINAVIA IN THE 12TH AND 13TH CENTURIES

Peter Landau

Introduction

Canon Law and its rules had great influence on the history of the Scandinavian countries, beginning in the early 12th century. The gradual penetration of canon law in Scandinavia was already noticed by German legal historians in the 19th century, especially by Konrad Maurer (1823-1902) whose lectures on *Altnordische Kirchenverfassung und Eherecht*, given in the University of Munich in 1887 and published only after Maurer's death in 1908, are still probably the most important publication on the subject.[1] Maurer and his disciple Philipp Zorn (1850-1928), who published a book on "Staat und Kirche in Norwegen" in 1875,[2] saw the beginning of the influence of canon law connected with the stay of the papal legate, Cardinal Nicholas Breakspear, in Norway in 1152.[3] Nicholas Breakspear, later Pope Hadrian IV, an Englishman and the only English pope until now, founded the metropolitan see in Nidaros (Trondheim) and abolished the submission of the Norwegian and Icelandic bishoprics to the

---

1. K. Maurer: „Über altnordische Kirchenverfassung und Eherecht" in *Vorlesungen über altnordische Rechtsgeschichte Bd. II*, Leipzig 1908. The preface by the editor Ebbe Hertzberg mentions that Maurer gave these lectures in summer 1887 in Munich.
2. Ph. Zorn: *Staat und Kirche in Norwegen bis zum Schlusse des dreizehnten Jahrhunderts*, München 1875.
3. Maurer (n.1); Zorn (n.2) 89-92.

archiepiscopal see of Lund.⁴ The new Norwegian archiepiscopal province extended to eight bishoprics in Norway, Iceland and even in Greenland.⁵ Lund kept its metropolitan status for the bishoprics in Denmark and Sweden. This great act of organisation for the Scandinavian churches was confirmed by Pope Anastasius IV in 1154.⁶ The mission of Nicholas Breakspear might also have contributed to the knowledge of canon law in Norway – e.g. Zorn presumed that Nicholas made the requirements of canon law very clear to the Norwegian clergy.⁷ It is true that our available sources do not antedate the second half of the 12th century. But we have some information that manuscripts concerning canon law might have come to Scandinavia already at the beginning of the 12th century.

Ivo of Chartres in Scandinavia

The Vatican library has in its rich collection of manuscripts the so-called Decretum of Bishop Ivo of Chartres (1040-1116), the most comprehensive canonical collection compiled before the Decretum of Gratian.⁸ According to our present knowledge, Ivo's Decretum was finished as a collection probably around 1095⁹ – it is now known from a small number of manuscripts in France and England,¹⁰ but was almost unknown in Italy. The Vatican manuscript concerning Scandinavia belongs to the Palatine fund of manuscripts in the Vaticana,¹¹ manuscripts brought to Rome during the Thirty Years War as war booty from the library of the Palatine prince electors in Heidelberg. The Codex has a note of property written around 1400 saying: "Liber Sancte Crucis de Dalby".¹² It obviously has connections to a place called Dalby, and one may identify that place with

---

4. See A. Bergquist: „The Papal Legate: Nicholas Breakspear's Scandinavian Mission" in: B. Bolton/A.J. Duggan,: *Adrian IV. The English Pope (1154-1159)*, Aldershot 2003, pp. 41- 48.
5. Cf. Zorn (n.2) 89.
6. JL 9941. Cf. Zorn (n.2) 89.
7. Zorn (n.2) 91.
8. For Ivo's Decretum see L. Kéry: *Canonical Collections of the Early Middle Ages*, Washington D.C. 1999, 250-253, with bibliography.
9. For the date of Ivo's Decretum see M. Brett: „Urban II and the collections attributed to Ivo of Chartres", *Proceedings of the Eighth International Congress of Medieval Canon Law San Diego 1988*, ed. S. Chodorow , MIC, Ser. C, vol. 9, Città del Vaticano 1992, 27-46, especially p. 44.
10. List of the manuscripts in Kéry (n.8) 251s.
11. MS Pal. lat. 587.
12. Cf. P. Landau: „Das Dekret des Ivo von Chartres", *ZRG Kan. Abt. 70*, 1984, 1-44, esp. 25s. - also in: P. Landau: *Kanones und Dekretalen*, Goldbach 1997, 117-160, esp. 141s.

Dalby near Lund, 10 km away. A monastery of the Austin canons had been founded in Dalby in 1066 and already by the end of the 11th century it had become an intellectual center for the nearby episcopal see of Lund.[13] The Palatine manuscript contains only the first six books of Ivo's comprehensive collection, leaving out books 7 to 17 dealing with the law of the monks and the law of the laity. These first six books provide a very comprehensive collection of canonical rules dealing with the law of the clergy. As a supplement to the fragmentary Ivonian collection, the manuscript contains a text of St. Augustine and the so-called Capitula Angilrammi, which belongs partly to the Pseudo-Isidorian forgeries of the ninth century and which stress the independence of the clergy from secular jurisdiction. There is also a text of the council of Guastalla under Pope Paschal II in 1106.[14]

The selection of texts may have been very useful for a collegiate chapter of Austin canons – the date of the last text may lead us to assume the years around 1110 as the date for the production of the manuscript. It might have been written especially for Dalby and come to that place immediately. Anyway, it was not very useful after the composition of Gratian's Decretum around 1140 - it is my opinion that it must have already been brought to Dalby before 1140. When the Dalby monastery was suppressed during the Reformation in Denmark, Ivo's manuscript probably was sold to Prince Elector Ottheinrich, a famous bibliophile of the 16th century. The Palatine manuscript offers some probability that canon law texts had already reached Scandinavia prior to Gratian. We have a parallel to that in the early transfer of an Ivonian canonical collection to Poland. The first canonical collection brought to this country was a manuscript of the so-called Collectio Tripartita, another collection compiled by the circle of Ivo of Chartres and brought to Poland by the papal legate Gwalo, bishop of Beauvais and disciple of Ivo in the year 1104.[15] Probably in the same decade both Poland and Denmark got first-hand knowledge of canon law.

---

13. For Dalby c.f. H. Kluger: *Series Episcoporum Ecclesiae Catholicae Occidentalis VI/II: Archiepiscopatus Lundensis,* Stuttgart 1992, 34-37. The first bishop of Dalby with the name of Egino became also bishop of Lund between 1067 and 1071. Then Dalby became a part of the diocese of Lund, whereas Egino founded a monastery of Austin canons in Dalby.

14. For the Capitula Angilramni in this manuscript see Kéry (n.8) 117. Council of Guastalla, c.4 - cf. U.-R. Blumenthal: „Decrees and decretals of Pope Paschal II in twelfth-century canonical collections", *BMCL N.S. 10,* 1980 15-30, here p. 29 - also in: U.-R. Blumenthal: *Papal Reform and Canon Law in the 11th and 12th Centuries,* Ashgate 1998, no. XII.

15. For the manuscript of the Ivonian Collectio tripartita cf. H. Fuhrmann: *Einfluss und Verbreitung der pseudoisidorischen Fälschungen. Teil III (MGH, Schriften, Bd. XXIV, 3)* Stuttgart 1974, 777, n.9.

The Norwegian Synod in Bergen

The first evidence of canon law in Scandinavia is the canons produced by a Norwegian synod assembly in 1164. It was the time of the coronation of King Magnus Erlingsson who had been a candidate for the throne of Norway from the party of his father, Jarl Erling, in the long struggle among several pretenders to the Norwegian kingship.[16] The child, Magnus Erlingsson, was crowned in Bergen in 1164 in the presence of the papal legate, Subdeacon Stephanus.[17] A national diet in Bergen at the time of the coronation changed the succession to the Norwegian throne from a hereditary system to an elective monarchy. I remind you that the regulation of the king's election can be found as the second statute of Gulathings-book's Christian Law[18] – the Gulathings-book being considered the oldest source of medieval Norwegian law.

In the statute the archbishop of Trondheim and his suffragan bishops are named the principal electors of the king - they should act as electors together with a group of laymen selected by the bishops in their dioceses to attend the assembly of election together with the bishops.[19] The nearest relative of the late king should be entitled to be elected if he was sufficiently qualified for kingship. If the relatives lacked the proper qualifications, the electors should vote for a candidate who would protect divine law and the law of the people.[20] Divine law as a special legal category can only refer to the Bible and to canon law in this time;[21] the protection of canon law is a major duty of the king in this election statute. This interpretation is confirmed by the text of the coronation oath sworn by King Magnus at the

---

16. Cf. Zorn (n.2) 98-103 and W. Holtzmann: „Krone und Kirche in Norwegen im 12. Jahrhundert", *DA 2*, 1938, 341-400, here 343.
17. Zorn (n.2) 103. See also B. La Farge: „Art. Magnus Erlinsson", *Lex MA VI,*1993, 98.
18. Cf. R. Meißner (ed.): *Norwegisches Recht. Das Rechtsbuch des Gulathings,* Germanenrechte, Bd. 6, Wsimar 1935, 3s.
19. Cf. Meißner (n.18): „dann soll der seiner Brüder vom gleichen Vater König sein, der dem Erzbischof und den Suffraganbischöfen am besten dafür geeignet erscheint und ebenso den zwölf verständigsten Männern aus jedem Bistum, die jene sich hinzuwählen ..."
20. Cf. Meißner (n.18) 4: „Und wenn der nicht geeignet erscheint, so soll es der sein, von dem die dazu ernannten annehmen, dass er am besten würde Gottes Recht und die Landesgesetze in seinen Schutz nehmen."
21. Cf. my remarks on lex divina in: P. Landau: „Die „Rhetorica ecclesiastica" - Deutschlands erstes juristisches Lehrbuch im Mittelalter", in: F. Theisen/W.E. Voß: *Summe - Glosse - Kommentar (= Osnabrücker Schriften zur Rechtsgeschichte Bd. 2.1,* Osnabrück 2000, 125-139, here p. 131s.

same time and preserved in an English manuscript of the 12th century.²² King Magnus swears to confer justice on all churches, ecclesiastical persons, poor people and orphans according to the law of the land and "sanctorum canonum statute".²³ He promises to be obedient "secundum instituta divinae et humanae legis".²⁴ This refers to canon law. Obedience to the king from the members of the church is restricted in the oath to concessions mentioned in the "sacri canones" dealing with the submission of churches to the authority of kings.²⁵

In the coronation oath of 1164, relations between the Church and the Norwegian kingdom are primarily defined by the regulations of canon law. Philipp Zorn, the German jurist and author of the book already mentioned about Church and State of Norway during the years of Bismarck's so-called "Kulturkampf" against the Catholic Church, called the oath of 1164 a pure "catastrophe" and a "Norwegian Canossa".²⁶ Avoiding any evaluation of those events according to the standards of modern state supremacy, we can conclude that by this oath the assembly of 1164 finally promoted the acceptance of canon law as a major part of valid law in the Norwegian kingdom.

The fields for the influence of canon law in Norway after 1164 can be easily determined by the decrees of a national synod assembled probably in Bergen at the same time. Those decrees are also preserved in the already mentioned Harley manuscript of the British library.²⁷ Most of these

---

22. *The coronation oath is preserved in MS British Library*, Harley 3405, fol. 3r - edited by Holtzmann (n.16) 367s.
23. Holtzmann l.c.: „Ego rex Magnus promitto et iuro ... quod iusticiam faciam ecclesiis, ecclesiasticis personis, populo mihi subdito maioribus et minoribus et precipue viduis et orphanis et pupillis tam pauperibus quam divitibus secundum patrias leges et secundum sanctorum canonum statuta ..."
24. Holtzmann l.c.: „in spiritualibus ecclesie, cum ab ea de sua iusticia requisitus fuero, respondebo et quod debitam reverentiam et debita obsequia secundum instituta divine et humane legis ecclesie Trundensis et totius regni Norwagie pro posse meo prestabo et ab ea nulla obsequia violenter exigam, nisi que sacri canones ecclesiam regibus parare concedunt, nisi gratis pro necessitate temporis ipsa prestare velit."
25. Cf. n.24.
26. Zorn (n.2) 103.
27. The decrees are edited by Holtzmann (n.16) 377-382, commentary by Holtzmann pp. 355-361. Some Norwegian authors (Oluf Kolsrud, Arne Odd Johnsen, Eirik Vandvik) claimed that the decrees originated with the establishment of the Norwegian ecclesiastical province by the legatine mission of Nicholas Breakspear in 1152/53 - cf. A.L. Johnsen: „The Earliest Provincial Statute of the Norwegian Church", *Mediaeval Scandinavia 3,* 1970, 172-197. V. Skanland, *Det eldste norske provinsialstatut,* Oslo 1969, claimed that the collection of decrees originated with a provincial council in the 1170s and was drawn up by Archbishop Eystein. I think that the date given by Holtzmann is the most probable, because 1153 seems too early for an influence of Gratian in Scandinavia and any date after 1170 does not

conciliar decrees of the oldest Scandinavian conciliar legislation deal with the constitution of the Norwegian church and with the legal duties of clergymen according to canon law. One of the most important decrees contains a general prohibition of lay investiture for bishops, abbots and any dignity in a church. A bishop allowing himself to be invested by a layman – "per laicam manum," – is threatened with deposition.[28] A text in Gratian from the Roman synod of 1078 is carefully used but also altered in some formulations by the council – so "per laicam manum" replaces "de manu imperatoris, vel regis, vel alicuius laicae personae, viri vel feminae" in the original.[29]

The prohibition of lay investiture is supplemented by another decree taking over the text of five chapters in Gratian defining the newly developed right of advowson replacing the old right of proprietary churches.[30] The founder of a church is denied any right of property – "proprii iuris potestas" – but should enjoy a privilege of offering a candidate to the bishop for ordination and also being supported by means of the church in a situation of distress.[31] The elements of the institution of advowson are already present even though the label "Ius patronatus", first developed by the canonist Rufinus in his Summa at the same time, is still lacking.[32] We can see the same influence of Gratianic texts in the the conciliar decrees on elections of bishops and metropolitans. A bishop should be elected by the canons of the cathedral assembled with clergy and people of the diocese and also with "religiosi viri" - a term used by the second Lateran council in 1139 and

---

    take account of the decretals of 1169 to Trondheim obviously supplementing the decrees of the council. See also S. Bagge, „Art. Canones Nidrosienses", *Lex MA II,* 1983, 1438, who accepts the date given by Holtzmann.

28. Holtzmann l.c. p. 378s. (c.4): „Constitutiones sanctorum patrum sequentes statuimus, ut quicumque clericorum ab hac hora investituram episcopatus abbatie vel cuiuslibet ecclesie seu ecclesiastice dignitatis per laicam manum acceperit, investituram ipsam auctoritate apostolica irritam esse cognoscat et tam se quam episcopum, qui sibi manus imposuerit, gradus sui periculo subiacere."
29. C.16, q.7, c.13.
30. Holtzmann l.c. p. 377s. (c.2). The chapter uses C.16, q.7, c.30-32, c.35-36.
31. Holtzmann l.c. (n.30): „Ipsis autem fundatoribus vel eorum heredibus in eisdem ecclesiis vel rebus earum non licet quasi proprii iuris potestatem preferre, non rapinam non fraudem ingerere nec violentiam quamcumque presumere; sacerdotes inde removere vel in eis ponere absque episcoporum auctoritate et consilio non presumant, set episcopis offerant ordinandos. Quod si ad inopiam fuerint devoluti, in cenobiis vel ecclesiis capitulis habentibus, quas ipsi construxerunt vel ditaverunt, si ibi manere voluerint, suffragium vite pro temporis usu percipiant."
32. Cf. my book „*Ius Patronatus"* *(Forschungen zur kirchlichen Rechtsgeschichte und zum Kirchenrecht Bd. 12,* Köln/Wien 1975, 11s.

included also in Gratian's Decretum.³³ The Bergen council also follows Gratian in giving the metropolitan the right of chairman's casting-vote in a situation of dissent among the electors.³⁴ The Bergen council finally adopted a Gratianic chapter from Leo I determining the right of the suffragan bishops to elect their metropolitan.³⁵ The reception of this text was made with two adjustments: the assembly can elect a bishop to the metropolitan see, so the prohibition of translations of bishops is no longer valid; and the consecration of the metropolitan should be reserved to the pope.³⁶

The other decrees of the council also demonstrate an intimate knowledge of recent developments in canon law. A decree about tithing prohibits any abstraction of tithes by laymen, again in connection with Gratian,³⁷ and the same decree also forbids any request of tithes from monks "de laboribus suis" – from land cultivated by friars, again a quotation from Gratian.³⁸ But in the manuscript preserving the decrees "de laboribus" is explained "id est novalibus", a remarkable restriction of monastic freedom of tithes, which should now only be granted to land newly cultivated by the monks. The restriction had been introduced by Pope Hadrian IV in 1155;³⁹

---

33. D.63, c.25 = 2 Conc. Lat. c.28, ed. J. Alberigo/C. Leonardi: *Conciliorum Oecumenicorum Decreta*, 3Bologna 1973, 203. The text was used for the Bergen Council c.6 - Holtzmann (n.16) 379s.
34. Holtzmann (n.16) 379s. (c.6): „Verum si vota eligentium in duas se diviserint partes, is metropolitano iudicio alteri preferatur, qui maioribus iuvatur studiis et meritis." This text depends on D. 63, c.36 (Leo I).
35. Holtzmann (n.16) 379 (c.5): „Metropolitano defuncto cum in loco eius alius fuerit subrogandus, episcopi suffraganei ad metropolim civitatem accedant et clericorum ac civium voluntate discussa vel ex ipsis episcopis aut presbiteris seu diaconibus eiusdem ecclesie vel alterius, si ibi inventus non fuerit, qui sanctior et peritior inventus fuerit, eligatur.." This text depends on D.63, c.19 (Leo I).
36. Holtzmann (n.16) 379 (c.5): „et cum solennitate decreti subscriptione omnium roborati litterarumve testimonio ad summum pontificem cum archidiaconibus et melioribus ecclesie sue clericis consecrandus accedat." This text depends on D.61, c.11 (Gregory I) - but the consecration of the bishop by the pope should take place in the case of a postulatio (irregular election).
37. Holtzmann (n.16) 382 (c.14): „Laici vel clerici et persone utriusque sexus, si proprietatis sue loca vel res alicubi delegaverint, decimationis proventum priori ecclesie legitime assignatum inde abstrahere nullam habent penitus potestatem." This text quotes C.16, q.1, c.42.
38. Holtzmann (n.16) 382 (c.14): „Monachi autem vel clerici communem vitam professi de laboribus et propriis nutrimentis suis episcopis vel quibuslibet personis decimas reddere minime compellantur" - a quotation from C.16, q.1, c.47 (Paschalis II).
39. For the gloss „id est novalibus" see Holtzmann (n.16) 382, n.b. For the restriction by Hadrian IV cf. G. Constable, *Monastic Tithes from their Origins to the Twelfth Century*, Cambridge 1964, 279. The text is JL 9972.

if the gloss "id est novalibus" had already been added to the text in Bergen, it would means, that in 1164 the Norwegians already knew about the most recent papal legislation on tithes.

Three decrees of the council deal with the marriage of clerics in Holy Orders. The rule of clerical celibacy, finally formulated by the second Lateran council of 1139,[40] is only prescribed with moderation. Clerics who were married before becoming priests should promise abstention when being ordained to priesthood, whereas canons of cathedral chapters are not allowed to marry at all or to live with concubines in their houses.[41] The strict prohibition of the Lateran council applied only to the cathedral clergy of Norway. Marriage of priests was formally not allowed for the Norwegian clergy, but the church did not struggle directly against the marriage of priests, still a widespread custom in Norway "deep in the 13th century".[42] If somebody had married a widow or a wife repudiated by a former husband, or had been married twice before ordination, i.e. that he had been living in what was known as "successive bigamy", he should never be admitted to ordination. The bishop responsible for such an ordination against the prohibition should lose his right to ordain.[43]

The tradition of prohibition goes back to St. Paul's Pastoral letters and to the Apostolic Canons of the fourth century, and it was also incorporated into Gratian's Decretum.[44] The council of Bergen added the most serious

---

40. 2Conc. Lat. c.7, ed. J. Alberigo/C. Leonardi: *Conciliorum Oecumenicorum Decreta,* Bologna 1973, 198.
41. Holtzmann: (n.16) 380 (c.7): „Clerici, qui ante adeptum sacerdotium duxerunt uxores, ad sacerdotium nisi promissa continentia nequaquam promoveantur" and c.9: „Ut lex continentie, que altaris ministris precipue necessaria est, in clero plenius observetur, apostolica auctoritate decernimus, quatenus canonici episcopalium ecclesiarum nec uxores ducant nec publicas concubinas in domibus suis habere presumant."
42. Cf. Maurer II (n.1) 334-337.
43. Holtzmann (n.16) 380 (c.8): „Precipimus, ut episcopi eos, qui viduam aut repudiatam, aut secundam duxerunt uxorem, nequaquam ordinare presumant. Sacri namque canones episcopos, qui tales ordinant, ordinandi dumtaxat potestate privandos esse sancserunt."
44. 1Tim. 3.2 and Tit. 1.6. Canones apostolorum c.17, ed. C.H. Turner: *Ecclesiae Occidentalis Monumenta Iuris antiquissima I/1,* Oxonii 1899, 15s. For the influence of the Canones in western Canon Law see my paper „Die Canones apostolorum im abendländischen Kirchenrecht, insbesondere bei Gratian", in: K.Th. Geringer/H.Schmitz (ed.): *Communio in Ecclesiae Mysterio. Festschrift f. Winfried Aymans,* St. Ottilien 2001, 269-283. Gratian used c.17 for D.33, c.1. For Gratian's immediate source see n.54 in my paper. „For ‚bigamy' in the history of canon law" cf. also the study by S. Kuttner: „Pope Lucius III and the Bigamous Archbishop of Palermo" in: J.A. Watt (ed.): *Medieval Studies presented to Aubrey Gwynn S.J.,* Dublin 1954 - also in: S. Kuttner: *The History of Ideas and Doctrines of Canon Law in the Middle Ages,* London 1980, no. VII.

sanction against a bishop violating the prohibition in as much as he should lose all power of ordination. The council tried to enforce the prohibition in Norway with remarkable rigidity.

Another attack on customary law is the prohibition against ordeals of hot iron being used as a means of proof against clerics. The "iudicium candentis ferri" should never be applied against clerics who should only be asked to offer a purgatory oath in cases of infamy with criminal acts.[45] This tendency to recommend the purgatory oath with seven compurgators in all cases of criminal procedure is totally in line with Pope Alexander's policy of reforming the standards of criminal procedure that can be seen in a letter from the pope to Archbishop Stephan of Uppsala in 1171/72.[46]

We cannot comment on all of the decrees of the Bergen council, but the acquaintance with Gratian and the zeal to bring canon law to Norway can be seen in each decree. The papal legate to the council, Stephanus de Urbe veteri (from Orvieto) might have had a major role for the formulation of the decrees. Stephanus is mentioned as a magister by a contemporary English chronicler.[47] Coming from the vicinity of Bologna, he could have already been trained in canon law. 1164 is probably the most important date for the introduction of canon law to Norway.

Papal Decretals in the Second Half of the 12th Century

The decrees of the Bergen council are supplemented by a remarkable series of 13 decretals sent by the popes to Norway between 1160 and 1200.[48] This is a comparatively high percentage compared to the output of papal decretal letters to other countries - for the same period we have approximately 30 decretals sent to Spain and probably only 10 to Germany.[49] 11 of those decretals are mainly preserved by two English manuscripts containing decretal collections. We are not exactly informed about the place of origin

---

45. Holtzmann (n.16) 382 (c.15): „Precipimus itaque, ut ignitum ferrum pro nulla emergente causa portare presumant. Indecens enim est et plurimum indecorum, ut manus domino consecrata candentis ferri vel aliud huiusmodi debeat subire iudicium. Set si a populo mala oppinione fuerit infamatus et legitimi testes vel accusatores defecerint, secundum decreta sanctorum patrum cum VII honestis sacerdotibus vel paucioribus, si episcopo visum fuerit, in sancto evangelio coram posito iuret, quod crimen sibi illatum non perpetravit, et hac satisfactione purgatus secure deinceps suum exequatur officium."
46. JL 12117 - P.L. 200, col. 854. Cf. Holtzmann (n.16) 371 and K. Maurer: *Altnorwegisches Staatsrecht und Gerichtswesen*, vol. 2 (Leipzig 1907) 237-241.
47. Holtzmann (n.16) 358.
48. See the editions of these decretals by Holtzmann (n.16) 383-400.
49. According to an estimate by myself.

of these manuscripts – but they were certainly written in the period between 1185 and 1195.[50] As we know, archbishop Eystein of Trondheim stayed as a refugee at the famous Benedictine monastery, Bury St. Edmunds, from 1180 to 1183.[51]

It seems very probable that these papal letters sent to Norway were brought to England during Eystein's exile. The famous archbishop, who had compiled a collection of legal texts – the so-called Goldfeather – wanted to have a textbook for his own use in the struggle against King Sverrir and he obviously aspired to defend the ecclesiastical claims with legal arguments guaranteed by written law.[52] To have the newest papal law at his disposal was crucial for him. He might well have had good reason to keep the precious decretals addressed to him personally in his luggage on his flight to England.

Some of those decretals used by Eystein are only preserved in minor English decretal collections from the end of the 12th century, but some of them were also transmitted to later canonical collections and finally found their way to the Liber Extra of Gregory IX[53] – the greatest codification of canon law in the Middle Ages and remaining the law of the Catholic Church until 1918. The remarkable influence and, as it were, career of the papal letters sent to Trondheim was promoted by Alanus Anglicus, an Englishman who lived as a professor in Bologna at the beginning of the 13th century and who was also active as a collector of papal decretals.[54] I don't want to go into details concerning the transmission of decretals from and to Trondheim

---

50. Those Collections are called *Collectio Cottoniana* (MS London, British Libary Cott. Vitellius E 13) and *Collectio Petrihusensis* (Cambridge, Peterhouse College cod. 193, 114, 203, 180). Both collections belong to the „Worcester family" of decretal collections - cf. Ch. Duggan: *Twelfth Century Decretal Collections and Their Importance in English History*, London 1963, 103-110 and my review in ZKG 76 (1965) 362-375, esp. 370s.
51. Holtzmann (n.16) 375s., n.2 and Duggan (n.50) 116s. For Eystein see also S. Bagge: „Art. Eysteinn Erlendsson", *Lex MA IV* (1989) 193s.
52. The contents of Eystein's collection „Goldfeather" are not known - cf. Holtzmann as in n.51.
53. Those are three decretals: 1.) JL 15750 (= WH 22 - Register by Walther Holtzmann); X 3.48.5; 2.) JL 14118 (= WH 622): X 2.9.3 and X 5.38.6; 3.) JL 14109 + 14204 + 14206 (= WH 833): X 2.9.2 + X 3.40.1 + X 3.3.4.
54. For Alanus Anglicus cf. P. Landau: „Art. Alanus Anglicus", *Lex MA I*, 1980, 267f. The transmission by the collection of Alanus can be seen as follows: 1.) WH 22: Alan. 3.23.2; 2.)WH 622: Alan. 2.3.3 = X 2.9.3 + X 5.38.6. 3.) WH 833: Alan. 2.3.2 = X 2.9.2, Alan. (MS Vercelli) 6.3.1 = X 3.40.1, Alan. 3.2.1 = X 3.3.4. For an analysis of Alanus' collection see R. v. Heckel: „Die Dekretalensammlungen des Gilbertus und Alanus nach den Weingartener Handschriften (ZRG Kan. Abt. 29), 1940, 116-357 and S. Kuttner: „The collection of Alanus, a concordance of its two recensions", *RSDI 26,* 1953, 37-53.

or from and to Bologna – I only want to point out that some details of papal decisions dealing with specific Norwegian problems travelled through Europe to become common law in the medieval Church.

The decretals received by archbishop Eystein were written by Pope Alexander III, some of them in December 1169 during the stay of the pope in Benevent.[55] Some decretals deal with the same or similar subjects as the decrees of the Trondheim council. Thus the pope repeats the prohibition of any investiture of bishops and abbots by the king who is allowed only to give his consent to a previous election.[56] The proof by hot iron is also once more forbidden by the pope in a letter sent to Eystein and all his suffrage bishops.[57] The Cistercians in Norway received a more extensive privilege of freedom from paying tithes than they had under Hadrian IV, who only conceded freedom of payment from newly cultivated soil, whereas Alexander granted it for all their agricultural labour.[58]

There are also some decretals dealing with new and difficult questions presented to the pope by Eystein and carefully answered by Pope Alexander III. I have called this type of decretals, very common to this period, "decretals upon consultations".[59] In one of them the pope begins his authoritative statement on canon law with the remark that difficult questions emerge in ecclesiastical lawsuits particularly about marriage. The pope stresses the principle of consent for the validity of any marriage and also the principle of lifelong marriage – two 'landmarks' in the notion of marriage found in canon law.[60]

---

55. Those are n.7-11 in Holtzmann (n.16) 391 - 395, all of them transmitted by the Collectio Cottoniana - WH 710, 100, 1086, 829,1014.
56. Holtzmann (n.16) 393 (no. 9): „Inde est quod auctoritate apostolica prohibemus, ne regi vestro vel alicui persone laice de regno episcopatus, abbatias vel ecclesias liceat aliqua ratione donare. Verumtamen in electionibus faciendis regium assensum inquiri et indulgeri minime prohibemus."
57. WH 100 = Holtzmann (n.16) 391s. (no.8): „Audivimus quod in partibus vestris per igniti ferri examinationem iudicia fieri sepius consueverunt, que tamen ecclesia Romana, quoniam contra sacros canones esse noscuntur, nequaquam admittit. Verumtamen nos huiusmodi nullatenus approbamus, que tamen in diversis ecclesiis secundum terre consuetudinem non sustinentur."
58. WH 829 = Holtzmann (n.16) 394 (no.10): „ In abbatiis vero Cisterciensis ordinis, que in parrochiis vestris consistunt, benedictionem abbatis, vocationem ad sinodum et alias in negotiis ecclesiasticis consilium episcopus diosesanus potest de iure exigere, set de laboribus quos propriis manibus aut sumptibus excolunt, nulle sunt ab eis decime dande ne aliquid aliud ab eis quamquam vestrum exigere licet, nisi quod ipsi ex caritate sponte sua voluerint conferre."
59. Cf. my paper "Rechtsfortbildung im Dekretalenrecht", *ZRG Kan. Abt. 86,* 2000, 86-131, here p. 99.
60. WH 1083 = Holtzmann (n.16) 385 (no.2): „Vestre discretionis providentiam non credimus ignorare, quod difficiliores questiones, que in causis ecclesiasticis

One decretal is specifically interesting for the situation of Christians in remote areas of the archbishop's jurisdiction and for his care to observe the rules of canon law. Eystein had sent ambassadors to the pope to confront him with a problem arising from the very rigid law prohibiting marriages between relatives up to the 7th degree of consanguinity. Eystein reported to the pope that all inhabitants of an island about 12 days travel by boat from Norway were related to each other so that they could not find a partner on the island, and even sometimes had no opportunity to find a wife by travelling to another country, particularly if they could not afford the travel expenses.[61] The distance of the island from Norway leads one to identify it with Iceland or Greenland. The pope allows the archbishop and his suffrages to grant dispensations to those people wanting to get married and being prevented from doing so because of the 5th, 6th or 7th degree of consanguinity.[62] The later legislation of the 4th Lateran council limiting the impediment to the 4th degree was first introduced to Iceland or Greenland 40 years before – these islands seem to have had a pioneering role in the development of canon law at that time.[63]

The preservation of church property was always of primary concern, and it is the subject of one of Pope Alexander's decretals to Eystein. In this letter the pope decides that no cleric may devise to his relatives or other secular heirs any property which he obtained through his church.[64] He

---

contingere solent, circa matrimonium emergere consueverunt. Quapropter de illis, qui post occultum concubitum a parentibus mulierum eas ducere compelluntur, vestram volumus prudentiam edocere, quod si ille, qui coactus fuit, ex quo facultatem habuerit dissentiendi, semel consenserit ex tunc ita dissentire non potest, ut factum valeat revocare."

61. S. Chodorow/Ch. Duggan (ed.): *Decretales ineditae saeculi XII* (MIC, Ser. B, vol. 4, Città del Vaticano 1982) 149 (no.86) = WH 406a: „Ex diligenti relatione nuntiorum tuorum nostris est auribus intimatum quod insula quedam a Norwegia per XII dietas et amplius distat, in qua episcopatus tibi metropolico iure subiectus existere perhibetur, cuius itaque parochiani ita sibi invicem dicuntur contingere, quod matrimonia inter se vix aut numquam legitime possunt contrahere, presertim cum difficile sit eis - et pauperibus fere impossibile - terram hac occasione exire et aliunde uxores quererere."

62. Chodorow/Duggan (n.61): „Verum tamen si ab aliis insulam prescriptam terris per XII dietas, sicut audivimus, constet distare et eius populo tantam in his necessitatem noveris iminere, tu ascitis tibi suffraganeis tuis cum suo et aliorum religiosorum virorum consilio poteris dispensare et supradicto populo ut in V' et VI' et VII' gradu contrahant matrimonium indulgere, donec omnipotens Dominus tantam ab eis aufert necessitatem. In quarto autem gradu et infra dispensationem fieri omnimodo prohibemus."

63. 4Conc. Lat. c.50, ed. Alberigo/Leonardi (n.33) 257 = X 4.4.8.

64. WH 49 = ed. Chodorow/Duggan (n.61) 153 (no.88): „Ad aures nostras perlatum fuisse cognoscatis quod quidam de clero vobis commisso non eam quam debent circa salutem suam sollicitudinem et curam adhibentes, ea que ipsis per ecclesias

should always be free to leave his inherited property to the church in which he served.⁶⁵ This decretal refers to the freedom to dispose by will in favour of the church, the most important change in the inheritance law achieved by the church in contradiction to all Germanic traditions of hereditary family rights.⁶⁶

The requirement that priests lead a celibate life was never easily accepted in Scandinavia, despite of the decisions of the Bergen council. This showed how impossible it was to control the way married priests conducted their lives, and even marriages after ordination were not unusual – the church being unable to enforce its prohibition. In fact, the pope permitted Eystein to restore priests who had lived in illicit marriages, allowing them to resume their service after a long period of penance, and thus providing the possibility for flexible responses to the permanent scandal of married priests.⁶⁷

The other decretals are particularly interesting because of their relationship to the regional necessities of a northern country. The pope gives permission to catch fish on Sundays and – during a period of penance with water and bread - allows for some kind of vegetable to replace the bread in those places where it was not available.⁶⁸ The concession to fishing on Sundays was welcomed as a privilege facilitating life in a northern climate and is mentioned as a special grace from the pope by the Frostathingbook,

---

    proveniunt magis volunt consanguineis et heredibus aliis suis secularibus relinquere quam eisdem ecclesiis de quarum bonis fuerant acquisita. Quidam etiam hec, etsi vellent, non possunt implere, quoniam legi vestre contraire noscuntur."
65. Chodorow/Duggan (n.64): „Si autem ea que iure hereditario possidet voluerit ecclesie cuius clericus fuit relinquere, id efficiendi liberam habeat facultatem."
66. For this principle cf. my paper "Die Testierfreiheit in der Geschichte des deutschen Rechts im späten Mittelalter und in der frühen Neuzeit", *ZRG Germ. Abt. 114* (1997) 54-72.
67. WH 833 (= JL 14206) = ed. Chodorow/Duggan (n.61) 155 (no.89): „Sane sacerdotes illi qui vetitas nuptias contrahunt, que non nuptie sed contubernia sunt nuncupanda, post longam penitentiam vitam laudabilem comitantem officio suo restitui poterunt et eius executionem ex indulgentia episcopi sui habere."
68. WH 622 (= JL 14118) = X 2.9.3 + X 5.38.6: „Inde siquidem eo est quod regionem vestram, quae non multis frugibus abundet, et mare, in quo populus maiorem consuevit habere sustentationem, sterilius solito effectum fuisse multorum relationibus cognoscentes, auctoritate B. Petri et nostra indulgemus, ut liceat parochianis vestris diebus dominicis et aliis festis, praeterquam in maioribus anni solennitatibus, si alecia terrae se inclinaverint, eorum captioni ingruente necessitate intendere, ita tamen, quod post factam capturam ecclesiis circumpositis et Christi pauperibus congruam faciant portionem. Si autem illi, qui aliquos dies in pane et aqua ex iniuncta sibi penitentia tenentur peragere, panem, quo vescantur, non habent: leguminibus aut piscibus aut aliis cibariis reficiantur, si necessitas id exposcat, discretione tamen adhibita, quod his non ad delicias, sed ad necessariam solummodo sustentationem utantur."

the famous law book of Norway.[69] In the Frostathingbook we can read that King Magnus Erlingsson, Jarl Erling, and Bishop Eystein had beseeched the pope to allow fishing for herrings on Sundays and that he granted that concession to the people.[70] The correctness of this information is confirmed by the decretal's text. Another decretal by Alexander that I have already mentioned develops some rules for the duration of festivities on feast days in the North, with its variability between extremely long or short days during the year. The pope concedes to Eystein and his bishops the right of discretion to fix the beginning and the end of feast days.[71] These rules formulated for special situations and customs in Norway later became two chapters out of five in the title 'De feriis' in the 'Liber Extra' of Gregory IX in 1234.[72] Norwegian regional canon law so became the model for universal canon law in observing Sundays and feast days in a Christian society.

We also know about some later decretals addressed to Scandinavian bishops by the successors of Alexander III. I only want to mention the decretal sent in 1198 by Pope Innocent III to the archbishop and the chapter of Lund.[73] The pope is giving his authoritative opinion on the question of formalities regarding the transfer of property in real estate to ecclesiastical institutions. Danish law required a ceremony of throwing clods as a sign of transfer; the ceremony is called 'scotatio' by the pope. The pope had been asked if such ceremonies could be accepted by canon law even if they were not known in Roman law. He gives a positive answer to the questioner from Lund by adding to this the distinction that such a ceremony of scotatio should not be considered as a necessary element of a donation to the church. It should be understood as a symbolic act of transfer of property or a symbol of traditio.[74] This decretal of Innocent III is probably the most important

---

69. Cf. R. Meißner: *Norwegisches Recht. Das Rechtsbuch des Frostathings* (= Germanenrechte, Bd. 4, Weimar 1939), 32 (II.26) mentioning the decretal by Alexander III.
70. Meißner (n.69): „auf die Bitte des Königs Magnus und des Jarls Erlingr, seines Vaters, und des Erzbischofs Eysteinn."
71. WH 833 (= JL 14109) = X 2.9.2, ed. Chodorow/Duggan (n.61) 154s. (no.89): „Inde siquidem est quod nos volumus prudentiam vestram certa cognitione tenere quod licet scriptum sit:" de vespera ad vesperam celebrabitis sabbata vestra", festorum principium et finis iuxta eorum qualitatem et iuxta diversarum regionum consuetudinem considerari debent et secundum dierum magnitudinem celebrari."
72. X 2.9.2 and X 2.9.3.
73. Po. 424 = X 1.4.2. The addressee was archbishop Absalon together with the chapter of Lund.
74. Innocentius III. l.c.: „Discretioni vestrae per apostolica scripta mandamus, quatenus donationes eorum, quae sub obtentu consuetudinis claustris, ecclesiis vel quibuslibet locis religionis pie ac provide conferuntur vel etiam sunt collata, faciatis irrevocabiliter observari, cum huiusmodi signum, quod scotatio dicitur, non tam factae donationis, quam traditae possessionis sit evidens argumentum ..."

text allowing toleration of regional customs in canon law - it is placed in the very beginning of the title 'De consuetudine' in the Liber Extra[75] and shows how the challenge of legal customs in Scandinavia influenced the structures of classical canon law.

Manuscripts of Canon Law in Scandinavia in the 13th Century

A survey of the distribution of medieval canon law all over Scandinavia is difficult and almost impossible because of the destructions during the Reformation period. Fragments from manuscripts were used for book covers – an estimate made in 1951 gives the number of 60 000 book covers made from recycled medieval manuscripts in Sweden. This information can be found in Stephan Kuttner's 'Repertorium der Kanonistik' and in Toni Schmid's two articles about Sweden.[76]

The Scandinavian manuscripts of Gratian appear rather late and date from the 13th century. They are usually connected with the later form of the Glossa ordinaria on Gratian, characterized by the supplement of Bartholomaeus Brixiensis to the text of Johannes Teutonicus.[77] This form of the gloss was completed in 1245 – that means that a great number of Gratian manuscripts in Scandinavia date from the second half of the 13th century or from the 14th century. One single manuscript of Copenhagen probably lacks the addition to the Gloss by Bartholomaeus and so it was perhaps written in the first half of the 13th century.[78] Nevertheless Gratian must have already been known in Scandinavia in 1164, as can be proved by the decrees of the Bergen council.

There are also some traces of an acquaintance with early decretist commentaries in Scandinavia. The Historical Institute of Oslo preserves a small fragment of the earliest Summa of Gratian written by his disciple Paucapalea about 1148.[79] In the late 12th and the early 13th centuries Scandinavia might have gotten some information about canon law through French and English centres – not so much from Bologna directly. A

---

75. X 1.4.2 after a text taken from the Register of Gregory I.
76. S. Kuttner: *Repertorium der Kanonistik,* Studi e Testi 71, Città del Vaticano 1937. T. Schmid: „Canon Law on Manuscripts from Medieval Sweden", *Traditio* 7 (1949/51) 444-449; T. Schmid: „Manuscripts of Canon Law from Medieval Sweden", in: S. Kuttner/J.J. Ryan (eds.): Proceedings *of the Second International Congress of Medieval Canon Law* Boston 1963 (E Civitate Vaticana 1965) 93-98.
77. Two manuscripts in Copenhagen: Gl. kgl. S.193 fol. and Thott 160 - cf. Kuttner (n.76) 104.
78. Gl. kgl. S. 194 fol. - cf. Kuttner (n.76) 104, but without autopsy according to the catalogue.
79. Cf. Kuttner (n.76) 126.

fragment of a decretal collection preserved in Oslo and containing English decretals antedating 1198 can prove the acquaintance with English decretal collectors (Fragmentum Asloense).[80]

Another important anonymous commentary on Gratian – the Apparatus "Ecce vicit leo" – written in Paris around 1205, was brought to Sweden and is preserved in a Swedish manuscript as an independent Summa without the Decretum.[81] The Compilationes antiquae spreading the new papal decretal law all over Europe between 1190 and 1234 also came to Scandinavia, usually with the Ordinary Gloss in the margin of the texts. So we can find the 3rd Compilatio – the great collection of Innocent III's legislative work – in a Copenhagen manuscript combined with the standard commentary by Tancred, written about 1220.[82] In the later 13th century canon law must have been known and studied in Scandinavia almost everywhere. The great Codes of the Liber Extra and the Liber Sextus were known and certainly studied, as is shown by many manuscripts.[83] The classical commentaries of canonists during this period reached Scandinavian places too. Let me enumerate a few authors: Innocent IV and his Apparatus, the Summa written by Cardinal Hostiensis, the Speculum of Duranti, the Apparatus written by Goffredus of Trani.[84] These authors wrote the most successful works in the field of canon law during the 13th century; they were read all over Europe and in Scandinavia too. In the first half of the 14th century there was even a Swedish clergyman who wrote a "Summa de ministris et sacramentis ecclesiae". The author was Dean Laurentius of Uppsala – his book is preserved by nine manuscripts in Uppsala and Stockholm.[85]

During the later Middle Ages – in the 14th and 15th centuries – canon law had its greatest influence in Scandinavia when secular codes no longer needed to have a section on Christian law incorporated in them because the legal rules of the church were universally applied by the ecclesiastical courts. Despite some resistance, mainly in the 12th century, there was no permanent opposition against the influence of canon law in the Scandinavian kingdoms. The mutual penetration of canon law and northern secular law could probably be studied in many fields of legal history by historians interested in the common legal heritage of Europe as well as in the Ius proprium of their own countries. As a historian of canon law I can only invite my Scandinavian colleagues to notice also the interrelationship

---

80. For the Fragmentum Asloense see Ch. Lefebvre, Art. Oslo (Fragment d), *Dictionnaire de Droit Canonique VI* (1957) 1180.
81. Cf. Schmid: *Manuscripts of Canon Law* (n.76) 95.
82. MS Copenhagen Gl. kgl. S. 196 fol. - cf. Kuttner (n.76) 359.
83. Schmid: *Canon Law* (n.76) 446; Schmid: *Manuscripts* (n.76) 95.
84. Schmid: *Canon Law* (n.76) 449; Schmid: *Manuscripts* (n.76) 96.
85. Schmid: *Manuscripts* (n.76) 95.

between canon law and your particular legal tradition during at least four centuries of the Middle Age.

THE GERMANIC CHARACTER OF THE OLDEST LAWS OF THE LOW COUNTRIES

Dirk Heirbaut

Introduction[1]

Every legal historian has been influenced by von Savigny and his pupils, the Romanists and the Germanists. For the former, studying legal history was quite easy, as they had at their disposal one of the greatest law codes ever, Justinian's *Corpus Iuris Civilis*. The Germanists, however, had more problems in finding their sources and, therefore, made an extensive study of Nordic laws, their idea being that the Nordic countries at the periphery of Europe had been able to preserve the original character of their laws for a much longer time. In a certain sense, Scandinavia was the Germanists' time machine. This retrogressive method has come under attack, as later scholars have shown that the high and late medieval texts the Germanists were using did not reflect the oldest laws of the Nordic countries, but were influenced by Roman and canon law.[2] Even if one does not agree with these critics of the romantic idea that in Scandinavia the original *Germanentum* is to be found, one should harbour some doubts and, at least, try to find out 'How Nordic the Nordic medieval laws are?'

---

1. G. Sinnaeve and P. Carson have read my text and I am grateful for their efforts in correcting my English. Prof. em. R C. Van Caenegem, after reading my draft, wrote me a long letter, which has made me, to the benefit of this text's readers, clarify my positions, for which I would like to express my sincerest thanks to him.
2. See, inter alia, the articles by Tamm in this book.

Dirk Heirbaut

The Low Countries: A Shared Name as Testimony of a Shared History

This article wants to make a contribution to answering that question by looking at the oldest laws of the Low Countries, i.e. today's Belgium and The Netherlands. In fact, for any comparison with the Nordic countries today, these two, or three if one includes Luxemburg, should come to mind. Like the Nordic countries they have a very extensive cooperation, in the Benelux, an organisation with its own parliament, its own court, and even some Benelux-laws. An indication of the close links between Belgium and The Netherlands is that long before the Schengen treaty, border controls had ceased to exist between these two countries. Like in the Nordic countries, today's closeness is the product of a shared history, in which, at times, the Low Countries were united under one prince. This happened most recently in 1815-1830, in the United Kingdom of the Netherlands. Though there were, in 1815, political motives among the great European powers for bringing this kingdom into life, another consideration was that they had already been united at a much earlier date in history, in the fifteenth and sixteenth centuries.

That unification had brought some major changes, as the divisions of the Carolingian empire had split up the territories that now form Belgium and The Netherlands between France and Germany, the river Scheldt serving as frontier. The German and French kings gradually lost power there, so that in the twelfth century the Low Countries were a patchwork of autonomous principalities, like Flanders, Hainault, Brabant, Namur, Luxembourg, Liège, Holland, Utrecht, Guelderland, and even a kind of farmers' republic, Frisia. Although these territories were united by cultural, economic, linguistic and, sometimes, dynastic ties, they did not coalesce into a larger unit in the twelfth and thirteenth centuries. However, from 1384 onward, the dukes of Burgundy gradually brought many of these territories under their control. The Habsburgs, who, through a marriage to a Burgundian heiress, succeeded the dukes of Burgundy as rulers, finished the process of unification in the sixteenth century. At that time their new 'state' was in humanist circles known as *Belgium*. This Belgium of sixteenth-century scholars was not today's Belgium. It roughly covered the territory of the modern states of Belgium, The Netherlands and Luxembourg and even a part of Northern France. Thus, the term Belgium in the sixteenth century has to be translated as Low Countries. The same is true for its equivalent in Dutch, the vernacular in most of the Low Countries: *Netherlands* (*Nederlanden*), which does, again, not mean today's Netherlands, but the Low Countries (which is in fact the literal meaning of the term Netherlands).

The political unity of the Low Countries did not survive the sixteenth century. Due to religious and other reasons, they revolted against their

Habsburg overlord, Philip II, king of Spain. The North, the so-called Northern Netherlands, achieved independence and came to be known as the United Provinces. The Habsburgs managed to keep the South, the so-called Southern Netherlands. Thereafter, the old name of Belgium was still used for both the North and the South. In the eighteenth century, however, it was almost exclusively used for the South, which, by then, had been from the Spanish to the Austrian Habsburgs. Consequently, when after their brief unification in 1815-1830, North and South split up again, the Latin name, Belgium, or rather its French form, Belgique, was used for the South and the Dutch name was used for the North. However, in spite of all that, both Belgium and Netherlands originally referred to the Low Countries. Thus, even their names show how close these countries are: they share a name, because they share a history.[3]

A Shared History, but not a Shared Legal Historiography

In these circumstances it is evident that historians in Belgium and The Netherlands have also been working together, though this was quite late in happening. In the nineteenth and even for most of the twentieth century, they were more influenced by their times' national realities, like Belgium's Henri Pirenne, who finally gave his country the national history it had so long craved for, than by the shared unity of the past.[4] However, Pirenne's students went in another direction altogether. To them, the canvas of their national histories was the Low Countries, which led to publications like the one from François-Louis Ganshof about the development of cities between Loire and Rhine[5] (thus even expanding the territory of the Low Countries in a way the Burgundain duke Charles the Bold would have liked), or the great masterpiece, the *Algemene Geschiedenis der Nederlanden* (General history of the Netherlands, Netherlands here in their original meaning of North and South, Belgium and The Netherlands; the shorter name is AGN), published from 1949 to 1958.[6] This AGN was so successful that the next generation of historians in Belgium and The Netherlands wanted to write their own AGN, fifteen volumes, published from 1977 to 1983, containing contributions by

---

3. See about this D. HEIRBAUT, "The Belgian legal tradition: does it exist?", in H. BOCKEN and W. DE BONDT (eds.), *Introduction to Belgian Law*, Antwerp, 2001, 1-9.
4. H. PIRENNE, *Histoire de Belgique des origines à nos jours*, Brussels, 1900-1932, 7 vol. and later editions.
5. E.g. F.-L. GANSHOF, *Over stadsontwikkeling tusschen Loire en Rijn gedurende de middeleeuwen*, Antwerp, 1941 (French translation, 1943; second edition, 1944).
6. VAN HOUTTE, J., NIERMEYER, J., PRESSER, J. e.a. (eds.), *Algemene geschiedenis der Nederlanden*, Zeist, 1949-1958, 12 vol.

about 400 scholars.[7] The whole project was so grandiose that it ruined the publisher, but even so there could no longer be any doubt about the fact that Belgium and The Netherlands have a shared history. Some universities even expressed this in the history curriculum, replacing national Belgian or Dutch history by 'History of the Netherlands' (once again in its original meaning of Northern and Southern Netherlands). All this does not mean that there is no historiography of Belgium and The Netherlands, or parts of them, separately, but that there is also a very strong tendency amongst historians to look at the Low Countries as a unity, something which may show up in very surprising ways. For example, Belgium's François-Louis Ganshof is well-known for his classic account of feudalism, *Qu'est-ce que la féodalité*. In the introduction to this work he states that the heartland of feudalism is to be found between Loire and Rhine, and most of all in Flanders and Lotharingia, the Low Countries.[8]

As Ganshof's example shows, legal historians have also been inspired by the enthusiasm for the old Netherlands, so much, that a 'national' legal history congress, like in France, Germany or the United Kingdom, does not exist. Instead, Belgian and Dutch legal historians are united by the *Belgisch-Nederlandse Rechtshistorische Dagen* (Belgian-Dutch Legal History Days). Legal history reviews, like the *Tijdschrift voor rechtsgeschiedenis* (Legal History Review) are also Belgian-Dutch and the same can be said of many organisations, the most remarkable here being the *Société des anciens droits des pays picards, flamands et wallons*, which brings together legal historians from Belgium, The Netherlands and Northern France.

Yet, these close links have somehow failed to result in a common historiography, as Belgian and Dutch legal historians do not write about the Low Countries in general, but about Belgium and The Netherlands separately. Likewise, the course of non-Roman legal history has never been called 'Legal history of the Low Countries', but, in so far as a reference to a certain territory was part of its name, *Oud-vaderlands recht* (Old national law). The division in historiography also becomes clear in the new AGN, where Belgian and Dutch legal historians have written separate articles about law and institutions in the Middle Ages.[9]

---

7. BLOK, D., PREVENIER, W., ROORDA, D. e.a. (eds.), *Algemene geschiedenis der Nederlanden*, Haarlem, 1977-1983, 15 vol.
8. F.-L. GANSHOF, *Qu'est-ce que la féodalité*, Paris, 1982, 15.
9. E.g. in vol III: D. VAN DEN AUWEELE, "De evolutie van het recht in het Zuiden. 12de-14de eeuw", 145-163; T. DE SMIDT, "De rechtsbronnen in het Noorden tot de 14de eeuw", 135-144.

A Difference in the Influence of Germanist Ideas

The division between Belgium and The Netherlands in the study of legal history is due to many factors, among them the tenacity of old national ideas, but also the influence of their legal education. Most leading legal historians in the Benelux were and are lawyers, and lawyers have been and are still trained differently in Belgium and The Netherlands. Both became part of France under Napoleon (The Netherlands some years later than Belgium), and the Napoleonic codes became law there. Their subsequent history, however, was very different. Belgium's elite was French-speaking and so were its lawyers. Therefore, at its worst, the French character of Belgium's laws was only a minor inconvenience. Belgian lawyers went so far in their fidelity to the Napoleonic code that it is not exaggerated to say that Belgium remained more faithful to Napoleon than France itself, at least until the 1949 amendment of the text of the 'Belgian' Civil Code. Henceforward, in this lawbook the country would no longer be called France but Belgium and likewise its head of state was no longer called emperor but king, finally recognising that Belgium had been an independent kingdom under its own king since independence in 1830, and not a French province.[10] Such subservience to France was not to be found in The Netherlands, where Dutch lawyers remembered that their country had a great tradition of legal scholarship, and gradually developed their own law, a process culminating in the 1992 *Nieuw Burgerlijk Wetboek* (New Civil Code), one of the major law texts of our time.[11] In doing so they were greatly influenced by the other great lawyers of Europe, their German neighbours. In short, whereas Belgian legal historians had more of a French view of law, the Dutch were more German.

In terms of legal history, this means that the German Historical School had little or no influence in Belgium, but was an important factor in The Netherlands.[12] Belgian legal historians have not bothered much about any division between Romanists and Germanists, the division of the *Savigny Zeitschrift* in Romanist, Germanist and canonist sections, being something of a source of amusement to them. In so far as the old non-Roman law was studied, this was largely free of any ideological component or animosity

---

10. See D. HEIRBAUT, "L'émancipation tardive d'une pupille de la nation française. L'histoire du droit belge aux 19ème et 20ème siècles", in A. WIJFFELS (ed.). *Le Code civil* (forthcoming).
11. See T. VEEN, '*En voor berisping is hier ruime stof*'. *Over codificatie van het burgerlijk recht, legistische rechtsbeschouwing en herziening van het Nederlandse privaatrecht*, Amsterdam, Cabeljauwpers, 2001.
12. See e.g. J. VAN DEN BROECK, "Het Burgerlijk Wetboek en de invloed van de Duitse rechtshistorische school in België tijdens de 19de eeuw", in: *Liber amicorum John Gilissen*, Antwerp, 1983, 417-425.

towards the professors of Roman law. That Belgian legal historians were mostly uncluttered by Germanist ideas has sometimes been to the good. For example, they like to point out that in vernacular Dutch in the Southern Netherlands the word *weer* (the *Gewere, saisine* of Germanist literature) has been absent.[13]

In The Netherlands, however, the distinction Romanists-Germanists was much more important, the course on national legal history being the preserve of the Germanists and Roman law of the Romanists. Thus, to a lesser extent, the Germanist-Romanist fight was also present in Dutch law faculties. Due to the pre-war differences in attitude between Dutch and Belgian legal historians, World War II affected them in different ways. In Belgium nothing much changed because of the war, but in The Netherlands it led, in the long run, to a weakening of the Germanists. Some of them had been on the wrong side during the war and lost their chairs and, in general, Germanism gradually lost its appeal, the result being that, nowadays, there is no-one among the active legal history professors in The Netherlands who is specialised in medieval non-Roman law. This, combined with the lack of enthusiasm for Germanism in Belgium from the start, has led to the strange fact that the earliest laws of the Low Countries, i.e. before 1000, have largely been neglected since the 1960's, when Immink was still writing regularly about Germanic law.[14] A question like *How Nordic are the Nordic medieval laws?* has not been asked for the Low Countries because no-one seems to be interested. The study of the oldest laws of the Low Countries is, for now, completely out of fashion.[15]

---

13. GODDING, P., *Le droit privé dans les Pays-Bas méridionaux du 12e au 18e siècle*, Brussels, 1987, 227.
14. See e.g. P. IMMINK, *Verspreide geschriften*, Groningen, 1967; P. IMMINK, *De wording van staat en souvereiniteit in de middeleeuwen*, Groningen, 1969.
15. It is significant that in F. FELDBRUGGE (ed.), *The law's beginnings*, Leyden, 2003 no article deals with 'Germanic' law, even though this book was written in the Netherlands. (There was, however, an article about Frisian law, which proves the point to be made in the next paragraph.) A recent book about pre-Christian culture in the Netherlands has an article about law (M. DE BRUIJN, 'Voetangels en klemmen: inheems en uitheems, continuïteit en discontinuïteit in de ontwikkeling van het Nederlandse recht', in STROUKEN, I. and RIETER, O. (eds.), *Inheemse erfenis. Continuïteit en discontinuïteit in de geschiedenis*, Utrecht, 2003, 41-46), but the author just indicates some problems in trying to study the subject, so that his article is about the dangers of anachronisms, and not about pre-Christian law in the Netherlands. However, there is some research about early medieval law by Dutch scholars, but it is not really interested in 'regional' history and, most of all, legal historians are not welcome to it (see e.g. the Leyden workshop on May, the 1st, 2004 about *Carolingian legal culture-the evidence of Leiden BPL 114/Paris BnF 4629*, for which in the best tradition of authors like Davies and Fouracre, no legal historians had been invited.)

The Frisian Exception

It is very remarkable that, contrary to the general trend, there has been something of a renaissance in the study of Frisian law (in The Netherlands and in Germany),[16] but Frisia (not to be confused with the actual Dutch province of *Friesland*, which is much smaller than the area from near Bruges to Denmark where Frisians were found in Carolingian times) is in a category of its own. The Frisians had their own law text in the Carolingian era, the *Lex Frisionum*, but unlike all the other Carolingian tribal laws, it is a preparatory document, meaning containing a lot of material which should have disappeared from the final version approved by Charlemagne. In later times too, Frisia was very rich in legal sources. Several documents from the twelfth to the sixteenth century survive which sometimes give us a glimpse into earlier times (e.g. references to persons kidnapped by the Vikings). Another element that sets Frisia apart, is that no medieval prince was able effectively to extend his power over this territory, which in theory meant that Frisia depended directly from the emperor of the Romans; in practice, that it was on its own. Therefore, Frisia shows what the rest of the Low Countries might have been without territorial princes and the like.

The special situation of Frisia is not always a boon to the legal historian. A lot of research has been done about Frisian legal texts, but most of the time by scholars who were more interested in Frisia and the Frisian language than in law. Consequently, many publications are written by specialists of Frisian studies for their fellows, not for legal historians.[17] The study of Frisian law seems to have taken off on its own, with little regard for the general study of legal history in the Low Countries, Frisian specialists not doing much for communicating the results of their research to other legal historians, nor these really being interested therein. Another problem is the sources. Frisian law in the high and later Middle Ages took its respectability from the myth that the Frisians had received their law from Charlemagne,[18] which was not such a bad idea if one thinks of the Lex Frisionum, but which was definitely not true for the later texts. The impression an outsider has is that sometimes specialists of Frisian law seem to follow this myth and project their texts further back in time than they should. Moreover, the general idea that Frisia remained more primitive and thus a good indicator of what a more pristine law of the Low Countries should have been, is to be rejected, as, certainly in Carolingian times, Frisia was a prosperous and rich region because of its trade. In short, Frisia deserves to be studied on its own, for its own merits. Even so, this article

---

16. See e.g. N. ALGRA, *Oudfries recht 800-1256*, Leeuwarden, 2000.
17. See for an example ALGRA, *Oudfries recht*, 5.
18. ALGRA, *Oudfries recht*, 16.

will sometimes mention Frisian law, without any claims whatsoever to being complete in this regard and it should be stressed that anyone who wants to take up the study of Germanic law could do worse than start in Frisia.[19] In fact, he would have a predecessor of note. Rudolf His, well-known from his book *Das Strafrecht des deutschen Mittelalters*, started his career by studying Frisia.[20]

The Problem of Finding the Oldest Laws of the Low Countries

Even if legal historians of the Low Countries have done little, if any, research about their oldest 'Germanic' laws, they wrote about it in their general handbooks or referred to it in studies about younger law. Most of the time, written sources were lacking and archaeology has not been much of a help either, legal historians of the Low Countries never having been much interested in the valuable insights archeology could offer them. Among the few written sources were Tacitus' *Germania* and the *Leges nationum germanicarum* as written down in the early Middle Ages. However, the first is not that reliable a source, because, as he wrote for a Roman public, his account of the Germanic tribes may in the end tell us more about Roman ideals than about Germanic realities.[21] Likewise the *Leges nationum germanicarum* may reflect certain princely ideals better than Germanic practices.[22] Moreover, for these one should take into account that only five of them can have had any influence in the Low Countries: the *Lex Salica*, the *Ewa ad Amorem*, the *Lex Saxonum*, the *Lex Frisionum* and the *Lex Ribuaria*. The impact of the latter though, is disputed and the *Lex Saxonum* can only have had importance for a small part of the Low Countries. However, the most important problem is the influence of vulgar Roman law. Although, there can be no doubt that some parts of the *leges* have not been 'corrupted' by vulgar Roman law (for example, the Malberg glosses in the *Lex Salica*), the latter has been very influential. Even the well-

---

19. There is already a good article about traces of old Germanic law in the Lex Frisionum: R. TIMMER, "Restanten van Oud-Germaans recht in de Lex Frisionum", *Pro Memorie*, II, 2000, 17-45.
20. R. HIS, *Das Strafrecht der Friesen im Mittelalter*, Leipzig, 1901.
21. See e.g. S. FANNING, "Tacitus, Beowulf and the comitatus", *Haskins society journal*, IX, 1997, 17-38; A. LUND, "Zur Germanenbegriff bei Tacitus", in H. BECK (ed.), *Germanenprobleme aus heutiger Sicht*, Berlin, 1986, 53-87; KROESCHELL, K., "'Recht', in 'Germanen, Germania, Germanische Altertumskunde", in *Reallexikon der Germanischen Altertumskunde*, XI, Berlin, 1998, 399-400.
22. Cf. P. WORMALD, *The Making of English Law: King Alfred to the Twelfth Century*, I, *Legislation and its Limits*, Oxford, 2001.

know exclusion of daughters from the inheritance of *terra Salica*, once seen as being typically Germanic, or at least typical for the Franks, has now been unmasked by Kroeschell[23] and Poly[24] as a rule of Roman generals for their Germanic soldiers. In these circumstances, new detailed research of the sources is needed to separate 'original' Germanic law from vulgar Roman law in the *leges*.

Because it is so hard to sift out the undisputedly Germanic elements from the *leges*, the easiest way for legal historians of the Low Countries of getting to know their oldest laws is to consult general studies of Germanic law and assume that, as the inhabitants of the Low Countries were, after the great invasions, Germanic, their law was the Germanic law set forth in these great books.[25] Problems for this approach now abound. First of all, the concept 'Germanic' itself has come under attack. Anyone browsing through current literature about the subject[26] can be certain only about the fact that there are no certainties anymore. For example, the tribes called Germanic in historical documents were, by the definitions of some modern scholars, not Germanic at all.[27] Concepts once very firmly entrenched in historiography like *Gefolgschaft*, *Sippe*, *Treue*, *Gemeinfreie*, *Friedlosigkeit* and so on are now being seen as constructs of the nineteenth century.[28] In their place has come the idea that, as soon as we have texts about 'Germanic' law, it is already influenced by Christian notions and vulgar Roman law. To the despair of the legal historian who wants some clarity, these new theories are

---

23. K. KROESCHELL, "Söhne und Töchter im germanischen Erbrecht", in G. LANDWEHR (ed.). *Studien zu den germanischen Volksrechten. Gedächtnisschrift für W. Ebel*, Frankfurt, 1982, 87-116.
24. J.-P. POLY, "Terra Salica. De la société franque à la société féodale: continuïté et discontinuïté", in *Les origines de la féodalité. Hommage à Claudio Sanchez Albornoz*, Madrid, 2000, 182-196.
25. See e.g. E. VAN DER HEIJDEN and B. HERMESDORF, *Aantekeningen bij de geschiedenis van het oude vaderlandse recht*, Nijmegen, 1968. For a more cautious attitude, see P. GERBENZON and N. ALGRA, *Voortgangh des rechtes. De ontwikkeling van het Nederlandse recht tegen de achtergrond van de Westeuropese cultuur*, Groningen, 1972, 35.
26. For an excellent introduction, see 'Germanen, Germania, Germanische Altertumskunde', in *Reallexikon der Germanischen Altertumskunde*, XI, Berlin, 1998, 181-438; W. POHL, *Die Germanen*, Munich, 2000.
27. Several articles about this can be found in H. BECK (ed.), *Germanenprobleme aus heutiger Sicht*, Berlin, 1986.
28. See e.g. K. KROESCHELL, "Germanisches Recht als Forschungsproblem", in K. KROESCHELL (ed.). *Festschrift für Hans Thieme zu seinem 80. Geburtstag*, Sigmaringen, 1986, 3-19; K. KROESCHELL, "Recht", 403-406; H. NEHLSEN, "Entstehung des öffentlichen Strafrechts bei den Germanischen Stammen", in K. KROESCHELL (ed.). *Gerichtslauben-Vorträge. Freiburger Festkolloquium zum fünfundsiebzigsten Geburtstag von Hans Thieme*, Sigmaringen, 1983, 7-16.

not undisputed either. What should one make of, for example, the influence of vulgar Roman law on the laws of the Germanic tribes, when specialists of post-classical Roman law are trying to show that Roman law in that era was less vulgar than Levy, its great specialist, once thought.[29] Legal historians of the Low Countries have not taken part in these debates, and these have influenced them little with the exception of the discussion about the origins of the *marken* (marca, commons) of which the Germanic origin was already disputed in French literature in the nineteenth century.[30] Thus, the new critical theories about Germanic law have had an effect on legal historians in the Low Countries, only by driving them away from the study of their oldest laws, because they do not want to enter this minefield. Instead of stimulating research into old law, the new debates have killed it in the cradle.

Regressive Legal History: Some Lessons from the Low Countries

Yet, all this does not mean that for an answer to the question 'How Nordic are the Nordic medieval laws?' the early legal history of the Low Countries is useless, as historians there have been devoting a lot of time and effort to their study of high and late medieval laws. In doing so they have, at times, made speculations about the origin and antiquity of the rules they studied and some results of that research can be valuable for anyone studying the Nordic medieval laws. One prelimary remark has to be made. It is absurd to speak of the law of the Low Countries, as this was one of the regions in Europe where the splintering of customary law had gone to the extreme. In the fifteenth and sixteenth centuries there were about six hundred different customary legal systems in the Low Countries.[31] If one takes into account that this was the situation after some mechanisms of unification had already been at work for centuries, one can only guess how much higher this number may have been in the high Middle Ages. This diversity makes it impossible for any statement about customary law in the Low Countries to be true in all of its regions and at all times.

---

29. A doctoral thesis about this is being prepared by S. Vandendriessche (Frankfurt).
30. A. DE BLECOURT and H. FISCHER, *Kort begrip van het oud-vaderlands burgerlijk recht*, Groningen, 1967, 116-117.
31. GILISSEN, J., *Historische inleiding tot het recht*, Antwerp, 1981, 282.

Customary Law is not the Same as Old Law

The traditional assumption underlying research into old law anywhere is that customary law is traditional.[32] Hence, when a historian knows a custom existed in the high or late Middle Ages, he can without any trouble at all project it back in time, like the Germanists did by using high or late medieval Scandinavian law texts as a source of early Germanic practices. Research in the Low Countries has shown that customary law is anything but unchanging. An example of that can be found in Flemish feudal law.[33]

In inheritance law it was evident that the eldest son should get the lion's share and that his siblings would have to be satisfied with less. That way, the riches and power of the family head could be assured for yet another generation. This general principle was the same all over Flanders, but it was realised in different ways:

- in central and northern Dutch-speaking Crown Flanders (i.e. the part of Flanders that was a French fief): the so-called *trientation*: the second son could demand a third of the fiefs from the eldest, but in turn had to hand over his non-feudal inheritance, the third son could then ask a third of that third from the second, if he turned over his share of the non-feudal goods and so on.

- in Aalst and Waas: the younger children received one third of the fiefs, in which they shared equally, and could keep all their non-feudal goods.

- in Lille and Tournai: if there were no daughters and the inheritance contained more than one fief, the eldest had the first choice of the fiefs, thereafter the second son could chose a fief and so on. In other cases, the younger children received a fifth of the feudal inheritance, which they had to share equally.

- Cassel, Bailleul, Warneton, Douai, Orchies: the younger children received a fifth of the fiefs which they had to share equally.

- Ronse: absolute primogeniture. The younger children get nothing.

- Dendermonde: either a system comparable with the one in Aalst and Waas or another in which all fiefs are equally divided among all children, including the eldest, who does homage for the fiefs to the lord, but receives no homage from his siblings (so-called *parage sans hommage*).

---

32. Cf. D. HEIRBAUT, "Europe and the people without legal history: on the need for a general history of non-European law", *Tijdschrift voor rechtsgeschiedenis*, LXVIII, 2000, 276.

33. Studied in D. HEIRBAUT, *Over heren, vazallen en graven. Het persoonlijk leenrecht in Vlaanderen, ca. 1000-1305*, Brussels, 1997; D. HEIRBAUT, *Over lenen en families. Een studie over de vroegste geschiedenis van het zakelijk leenrecht in het graafschap Vlaanderen (ca. 1000-1305)*, Brussels, 2000; R. OPSOMMER, *'Omme dat leengoed es thoochste dinc van der weerelt.' Het leenrecht in Vlaanderen in de 14de en 15de eeuw*, Brussels, 1995, 2 vol.

If one should follow Eduard Maurits Meijers, inheritance law is the most conservative part of the law and nowhere is that more visible than in feudal inheritance law in which, according to Meijers in a book about Western Flemish inheritance law, the old Germanic law still lived on.[34] However, the reality is very different. Feudal inheritance law has no traces of old Germanic law, and it was anything but conservative. In fact, research of the sources shows a lot of evolution. Feudal law only broke through in Flanders around 1000. At that time, feudal inheritance law gave all the fiefs to the eldest son. This changed after the middle of the twelfth century: absolute primogeniture was replaced by a vaguer principle which laid upon the eldest son the obligation to provide, one way or another, for his younger siblings. Only at the end of the thirteenth century this vague rule received more precise formulations in the rules mentioned above. Even these were not stable, as some of them already underwent transformation in the next thirty years. For example, the rule that the younger children received a fifth was originally meant to be applied only once in the history of a fief, but already in the middle of the fourteenth century this rule was changed to 'once in every generation'.[35]

In short, what this shows is that, if anything, customary law was ever changing, adapting itself to new circumstances. Other examples of this can be given, from the Low Countries, but also from studies of African law.[36] They all show the fallacy of the idea that customary means traditional. This is in fact what critics of the Germanists who used medieval Scandinavian laws as a window into ancient Germanic law, have always said. The data from the Low Countries are just one more additional argument for their theories.

'Not-Roman' does not necessarily Equal 'Germanic'

An easy way of finding Germanic traces in later medieval law used to be discarding anything influenced by learned law: if it is not Roman or canon law, it has to be Germanic. In the legal history of the Low Countries this 'method' received a death-blow in some studies of, once again, E. M. Meijers, though not in the way he intended. Meijers and scholars of his generation, like Jean Yver,[37] were fascinated by the 'customary geography'

---

34. MEIJERS, E., *Het Ligurische erfrecht in de Nederlanden*, II, Haarlem, 1932, 30.
35. D. HEIRBAUT, "Weduwen, erfgenamen en lenen. Het feodale erf- en huwelijksvermogensrecht in Vlaanderen (1000-1300)", in *Jaarboek voor middeleeuwse geschiedenis*, I, 1998, 7-26.
36. HEIRBAUT, "Non-European law", 276.
37. J. YVER, "Les deux groupes de coutumes du Nord", in *Revue du Nord*, XXXV, 1953, 197-220; XXXVI, 1954, 5-36.

of the Low Countries and Northern France.[38] These regions had lots of customary legal systems, but this diversity hid some common characteristics. Yver distinguished two groups of customs, the Flemish, where the interests of the larger family group dominated inheritance law, and the Picard-Walloon customs, in which the couple was more important than the relatives. Yver was right in making these distinctions, but failed in finding a convincing explanation, as he thought they were determined by the linguistic frontier between Dutch- and French-speaking peoples, which they clearly were not.

Yver had been influenced by Meijers[39] (it is a tribute to Meijers's scholarship that the Frenchman Yver learned Dutch so that he could read Meijers's books), who had gone much further in bringing together local customs and explaining their similarities. Meijers was convinced that regions as diverse and far-flung as the high valleys of Switzerland and Austria, Brittany, the Basque lands, Southern Holland, Zealand, Dutch-speaking Flanders, northern Artois and western Brabant shared some common principles about inheritance law: relatives in the ascending line could only inherit, if there were no survivors in a collateral line; inheritance by right of representation was very generally applied and, when a person died without issue or siblings, his goods reverted to the lineage from whom he had inherited them.

Meijers deemed that these principles were not Roman, not even Germanic or Celtic, but went back to a pre-Celtic, pre-Germanic law, which he called 'Ligurian' (this name being less important than the 'pre-everything else' character it should imply). This Ligurian law was best preserved among the serfs, the oppressed population, whereas the law of the nobility was, according to Meijers, Germanic. (At the end of one of his books he relates the story of a young wife in Western Flanders, who was scorned by her mother in law for having hair like the ravens. Meijers saw that as an indication of the survival of ethnic distinctions between his dark haired Ligurians and the fair haired Germanic invaders, and thus as a slur upon the nobility of the daughter in law.[40] At the time he wrote this, Meijers did not realise that his own ethnic origin would put him in a camp, an experience which he, unlike the heroin of his story,[41] managed to survive.) That the law of the nobility was more recent than Meijers thought has already been shown. His theories about the former have also been discarded. His critics,

---

38. See about the 'customary geography' of the Low Countries and Northern France the article by P. Godding in *Sartoniana*, XVI, 2003 (forthcoming).
39. E. MEIJERS, *Het Ligurische erfrecht in de Nederlanden*, Haarlem, 1929-1936, 3 vol.
40. MEIJERS, *Ligurische erfrecht*, II, 107-108.
41. She was killed by her in-laws (DROGO OF BERGUES, *Vita Godeliph*, ed. N. HUYGHEBAERT and S. GYSELEN, Tielt, 1982).

like John Gilissen[42] or Robert Jacob,[43] have been able to prove that the non-noble inheritance law he found in the high and later Middle Ages was formed in the tenth to twelfth centuries. Thus, Meijers was right in stating that non-Roman does not equal Germanic, but he was wrong in seeing in this an indication of an even older, instead of a much younger law.

None of Meijers's colleagues, in his time or later, accepted his theories, though he was greatly admired and is, deservedly, still seen as the greatest twentieth-century jurist of The Netherlands.[44] (At the end of his life, he single-handedly wrote about one half of the New Dutch Civil Code in seven years, whereas it took his successors almost four decades to complete it.) It may be, however, that his idea of a pre-Celtic, pre-Germanic law is less absurd than it seemed to his contemporaries during the interbellum. A few years after Meijers's death, from 1959 on, Hans Kuhn started to defend the idea of a Northwestern Block, an area from the Somme to the Weser in which not a Celtic or a Germanic, but another Indo-European language had been spoken. In the Northwestern Block germanisation was only a later phenomenon.[45] Kuhn's theories are not undisputed,[46] but if one is willing to follow him and allow for a pre-Celtic, pre-Germanic language, which left some traces, why not allow also for the possibility that this Northwestern Block may have left some traces in law? So far, however, no evidence of that has been found, but honesty insists that Meijers may be owed something of an apology. After all, his ideas were not that farfetched.

Not-Roman can be an Original Creation of the Middle Ages Without Canon Influences

Not-Roman in Meijers's story was meant by him to be prehistoric, but it turned out to be high medieval (i.e. it came into existence between 1000 and 1300). In many cases these original creations of the Middle Ages turn out to be less original than was first assumed. Not-Roman in many cases seems to

---

42. See e.g. J. GILISSEN, *Historische inleiding*, 632.
43. R. JACOB, *Les structures patrimoniales de la conjugalité au moyen âge dans la France du Nord. Essai d'histoire comparée des époux nobles et roturiers dans les pays du groupe de coutume 'picard-wallon'*, Paris, 1984, 7 vol. (unpublished doctoral thesis, Paris IV).
44. See the special issue of the *Weekblad voor privaatrecht, notariaat en registratie* to commemorate the centennial of his birth (*WPNR*, CXI, 1980, 13-120).
45. For the name 'Nordwestblock', see H. KUHN, "Das Zeugnis des Namen", in R. HAMANN, G. KOSSACK and H. KUHN (eds.). *Völker zwischen Germanen und Kelten*, Neumünster, 1962, 105-128).
46. W. MEID, "Hans Kuhns "Nordwestblock"-Hypothese. Zur problematik der "Völker zwischen Germanen und Kelten" ", in BECK, H. (ed.), *Germanenprobleme in heutiger Sicht*, Berlin, 1986, 183-211.

mean only 'not derived from the Corpus Iuris Civilis or the learned law based upon it'. However, there is also vulgar Roman law and canon law. Late Roman law sometimes had an impact. In fact, in French historiography a few authors even claim that Roman patterns were influential until about the year 1000, when they were swept away by the feudal revolution.[47] This theory seems to have no adherents in the Low Countries,[48] and legal historians there refer only very exceptionally to vulgar Roman law. It is different with the influence of the Church, which has found more recognition. For example, in the South of the Low Countries, when ordeals lost their appeal, sometimes juries were used as an alternative, for which the model had been the *testes synodales* of canon law.[49]

However, it is not always clear whether something has been touched by Christianity or not. A case in point is the so-called *zeventuig* ('seven-witnesses'), another alternative for the ordeals. A group of seven upstanding persons had to examine the facts and their findings were binding for the judges. The number seven may be biblical in origin, but another explanation is also possible. The seven were originally twelve, but that meant that seven, the smallest possible majority, was enough.[50] One should be a bit cautious here. The pitfall is that vulgar Roman law and canon law, or at least the Bible, are better known to legal historians than contemporary legal practices, and, therefore, more available for an explanation. One should also not forget that sometimes popular practices influenced the Church and not the other way round. An example of this is the so-called old-Germanic system for determining kinship. In some regions of the Low Countries this system led to including in the family only persons related within the fourth canonical degree. Thus, only they could inherit or share in the *wergeld*. One might be inclined to see a canon influence here, as the Church from 1215 considered only marriages within the fourth canon degree to be incestuous, i.e. the family was limited to the persons related within the fourth canon degree. However, this was influenced by the so-called 'old-Germanic' system which limited the family to persons related in the third 'degree', the equivalent in that system of the fourth canon degree.[51]

---

47. See e.g. J.-P. POLY and E. BOURNAZEL, *La mutation féodale, Xe-XIIe siècles*, Paris, 2004.
48. See however for a neighbouring region R. FOSSIER, *La terre et les hommes en Picardie jusqu'à la fin du XIIIe siècle*, Paris, 1968, 2 vol.
49. LAMBRECHT, D., *De parochiale synode in het oude bisdom Doornik gesitueerd in de Europese ontwikkeling. 11de eeuw-1559*, Brussels, 1984.
50. Cf. ALGRA, *Oudfries recht*, 208.
51. HEIRBAUT, *Over lenen en families*, 92-93.

In many cases, canon law influence should be excluded. The best example of that is the attitude towards bastardy.[52] The medieval Church wanted to discriminate against bastards for moral - they were born out of wedlock -, and financial reasons (as a bastard could not inherit, there were more chances that a family died out, so that its last scion would be likely to make a gift to a church). Contrary to this, there was a widespread rule in the Low Countries stating: *Moeder maakt geen bastaard* (A mother does not 'make', i.e. procreate, a bastard). This did not mean that, unlike their sisters elsewhere in Europe (except for Scandinavia, where a like rule existed; something which needs further exploration), women in the Low Countries were so virtuous that they had no sex outside marriage, but only that, when they had, bastardy did not bar their children born out of wedlock from inheriting from their mothers or even the latter's relatives. One can hardly imagine such a rule having been to the liking of the medieval Church. In this case, an older notion successfully resisted, up to a point, clerical ideas. In general, as far as landed property was concerned, the Church could hardly influence the evolution of the law. The supreme principle seems to have been the protection of the interests of the couple or the larger kin group, but not the interests of the Church.[53] Even when the testament resurfaced in the thirteenth century law of the Low Countries, it could only to a very limited extent be used to transfer landed property, the only property that really mattered, to others than one's lawful heirs.[54]

If not the Church, what was then the major factor for creating original rules in the Middle Ages in the Low Countries? Princes and courts seem to have been the major agents of legal change. If one looks for borders influencing the customary geography of the Low Countries, it turns out that most of them, like for example the linguistic border between Dutch and French, or the political border between France and the Empire, had little or no impact. (This becomes very clear when one consults the maps at the back of Philippe Godding's book about private law in the Southern Low Countries).[55] Political divisions between the principalities seem to have been more important, which, once again, shows that many legal rules were quite recent, as the principalities are post-Carolingian.[56] However, the political divisions do not explain everything and an even more important factor were the courts within the principalities. The diversity of rules about the share of a feudal inheritance the younger children received in Flanders

---

52. See for an extensive study, M. CARLIER, *Kinderen van de minne? Bastaarden in het vijftiende-eeuwse Vlaanderen*, Brussels, 2001.
53. D. HEIRBAUT, *Europese juristen en oud recht*, Ghent, 2000, 201.
54. GODDING, *Le droit privé*, 393-398.
55. GODDING, *Le droit privé*, 569-582.
56. See the article by P. GODDING in *Sartoniana*, XVI, 2003 (forthcoming).

illustrates this very well. This diversity of legal rules came into existence one generation after local feudal courts took over the competence for inheritance disputes from a central feudal court.[57] That courts were a major factor in the development of customary law should not surprise us as, after all, a custom only comes to life in a court.

Sometimes Older Tribal Differences May have Left Traces
Political differences or the influence of courts apart, sometimes older tribal divisions may have left traces. One can, for example, think of the procedures used for transferring rights in land. The *effestucatio* in which a straw was used to symbolise the land, is seen as being typical for the regions where Franks settled, although that should not be exaggerated, as it can sometimes be found in non-Frankish regions.[58] Also in the organisation of the courts one can at times see the differences between Frankish and Frisian origins at work. The typically Frisian *asega*, a specialist of the law who proposed a judgement to the court, can also be found in the North of Holland, but not in the South. The difference Frankish-Frisian also is evident in the division of the money awarded to the relatives of victims of murder or manslaughter, and the same holds for the computation of consanguinity.[59]

Most of the time the influence of older tribal origins can be suspected, but not really proven and in many cases has to be discounted. An example is the well-known distinction in the inheritance law of the county of Holland between *schependomsrecht* and *aasdomsrecht*, terms which refer to courts either composed of *scabini*, who held their function for a certain time and thus were more knowledgeable about the law, or of persons chosen ad hoc, 'neighbours', who were not so familiar with the law and therefore were advised by an *asega*. The *schependomsrecht* is to be found in Holland south of the Yssel, the *aasdomsrecht* north of it. Their main difference is the importance they attach to the origin of the goods. In the *aasdomsrecht* it does not matter: the nearest relative ('nearest blood') inherits, regardless of the origin of the goods. In the *schependomsrecht* the goods revert to the lineage from whom the deceased had inherited. As *schependomsrecht* and *aasdomsrecht* appear together with the Frankish *scabini* or the Frisian *asega*, it is easy to think of an ethnic origin for this distinction. An inconvenience then is that the *schependomsrecht* belongs to Meijers's

---

57. HEIRBAUT, *Over lenen en families*, 81-87.
58. DE BLECOURT and FISCHER, *Oud-vaderlands burgerlijk recht*, 155-156.
59. S. FOCKEMA ANDREAE, "Ueber den Ursprung der niederländischen Rechte mit Rücksicht auf ihre Stammeszugehörigkeit", in S. FOCKEMA ANDREAE (ed.). *Bijdragen tot de Nederlandsche rechtsgeschiedenis*, V, Haarlem, 1914, 320-337.

'Ligurian' laws, which are believed to go back no further than the tenth to twelfth centuries.[60]

The South-North Axis: From Progressive to Conservative

Change in the laws and institutions of the Low Countries during the high and late Middle Ages seems to have run more or less along a South-North axis. New rules and institutions came earlier and developed faster in the South. The county of Flanders, close to France and having some of the greatest cities in Europe, was the forerunner, whereas some northern territories, like Drenthe, were rather backward. An example of this is the composition of the courts, where Flanders was the first in ensuring more professionalisation and the others lagged behind.[61] Another example is the spread of legal rules. Flanders had a great impact on the *keuren* (law charters) of Zealand in the thirteenth century.[62] This influence from the South did not always start in Flanders. The great success of the city law of Louvain, which spread to other cities in the duchy of Brabant in the twelfth and thirteenth centuries, is well-known. From one of these, Den Bosch ('s Hertogenbosch, i.e. the duke's forest) it was exported to Haarlem in Holland, and subsequently to lots of other cities in Holland.[63] The South-North axis is not always at work. The Flemish cities, which generally had a very progressive law, seem to have preserved ordeals longer in their city laws than the cities of Holland.[64] In general, however, southern means more progressive. This suggests that, for any research into the oldest laws of the Low Countries, the northern regions may offer a better starting point than the southern, though this can only be proven by more detailed research

Stable v. Unstable

Change and conservation are not only determined by geography, but also by the field of law. Some areas were more stable than others. In public law changes came very rapidly, as already in the early Middle Ages many had

---

60. DE SMIDT, *Rechtsbronnen*, 143-144.
61. Cf. D. LAMBRECHT and J. VAN ROMPAEY, "De staatsinstellingen in het Zuiden van de 11de tot de 14de eeuw", in *Algemene geschiedenis der Nederlanden*, III, Haarlem, 1982, 77-134; P. VAN PETEGHEM, "La justice populaire médiévale aux Pays-Bas septentrionaux. Quelques remarques sur des questions débattues", in *Justice populaire. Actes des journées de la société d'histoire du droit, tenues à Lille, 25-28 mai 1989*, Hellemmes, 1992, 77-91.
62. Cf. HEIRBAUT, *Over lenen en families*, 52-54; J. KRUISHEER, *Het ontstaan van de dertiende-eeuwse Zeeuwse landkeuren*, Hilversum, 1998.
63. C. HOOGEWERF, *Het Haarlemse stadsrecht (1245)*, Amsterdam, 2001.
64. Cf. K. DE VRIES, *Bijdrage tot de kennis van het strafprocesrecht in de Nederlandse steden benoorden Maas en Schelde vóór de vestiging van het Bourgondisch gezag*, Groningen, 1955, 207-208.

taken place, like the introduction of kingship. In so far as there were changes in the early Middle Ages there is little use in studying these separately (although there are some nice chapters about it in both the old and new AGN by Ganshof[65] and even a book by him about local institutions in the Southern Netherlands in Carolingian times, called *La Belgique Carolingienne*),[66] as they may teach us a lot about Carolingian institutions, but not much about earlier periods. The post-Carolingian era is not that interesting in that respect either, because the principalities of the Low Countries all developed their own original institutions, which because of their originality are less interesting for a student of early Germanic law. More persistent was the organisation of the courts, where sometimes, in the North, older traditions than the Carolingian *scabini* still managed to hold on, in one case (Drenthe) even until the seventeenth century.[67]

Stability was more present in private law,[68] though not always in those areas where one might expect it. Inheritance law and matrimonial property law, nowadays, among the most conservative, were anything but so in the medieval Low Countries. The high Middle Ages seem to be the period of major change here. The same, in all likelihood, seems to be true of wardship too. The systems for determining consanguinity, the subordinate position of the married woman and the children, or the idea that bastards could inherit from their mother were more persistent elements of family law. As far as property rights are concerned, some ideas are older, e.g.: the distinction between land, which was a constant source of revenue, and non-productive, perishable chattels; the distinction between inherited and acquired land; allods; the interest of the family in the land one had inherited or the idea that chattels, of which one had lost possession, could not always be reclaimed. Other institutions seem to be more recent, like fiefs, which even in Flanders only became popular around 1000.[69] In the law of obligations Roman law

---

65. F.-L. GANSHOF, "Het tijdperk van de Merovingen. Het tijdperk van de Karolingen. Het laat-Karolingisch tijdperk", in *Algemene geschiedenis der Nederlanden*, 1949, 252-366. In 1981 these articles were the only ones to be reprinted, though in a slightly updated version, in the new *Algemene geschiedenis der Nederlanden* (cf. BLOK, D. and VERHULST, A., "Inleiding", in *Algemene geschiedenis der Nederlanden*, I, 1981, 20), which shows both Ganshof's genius and also the stagnation of early medieval studies in the Benelux. See also D. HEIRBAUT and A. MASFERRER, "François-Louis Ganshof: a Belgian view of the Middle Ages" (forthcoming).
66. F.-L. GANSHOF, *La Belgique Carolingienne*, Brussels, 1958.
67. See about the courts in Drenthe, F. KEVERLING-BUISMAN, *Ordelen van de Etstoel van Drenthe*, Zutphen, 1987-1994, 2 vol.; H. BECKER, *De etstoel van Drenthe* (forthcoming).
68. See for a very good survey, GODDING, *Le droit privé*.
69. D. HEIRBAUT, "Flanders: a pioneer of state-oriented feudalism? Feudalism as an instrument of comital power in Flanders during the High Middle Ages (1000-

came to dominate, so that few traces can be found of older notions, except for the formalities accompanying the conclusion of a contract, though these had been degraded from being necessary for a contract's validity to only being required to prove its existence.[70] The same survival of formalities can also be found in the procedures for transferring property. Whereas its venue had changed, the transfer of property no longer being on the land itself, but before the competent court, its formalities, like the *effestucatio*, managed to survive.[71] In short, there was certainly more stability in private than in public law, but in many cases in other areas than today's lawyers would expect.

The greatest stability is to be found in criminal law.[72] This cannot be said for criminal procedure, where changes abound: of the courts, the methods of proof or of prosecution (from accusatorial to inquisitorial), though, again many formalities managed to live on and the traditional method of the parties seeking reconciliation themselves was even in the fifteenth century more popular than the alternative of going before a court, although this would drastically change thereafter. In the rest of criminal law almost nothing but older notions (the list of them that follows is long): the idea of outlawry; the idea that the whole community has to make good the damage caused by one of its members; the importance of the feud and the rituals of peace making; the solidarity amongst the members of a kin-group in taking revenge or receiving compensation for a slain member; determining the criminal character of an act by looking at the effects of an act instead of the guilt of the actor (*Erfolgshaftung*); the fact that an attempt at a crime in itself was not punishable; special peaces for certain places, persons and periods; heavier punishment for thieves who were repeat offenders; a harsher treatment of criminals caught in the act; the close link between the crimes of raping and kidnapping a woman; the possibility for the kidnapper (and exceptionally even the rapist) of escaping the death penalty if his victim consented to marry him; the distinction between manslaughter (openly) and murder (in secret); the 'atomisation' of wounds and other injuries (i.e. instead of a general principle for bodily harm, a rule

---

1300)", in A. MUSSON, *Expectations of the law in the Middle Ages*, Woodbridge, 2001, 24-25.
70. GODDING, *Droit privé*, 421-424.
71. See D. HEIRBAUT, "De procedure tot overdracht van onroerende goederen in het oud-Vlaamse recht: enkele voorbeelden uit de dertiende eeuw", in: *Handelingen van de Maatschappij voor Geschiedenis en Oudheidkunde van Gent*, LI, 1997, 37-59.
72. What follows is based on R. VAN CAENEGEM, *Geschiedenis van het strafprocesrecht in Vlaanderen van de XIe eeuw tot de XIVe eeuw*, Brussels, 1956 and R. VAN CAENEGEM, *Geschiedenis van het strafrecht in Vlaanderen van de XIe tot de XIVe eeuw*, Brussels, 1954.

needs to provide for every single possibility, even the loss of one joint of a finger); crimes like witchcraft, poisoning or blasphemy; crimes with names that refer to their antiquity: *donslach* (when someone had been hit, but no blood had flown), *wapeldrink* (throwing someone in the water), *reroof* (robbing a corpse); punishments like hanging, burying alive, branding and confiscation; certain rituals accompanying executions (like letting the body hang on the gallows).

The long list above could even be longer, but even as it is it should be clear that the survival of older notions in medieval criminal law in the Low Countries was substantial. One should take into account here that there were many regional variations. For example, in the city of Ghent, not only the kidnapper, but also the rapist, could escape execution if his victim consented to marry him. There were also some changes over time. Self-defence, originally, was no justification for manslaughter, but later was accepted as such. The ritual of the *Wüstung*, the destruction of the criminal's house gradually disappeared because the authorities preferred confiscation or fines to an unprofitable destruction. Just as financial considerations also played a role in the increase to 60 pounds of the original 60 shilling fine of the Carolingian era which the princes of the Low Countries could have as successors of the Carolingian kings in their territories, but it is remarkable that although the shillings became pounds, the number remained the same. In general, the new changes of criminal law accreted to the old rules and institutions, but did not replace them. Like, for example, the new punishment of executing criminals by boiling them alive, they only joined, but did not replace older punishments.

The old rules of criminal law are interesting in that, though a few of them like burning sodomites or punishing blasphemers, heretics or the corpses of suicides originated with the Church, most of them did not. In fact, some elements seem to be older than the Carolingians, like certain methods of executing criminals or rituals accompanying them (e.g. hanging a dog next to a hanged criminal), which went underground in the Carolingian era, but resurfaced thereafter. The failure of the Carolingians to change criminal law is most evident in the lack of success of their efforts to restrict feuds, which did not survive them.[73]

Conclusion

What can the data from the Low Countries contribute to answering the question 'How Nordic are the Nordic medieval laws?' First of all, the above makes clear that not only in Scandinavia legal historians are confronted with

---

73. Cf. ALGRA, *Oudfries recht*, 185-199.

doubts about the antiquity of their non-Roman laws. If anything, these doubts are much stronger in Belgium and The Netherlands where they have made legal historians shy away from any research into their oldest laws. For the rest, the data from the Low Countries seem to agree with the critics of the idea that high and late medieval laws which are not based on learned Roman or Romano-canonic law, are not necessarily Germanic, or even old. The high medieval era is the point of origin of many rules which are found in high and late medieval texts. However, the Low Countries' data do not entirely confirm the theories of the Germanists' critics. For example, canon or late Roman influences are awarded much less importance by legal historians from the Low Countries. Even when stability of legal rules was present, it is not always to be found where one might expect it, and certainly not in inheritance and matrimonial property law. Only in the criminal law of the Low Countries are there enough indications of stability to make its study worthwhile for anyone who wants to learn more about Europe's oldest non-Roman law.

SOME DARK ASPECTS OF *IUS COMMUNE*

Mario Ascheri

An Introductory Approach

I am not here for deconstructing anything, even if I certainly have a good topic to advice for a future strong deconstruction: for example, the myth of the 'consuetudo'.[1] My actual paper, anyway, will be focused on very different topics comparing with the previous ones. Not on territorial and personal laws in Italian experience, let's say on the heritage of Lombard law, or on the specific features (if there were any) of thousands of local Italian laws during the Late Middle Ages, with the problems of the relationships among German and Italian law[2] (which should require to start with Tacitus...).

   Ius commune was the general context of our conference and therefore I felt free to move within this theme; not for reporting a work in progress, but just to give an idea of a problem I am now feeling as such. So, let's introduce to it, without many preliminary notes. Certainly I have not to stress in this conference, among scholars so learned in European jurisprudence, the positive aspects of *ius commune*. How great was this tradition, how creative, how important for European culture and institutions

---

1.   I am referring e.g. to the 'ideological' use of it – all to be studied in its implications - made by part of Italian legal history: see my review to P. Grossi: "Un ordine giuridico medievale", Rome-Bari 1995, in *Rechtshistorisches Journal*, 1996.
2.   Many good reflections in E. Cortese: "Il diritto nella storia medievale", I: *L'alto medioevo*, II: *Il basso medioevo*, 2 vols. Rome 1995; see also the recent A. Padoa Schioppa, *Italia ed Europa nella storia del diritto*, Bologna 2003, and my *I diritti del Medioevo italiano (secoli XI-XV)*, Rome 2000.

many centuries along: during the later Middle Ages and early modern history. For instance Peter Stein has even recently summarized it.[3]

It could be possible now to discuss about its heritage; to discuss how far Europeans should include this heritage in their new and future unified law; scholars can discuss how many and how deep were the gaps in this tradition many centuries along. I can refer of course to many recent interventions by Zimmermann, for instance, and to the many others with different preference, from Monateri in "Haskins Law Review" up to the recent notes by Mazzacane and Caroni published in the journal of Roman Law "Index", edited by Neapolitan colleagues.[4] These are examples of particular interest of a large debate now at stake. But, whatever can be thought looking to the future, it's impossible to deny that the *ius commune* tradition was widely operating, and that was very important both at a theoretical level and at a practical one. Equally impossible is to deny that it was a cultural tradition that contributed largely to the unification of the European culture in the past – what is often forgotten.

However, it is very easy to remember, for instance, the different outcomes of the legal culture and, on the other side, of the religious culture. Within the Middle Ages, before the Reformation, many areas in Europe were reached from the *ius commune* culture. Few universities and the strong presence of vernacular, territorial or 'national' law explain the different speed of its spreading, but it was intense – as well proved also during this meeting. So, a European religiously unified by institutional strength of the Papacy faced another Europe, still divided by different legal traditions: the medieval Europe is that one of different speed in receiving the Roman Law tradition, the learned tradition of the universities – which were for long time mainly southern foundations.

If we refer to the second half of the sixteenth century-beginning seventeenth century the situation is very different: no more religious unity, but a wide presence of learned law, either ready to be applied in the practice of the courts, or present everywhere at least as *ratio scripta* to operate as

---

3. P. Stein, *Roman Law in European History*, Cambridge 1999.
4. For all, even for other bibliography, see P. Caroni: *Saggi sulla storia della codificazione*, Milano 1998, P.G. Monateri: "Black Gaius. A Quest for the Multicultural Origins of the "Western Legal Tradition" ", in *Hastings Law Journal, 51* (2000), pp. 472-555; L. Peppe: "Alcune riflessioni sulla storia del diritto ovvero: della rottura della tradizione (giuridica)", in *Diritto romano attuale*, 4 (2000), pp. 61-88, and A. Mazzacane: ""Il leone fuggito dal circo': pandettistica e diritto comune europeo", in *Index, 29* (2001), pp. 97-111. Well balanced R. van Caenegem: *European Law in the Past and the Future. Unity and Diversity over Two Millenia*, Cambridge 2002.

guideline for legal operators with the new powerful presence of northern universities as well.[5]

Even at political level the gap is very evident: when the imperial power was declining, completely new shaped and limited at the Westfalian peace, on mid-seventeenth century, the Roman Law culture was strongly operating throughout European universities even if with different ways of approaching to it and with different weight. Not to say, the *ius publicum Europaeum* which was a product of the new divided religious and political European situation was largely built thanks to learned materials and rules: jurists were still able to help facing new situations. Different monarchic dynasties and Nations of the future could fight each other even with global wars, but they spoke a common legal language and they built national legal codes with common legal concepts: they were generally the concepts of European *ius commune* in a larger or more narrow way, according to local tradition and cultural and political choices of different codification time.

All things very well known. Now, for entering finally my topic, I would say that it is difficult – if we except the polemical writings of the *philosophes* and those of the other thinkers of Enlightenment –, to find out modern works on the dark aspects of *ius commune*, but many different critics of Roman Law and of single schools of interpreters of it: against glossators or commentators or *consiliatores* and so on. But the general tradition is generally over critics now, because it is felt as a moment in the process of modernisation and homogenisation of the different areas in Europe. There is a general good acceptance towards *ius commune*, even if we can be not always in agreement about the space to reserve to the Western legal tradition in building the new European unified law. And this is also the reason why here we are, eventually...

Some First Points of View

I would like therefore to try to isolate some aspects not so positive or not so commonly considered, not only because it is right to do so, but because even the shadows can be useful to clarify the brightening areas; moreover, they can also contribute to the general discussion on the future of European law. I shall present only some ideas very tentative, very temporary, ideas which will require still a lot of work about: I recognize this, but I would not lose an occasion like this to present some scattered ideas just to get your advices. I submit myself 'saniori consilio' while asking if in these considerations it is all to be put in a drawer or there is something to be

---

5. It is not necessary to refer in details to the writings by Franz Wieacker and Riccardo Orestano, e.g.

retained, improved and developed. My point of departure is that the continental common law tradition is a tradition in large part of private law – besides a tradition concerning international law, private included. Helmut Coing – a scholar perhaps too much forgotten now – has produced his great volumes as a ripe fruit of a long life work and they were dedicated to private law.[6]

As it happened for Roman lawyers, European academic jurists essentially were scholars working on private law. Constitutional law on one side, and criminal law on the other side, were not neglected, but largely understated if we compare their efforts on these fields with the amount of work done for solving private law cases, whilst constitutional and criminal laws were strongly affected by local territorial tradition and political developments.[7] But I certainly know that exactly working on private law principles, they developed very important rules for constitutional law; for all I only remember the question of 'quod omnes tangit ab omnibus adprobari debet' and the space it deserves in the developments of European parliamentary institutions; the maxim 'rex in regno suo est imperator' at the very origin of the modern national sovereignty is not bound to private law but was equally brought to consequences in ius commune sources. Their meaning all over Europe is very well known.[8]

As I know that we can find in continental common law writings some principles of equality among litigants or of guarantee for accused persons, like hints to the future 'in dubio pro reo' or similar propositions[9]. But the developments of constitutional and criminal laws were in the direction we can find in the late *ius commune* writings, during the centuries later qualified as period of the *Ancien régime*. This means that in some European areas the spaces for estates were limited because of political absolutism, and almost everywhere the powers of judges were increasing. The increasing professional aspects of the legal offices and their inclusion in the growing

---

6. H. Coing: „Europäisches Privatrecht 1500 bis 1800, In: "*Älteres Gemeines Recht, II: 19. Jahrhundert. Überblick über die Entwicklung des Privatrechts in den ehemals gemeinrechtlichen Ländern,* 2 vols., München 1985-1989 (there is a Spanish translation: „Derecho privado europeo", ed. by A. Pérez Martín, Madrid 1996).
7. Of course, a keen scholar like Giovanni Tarello felt the difference: see his "La crisi del diritto commune nel secolo XVIII: un problema storiografico", in *Il diritto comune e la tradizione giuridica europea*, Perugia 1980, pp. 435-441.
8. See e.g. R. van Caenegem: *An Historical Introduction to Western Constitutional Law*, Cambridge 1995; I find still very useful B. Tierney: *Religion, Law and the Growth of the Constitutional Thought 1150-1650*, Cambridge 1983.
9. See e.g. K. Pennington: "Innocent Until Proven Guilty. The Origins of a Legal Maxim", in *A Ennio Cortese, a cura di I. Birocchi, M. Caravale, E. Conte, U. Petronio, III*, Roma 2001, pp. 59-73.

bureaucratic system led to powerful judges who were felt as part of a Unitarian governing public power.[10] While doubts towards some traditional beliefs were increasing within the highest courts along the seventeenth century, like those on witchcraft, for instance[11], the formalities and complexity of procedure and of the different overlapping jurisdictions were growing: and they gave judges new and larger powers[12].

Uncertainty of law became a common and blamed feature: learned law brought sophisticated reasoned legal thoughts, but many doubts as well. For instance, with the treatises on nullity of sentence or on *arbitrium iudicis*.[13] Again, learned law brought to publication of too many collections of judgments which were consulted everywhere in Europe, even outside the borders of the jurisdictions they referred to, and therefore they opened too many possibilities of choosing arguments over arguments and among arguments. Collections of decisions[14] which were also introduced as a mean to avoid uncertainty, with their growing number became another reason of uncertainty! Things again well known and generally thought by historians as results of late criticism against medieval interpreters.

---

10. Useful are recent collections of researches like *Le juge et le jugement dans les traditions juridiques européennes*, sous la dir. de R. Jacob, Paris 1996, and *La conscience du juge dans la tradition juridique européenne*, dirigé par J.-M. Carbasse et L. Depambour-Tarride, Paris 1999 ; of course, the series of *Comparative Studies in Continental and Anglo-American Legal History* should be meant as known.
11. See e.g. *The Inquisition in Early Modern Europe*, ed. by G. Henningsen, J. Tedeschi, Ch. Amiel, Dekalb Ill. 1986.
12. Many Italian jurisdictions have been studied during last few decades; for Neapolitan kingdom under Spanish government, the series edited by Raffaele Ajello: *Storia e diritto* (Jovene publisher in Naples), is of great importance, as the Venetian studies by Gaetano Cozzi (classic his book *Repubblica di Venezia e Stati italiani. Politica e giustizia dal secolo XVI al secolo XVIII*, Torino 1982) and his school. Even the Milanese duchy had an important central court, called 'Senato', now under deep examination f. i. by L. Garlati Giugni: "Prima che il mondo cambi. La Milano dei senatori nel Transunto del metodo giudiziario" (1769), in *Studi di storia del diritto*, III, Milano 2001, pp. 521-639, and A. Monti: *I formulari del Senato di Milano (secoli XVI-XVIII)*, Milano 2001. For a general survey on Italian central court during this period, see my "Höchste Gerichte in Italien zur Zeit des Ancien Régime", in *Frieden durch Recht. Das Reichskammergericht von 1495 bis 1806*, hrsg. von I. Scheurmann, Mainz 1994, pp. 412-434.
13. Among the works of *ius commune* on this topic, see especially Iacobi Menochii Papiensis: *De arbitrariis iudicum questionum et causis* (many editions; see e.g. Venetiis 1613).
14. The most important general overview of these collection is still in *Handbuch der Quellen und Literatur der neueren europäische Privatrechtsgeschichte*, hrsg. von H. Coing, Band II 2, München 1976.

The Primacy of Renaissance Florence

But really was this widespread feeling a creation of eighteenth century? I think we can find the very beginnings of these developments already in the core of the *ius commune* system, going back to Renaissance Florence[15] even without relating once more to the humanistic world, Italian, French and German, always under investigation.[16] Indeed, there is not only to remember a jurist like Johannes Nevizanus, from Piedmont, an Italian northern region far from the traditional academic world, who wrote at the beginning of sixteenth century against the incredible amount of legal books on sale, and who began to ask how to get rid of them; we can better move also to Renaissance Florence, where we shall find a well known writer, the first modern historian of Italy, Francesco Guicciardini, who wrote at same time of Rabelais, better known than him for the attacks against jurists of *ius commune*,[17] and the great Montaigne of the *Essais*.

Guicciardini was a political writer in correspondence with Niccolò Machiavelli, a little older than the former, but he was also a jurist, and so he could speak at light of a large experience as attorney and judge, or governor in the papal State as well.[18] So he could characterize the system very keenly. We can therefore read in his notes known as *Ricordi*, personal memories like a diary:

> "I do not condemn entirely the civil justice system of the Turks, which is hasty rather than summary. For even a man who judges with his eyes closed will probably decide half of the cases justly and free both sides from expense and waste of time. But our judges carry on in such a way that often the winning side would have been better off with an unfavorable judgments on the first day rather than a favorable one after so much cost and trouble. Moreover, our judges are so wicked and ignorant, and our laws are so obscure, than even among us white is all too often made to seem black."[19]

---

15. Many recent works have been done by Julius Kirshner, Osvaldo Cavallar, Thomas Kuhen and others at the same time and after the basic book by L. Martines, *Lawyers and Statecraft in Renaissance Florence*, Princeton 1968.
16. Among recent studies, see f. i. those gathered in *A Ennio Cortese* (see note 9), I-III: by J.-L. Ferrary (François Hotman), J. Krynen (*Parlement de Paris* as Senate of France), A. Mattone (on the jurist and historian G. F. Fara), M. Montorzi (M. Wesenbeck), D. Osler (A. Alciatus), R. Savelli (on catholic censorship of books), R. sorace (on the Sicilian jurist G. Cumia).
17. E.g. it is possible to refer to E. Nardi: *Rabelais e il diritto romano*, Milano 1963.
18. But studies on these aspects of his activities are not many; see however O. Cavallar: *Francesco Guicciardini giurista. I ricordi degli onorari*, Milano 1991.
19. This is the 'thought' number 67 in F. Guicciardini: *Maxims & Reflections of a Renaissance Statesman*, ed. by M. Domandi, New York 1965, p, 112 s.

Some Dark Aspects of *Ius Commune*

As it clear, learned law – even with its 'summary' procedure[20] – did not solve any problem for the litigants, even in the mercantile courts;[21] as a model, it was much better the 'rash' procedure of Turkish judge, who finished well around half of cases judging with closed eyes!

In the following piece of his memories,[22] Guicciardini continues giving technical reasons of arbitrary conduct of judges as well:

> "It is a mistake to believe that cases left by law to the discretion of a judge are placed before his will and whim. The law did not give him power so that he might show favor. Rather certain cases are left to his discretion – that is to say, to his synteresis, to his conscience – because the law cannot cover every single case, given the differences in circumstances. And so the judge must consider all the facts and do what seems just. This latitude in the law absolves him from having to account *in sindicatu*, for since his decision is not determined by law, he can always excuse himself. But it does not empower him to give away other people's property".

Here Guicciardini introduces another topic very important to us, which he will consider again in a project of constitution for the Republic of Florence,[23] where he wrote:

> "In criminal cases law should be respected, but sometimes it is possible to use a discretional, free power ("con più larghezza" says the original text), while in civil cases it is necessary to follow a narrow rule (what we call *strictum ius*), so that cases will be solved in a clear way; moreover it is necessary that who is governing doesn't have any interference in them, because civil cases refer to personal welfare (in Italian: "sicurtà"), and people should be sure that judges don't take away what they keep rightly or they can get what they un-rightly lost".

Here, I think, a common feeling – very well spread among the leading elites of *Ancien régime* – becomes clear: public order and repression of criminality require even exceptional interventions and powers, which are forbidden on the contrary where and when it is question of private economic interests, since civil procedure generally affects wealthy people, beloved or

---

20. I would like to remember my "Il processo civile tra diritto comune e diritto locale da questioni preliminari al caso della giustizia estense", in *Quaderni storici*, 34 (1999), pp. 355-387.
21. With their trend to become 'learned' jurisdiction: see the Sienese case studied in my *Tribunali giuristi e istituzioni dal medioevo all'età moderna*, Bologna 1996.
22. *Ricordi* I, 69, and cf. II, 113.
23. Used by Cozzi: *Repubblica di Venezia* (note 12).

in any case necessarily with large audience or close to the heart of governments.

Guicciardini here was probably giving expression to deep feelings which were interpreted when politic powers on 1502 established in Florence the Supreme Court named Council of Justice and later Rota – following the Roman Catholic example. The choice made at that time was to establishing a learned court, which should be independent by political power and working with a 'clean' procedure,[24] since the judges were exceptionally bound to give reasons of their judgments – what was not required by *ius commune* tradition.[25]

Florentine Rota should be only a judicial institution just to give citizens guarantees of good justice administration. And certainly its decisions were generally felt as good ones during Ancien régime till the arrival of French troops at the end of eighteenth century – and later, in the post-French period, during the early nineteenth century. Apparently, here things went on exceptionally well, even because – we would like to think – Rota continued to be filled, as in Medieval and republican practice, with foreign judges, who were appointed for short periods (some years only) exactly like the university professors of the oldest tradition. But however there is a… 'but'!

We read in a report preserved in Florentine State archives under the title *Notes on the administration of justice*, and written around mid-seventeenth century probably by a secretary of the Tuscan grand-duke, that

> "some judges of Rota live in villas of Florentine citizens owners of them even if these, the latter, have frequent cases in front of those judges; some others make their profits doing business with goods products of their countries with Florentine merchants litigating in front of their court, and so, e.g., they make longer the litigation till the conclusion of the business; some others play the role of godfathers for families with good acceptance at court; finally, others enter at order and in the favours of the ministers".[26]

---

24. 'Clean hands' – the famous definition given by Milanese judges on the Italian political crisis during the years '90 of the twentieth century – are already mentioned in Sienese official documents during the sixteenth century: see my *"La Siena del "Buon Governo"" (1287-1355)*, in *Politica e cultura nelle Repubbliche italiane dal Medioevo all'età moderna: Firenze – Genova - Lucca – Siena – Venezia*, ed. by S. Adorni Braccesi-M. Ascheri, Roma 2001, pp. 81-107.
25. See again my *Tribunali giuristi e istituzioni* (note 19) and, more detailed, F. Mancuso: *Exprimere causam in sententia. Ricerche sul principio di motivazione della sentenza nell'età del diritto comune classico*, Milano 1999.
26. First published in E. Fasano Guarini: "I giuristi e lo Stato nella Toscana medicea cinque-seicentesca", in *Firenze e la Toscana dei Medici nell'Europa del '500*, I, p. 229 ff.

Of course we can think that they were expected to be ready to obey in any necessity. What was obvious even because there was always the possibility for temporary judges - like they were – to be fired or, on the contrary, to be appointed for leading new and higher offices at the end of the term in Rota. These few lines – better than any book – make clear an entire world; they are very precious since they appear in a writing which should be certainly kept secret, and therefore should be considered highly true.

Other More General Features of the *Ius Commune* System

But with Guicciardini and Florentine Rota we still are in a single State, and so we could think to an exceptional situation. Nevertheless, I suppose Florentine thinkers had only more consciousness thanks their extraordinary political and cultural experience. Anyway, we can consider also other more general aspects of that legal system, which was enriched with too many ideas and practices fighting with the 'modern' political systems, which required stronger and stronger powers to modernize their countries.

In Catholic countries there are to be considered of course the walls political choices always encountered when tried to rule or to limit ecclesiastical interests – like evident, typically, in Neapolitan experience[27] – or the weight of *periculum animae* even in civil matters where f. i. a sentence could not become *res iudicata*.[28] Among other handicaps, seen from outside the catholic world, *ius commune* was a legal system too deeply involved with canon law, i.e. with 'papist' law, and in itself it was the law of a tyrant and foreigner emperor like Justinian.

In fact, it had allowed the development of ecclesiastical privileges, Inquisition and of other tools of repression typically used by ecclesiastic powers.[29] But we can even consider other more general aspects. So, e.g., we can refer to the idea that "statutum interpretandum est secundum ius commune", a rule which stops any attempt to reform established principles by way of legislation; or to the other idea, of course criticized by an humanist like Connanus, that a new law should be interpreted at the light of the old ones, principle again difficult to accept for a political willing looking

---

27. See e.g. Raffaele Ajello in many articles published in *Frontiera d'Europa*, I-, 1995-, a review mainly dedicated to institutional and legal problems of Kingdom of Naples in XVII-XVIII centuries. Attention to more general Italian problems in the serial "Storica" (especially by Marcello Verga), curiously appeared beginning on 1995 too.
28. See my *Diritto medievale e moderno. Problemi di storia del processo, della cultura e delle fonti giuridiche*, Rimini 1991, p. 181 ff.
29. It is sufficient just to refer to the French *Encyclopedie*, or for Italy to brothers Verri and their review "Il Caffè".

to introduce some discontinuity in the legal system. More in general is was very common the idea – spread inside common law world as well – that *ius commune* should be meant as a rational and perfect legal treasure that 'local' law should only modify as little as possible, because to jurists local law generally appeared to be not a rational law, being only the answer to needs of the moment and not to permanent reasons of justice like *ius commune*.

Other examinations could find also that *ius commune* gave space even to large contradictions: liberty and slavery were equally found on it, exactly as equality and privileges, or again as an absolutist and a completely republican power of government.

Anyway, in spite of its flexibility, which favoured its spreading everywhere under different political regimes, *ius commune* generally finished to be thought as the law which authorized the leading positions of privileged people, including legal professionals besides clergy and nobility: inside *ius commune* found legitimacy and development not only judicial torture, or arbitrary powers of judges in criminal cases or procedure rules enacted by the same judging courts, but even private law institutes which deserved strong reforms. Like the *fideicommissum*, a legal institution very important for the survival of nobility, or any form of feudality, or any form of perpetual census, which excluded estates from the free market of business.

If we refer to procedure, we see litigation without end, with a lot of reasons of nullity for the judgements, manifold ways to cancel the judgements and judgements without reasons just because – as *ius commune* learned – iudex who gives reasons of his sentence is a *fatuus iudex* (Durandus, *Speculum*). But I don't want – I told already – to go on listing the many faults humanists like the Dutch jurists of elegant school or English and French *philosophes*, or 'Enlightened' German jurists like Thomasius or Italian polemists found in *ius commune* tradition: it would be a long list out of place here.

For our purpose it is sufficient to remember that *ius commune* finished to appear – rightly or not – as the law of jurists and judges who did not want to reform anything of traditional world of privileges, the law of people hindering the reforming efforts of Enlightened princes or *philosophes* who stressed the role of legislation in building a brave new world at light of a new reason, based on practical experience of natural sciences.

Therefore, the darkest aspect perhaps of *ius commune* was the negative *image* the system showed to the public, to people of 'common sense' and to their contemporary interpreters: the intellectual and political elites striving for reforms. The eternal and old (on sixteenth century, e.g.) claims towards codification and for a simpler legal system should be now considered under a new look. There was the necessity to re-establish the legal system showing a good will of political authorities – and even downloading any responsibility for the wrongs of the past due to the legal profession.

So, the darkest aspect of *ius commune* system in eighteenth century was more a question of difficult communication of its 'true' nature than an internal, objective and unsurpassable fault. Uncertainty of law could be healed with good restatements of uncertain doctrines and the use of vernacular law could stop polemics of ordinary people: the German 'enlightened' way which was tried.[30] But in other countries generally the answers given by jurists to all efforts of the reformers were wrong, and therefore secondary aspects were thought on the contrary as *essential* features of *ius commune*. Even stressing the rational (*ratio scripta*) or the 'natural' (*ius naturale*) character of *ius commune* they did not provide a good service to it, since this was a way to make it more perfect and practically and culturally untouchable by reforms.

Look, for instance, at what happened in Italy to the moderate critics to traditional legal world[31] written by Lodovico Antonio Muratori, a priest who was an important historian of Italian Middle Ages, a reformer active in Modena besides the duke.[32] His critics were rejected by Neapolitan jurists[33] even writing still in Latin on mid- eighteenth century! In the same Naples even the efforts to have reasoned judgements in the Seventies of eighteenth century were defeated.[34] Traditional jurists were the worse defenders of *ius commune* – like the conservative *Parlement de Paris*, pratically liable for the outbreaking of the *Grande Revolution*! They prepared in this way the triumph of codification.[35] The 'new' continental Europe was built as well known *against* the judges and legal professionals, even if and when the political elite was leaded by jurists – as French revolution shows.

Abolition of *ius commune* went on together with the cancellation of the feudal system: they – *ius commune* and the feudal 'system' – became

---

30. In Italian literature a book writttten by a philosopher of law opened new researches: G. Tarello: *Storia della cultura giuridica moderna*, I, Bologna 1976; in the recent literature see I. Birocchi: *Alla ricerca dell'ordine. Fonti e cultura giuridica dell'età moderna*, Torino 2002, and U. Petronio: *La lotta per la codificazione*, Torino 2002.
31. In *Dei difetti della giurisprudenza*, printed many times since its first appearance on 1742.
32. His legal *pamphlet* has been many time studied; see now f. i. U. Petronio: *Una critica araldica di Lodovico Antonio Muratori ai difetti della giurisprudenza*, Rome, Ministero della Giustizia, 1999.
33. See f. i. I. Birocchi: Giurisprudenza umnaistica e diritto patrio in Francesco Rapolla (1701-62), in *Iuris vincula. Studi in onore di Mario Talamanca*, I, Napoli 2001, pp. 237-282.
34. Here again there is only to quote Raffaele Ajello's works.
35. Inside a large literature, it is possible to look at my "A Turning Point in the Civil Law Tradition: from Ius Commune to Code Napoléon", in *Tulane Law Review*, 70, 4 (1996), pp. 1041-1051.

landmarks of the *Ancien regime* while the *interpretatio doctorum* appeared to be the proof of the compromise of the legal world with nobility. Cultural discontinuity wanted a battle against old legal system. The polemical milieu could not preserve the old judiciary and its law. Montesquieu's idea of the judge as *la bouche de la loi* implied a strong doctrine of division of powers unknown to Anglo-American world. Only during the nineteenth century, as recently stressed by Ugo Petronio working on Napoleonic and French legal world,[36] grew up the idea that was *impossible* to integrate law codes referring to customs or to *Professorenrecht* and therefore that jurists should only discover what was already *inside* the law – as generally told (later) by legal positivism.

Constitutional thought and the reforms in progress – especially affecting ecclesiastical privileges - required a strong legislative power, which sometimes had to claim the power of interpretation just like in Justinian's texts. Look e.g. at the first constitution enacted on 1848 in Piedmont and that later became the Italian constitution till 1948. In its article 73, *pour cause* speaking about judiciary, enacted that "the interpretation of the statutes in a mandatory way for everybody was reserved exclusively to legislative power" (shared by the king with the two chambers). Hence the *école de l'exégèse* even in late nineteenth century, while in Germany *Pandektenrecht* had such a large development. Its success shows that one of the (former) darkest feature of *ius commune*, the previous blamed primacy of jurist over the law, could be forgotten or that it was no more felt like a danger in German common sense and elsewhere, wherever its doctrine was largely spread and received.

The fear against *interpretatio doctorum* ceased in fact (not in theory: legal positivism) when codes strengthened their presence. That is why the brightest aspect of *ius commune* – the international effort *doctorum* toward a new *ius commune* – can operate and can develop again: the jurists have again this responsibility. Therefore it is a *Beruf unserer Zeit* a reconsideration of any wrong in *ius commune* tradition and a new start again with the medieval 'clean hands'!

---

36. U. Petronio: "La nozione di code civil fra tradizione e innovazione (con un cenno alla sua pretesa "completezza"", in *Quaderni fiorentini*, 27 (1998), pp. 83-115.

The Nordic Medieval Laws in the Legal History of the 17th and the 18th Centuries

Lars Björne

Introduction

"How Nordic are the Nordic medieval laws?"[1] If you had asked this question to a Nordic legal historian in the 17th century, you would probably have got an astonished look and perhaps, instead of an answer, a counter question: "Do you mean, how Nordic are the other laws of the ancient world?" Furthermore, the epithet 'Nordic' would have sounded strange. In the 17th century the Danes and the Swedes had been arch-enemies for centuries, and the main task of historical research was to demonstrate the superiority of its own people compared to its neighbour. The few Nordic legal scholars were, or at least pretended to be, loyal patriots and devoted subjects of their king and country. Also the term 'Middle Ages' was unknown, being an invention of later times, i.e. the Enlightenment in the 18th century. In other words, the problem, which we have been discussing during this symposium, had no relevance until the late 18th century when the first signs of a scientific historical method began to appear.

---

1. This lecture is mainly based on the first part of my History of Nordic Legal Science, *Patrioter och institutionalister* (1995). Unfortunately I have had no possibility of re-examining the sources.

Sweden

Sweden held a position as a Great Power in the 17th century. Her leading role was manifested in legal history, too. The glorious old Swedish society depicted by historians is for a modern reader a strange world, indeed. Some Swedish scholars formed an early 'Uppsala School', dominated by the famous polyhistor Olavus Rudbeckius (1630-1702) and his brother-in-law, the legal scholar and historian Carolus Lundius (1638-1715). Rudbeckius's creative imagination had no limits in his historical works: in his *magnum opus* "Atlantica" the author asserted that Sweden was the lost Atlantis and the original home of all nations, and he was at pains to explain that Paradise had been situated in the area of the town of Uppsala. By the standards of that time, Rudbeckius's theses were acceptable science, and his work got an astonished, however, not entirely negative reception in Germany. It is of course difficult to estimate to what extent Rudbeckius's Swedish contemporaries believed in his theses, but he was anyhow protected by the censorship of Carolinian absolutism.

Lundius and his pupils in the Faculty of Law focused on legal history. Lundius's most famous work was a dissertation entitled "Zamolxis Primus Getarum Legislator", published in 1687 with a humble dedication to King Charles XI. In his work Lundius tried to show that Zalmoxis or Zamolxis, who, according to Herodotus, was a disciple of Pythagoras and wrote laws for the 'Geatas', also had been the first lawmaker in Sweden. The evidence presented is a chain of conjectures; Lundius claimed that the 'Geatas', the 'Scythians', the 'Goths' during the Great Migration and the later Swedish 'Geats' (götar) were all one and the same people. Significant for Lundius's proof was the reference to old documents, which he refused to let other scholars see. When he was forced to present some evidence, he at last published a fragment of six words from the alleged ancient Swedish law, 'Vigers flockar'. This fragment was immediately dismissed as a fake.

Some of Lundius's pupils presented even more astonishing theses in the spirit of Rudbeckius. In the dissertation "De legibus Hyperboreis", also published in 1687, the author, "juris & antiquit. Studiosus" Laurentius Welt, disagreed with his teacher Lundius and presented the king of Crete Minos (whose name of course was Swedish, i.e. 'man' or 'minnur', gen. 'minnurs') as a former Swedish king, who had ruled in Uppsala. This etymology and a reference in the sources that Minos had been a foreigner were the only evidence. Furthermore Minos had been assisted by his brother Radamanthus, whose name according to Welt was even more Swedish (Rademan = 'rådman', a name, which later became an official rank).

Rudbeckius may have been in good faith, but one cannot assert that of Lundius, with his hidden documents and obvious fakes. Lundius's 'historical' studies were probably only written to promote his career during the period of Carolinian absolutism. The great fire in Uppsala in 1702 was for Rudbeckius a disaster. He lost his home, his library, his valuable manuscripts and his huge collection on natural history. On the other hand, the fire may have saved the last remains of Lundius's scientific reputation: now he could tell his critics that he would be happy to show his sources, but, alas, they had all been destroyed.

For a modern reader it is easy to belittle the achievements of Swedish legal history in the 17th century, developing works, in which ignorance competed with arrogance and homemade fantastic etymologies were presented as comprehensive evidence. However, one must remember that the historians were not so much concerned with historical truth as with the greatness of the king and realm. Besides, why spoil a good story through some impertinent critique of historical sources? This last point of view was in fact largely accepted by some legal historians until the early 20th century.

How was it then possible to present such theories by Rudbeckius and Lundius? Firstly, these historians were not creators of an entirely new theory, but they could rely on an old tradition of medieval origin. The Swedish delegate at the Council of Basel in 1434, the archbishop Nicolaus Ragvaldi, had tried to impress his colleagues by inventing a glorious Swedish past, and this story was later repeated by the famous Swedish 16th-century-historian, the Archbishop Johannes Magnus, who lived after the Reformation in exile in Rome. Secondly, there was yet no scientific critique of historical sources, except for the fact that the age of a source seemed to increase its credibility.

On the other hand, in 17th century Sweden there were also alternatives to the phantasmagoria of a Rudbeckius or a Lundius, even in Uppsala. Johannes Loccenius (1598-1677), professor at the Faculty of Law and librarian of the university, refused to begin his political history of Sweden earlier than with the alleged reign of King Björn I in Birka in the ninth century. Johan Dalekarlus Stiernhöök (1596-1675), who in 1672 published the for a long time internationally well-known study on Swedish legal history "De jure Sveonum et Gothorum vetusto", carried out critical research, which was far more advanced than many works in the 18th century.

In his discourse on the oldest laws in Sweden, Stiernhöök abandoned all patriotic wishful thinking. He denied naming a first legislator, because in his view the first legal system had been an example of a gradually developing system of customary law. He had no sympathy with the theory of Zamolxis as the first lawmaker in Sweden. Stiernhöök stated that no one knew anything about Zamolxis's alleged laws for the ancient 'Geats' and that it was very doubtful that these 'Geats' had been identical with the 'Goths' who had left Sweden. The Gothic laws in the period of the Great Migration shared, according to Stiernhöök, more similarity with contemporaneous Roman or Gaulish laws than with Swedish provincial codes.

One must of course not overemphasize the modernity of Stiernhöök's research. Writing a time long before the development of a scientific critique of historical sources, he had no possibility of evaluating the credibility of medieval narratives. Basing his argument on information in the provincial codes, he created a theory of the oldest written Swedish laws, which was widely accepted by many historians until the 19th century. Viger Spa and Lumber, two 'lagmen', who allegedly lived in the ninth century, laid down the first laws for the Swedes and the Geats. Stiernhöök, too, was fond of homemade etymologies. Unlike Loccenius, who stated that the feudal terminology was generally of Germanic origin, Stiernhöök claimed that it was purely Swedish and partly based on the dialect of his home province, Dalecarlia.

Denmark

Compared to their Swedish colleagues, the Danish historians of the 17th century were modest, or at least they had an older and more accepted tradition to rely on. The 'Bible' for Danish historians, including legal historians, until the late 19th century was the Latin chronicle of Saxo Grammaticus, "Gesta Danorum", probably written in the early 13th century. At any rate, you cannot speak of any legal history in Denmark in the 17th century, since there was hardly any Danish jurisprudence at that time. A rare exception is Cristen Ostersen Veile's legal glossary. In its historical survey the author was completely dependent on Saxo: Skiold, the apparently King of Denmark, who allegedly ruled in pre-recorded times, was mentioned as the first legislator.

Nordic Connections

With the loss of Sweden's position as a Great Power Swedish historians became more sober, and the vainglorious theses of Rudbeckius turned into a common joke. Swedish legal history suffered a loss of at least a thousand years from the 17th to the 18th century. After the Great Northern War in the early 18th century the old animosity between Danes and Swedes almost disappeared, and there was no use for a glorious national past aiming at diminishing the image of one's Nordic neighbours. In spite of the continuing sporadic wars between the Nordic kingdoms, some personal relations between legal scholars had already been established in the 18th century. The Swede David Nehrman (1695-1769) visited Copenhagen in 1726 and was later in correspondence with Danish colleagues. The Dane Peder Kofod Ancher (1710-1787) stayed one year in Stockholm in the early 1770s to conduct research on medieval Danish manuscripts (which the Swedish forces had plundered during their occupation of Denmark in 1658), and he was very impressed by the warm reception he received. Legal science in both kingdoms also became 'Nordic' in the late 18th century, in the sense that an early Scandinavian movement - which was still a cultural movement as opposed to the later political Scandinavism of the mid-19th century – influenced legal science. Legal scholars became especially aware of a common Nordic legal history, and their earliest interest in the laws of their neighbours was primarily historical.

Although Swedish historians in the 18th century abandoned the extreme Rudbeckian approach to history, one cannot talk of a legal history in any modern scientific sense. The new lawmaker heroes were not the more well-known legislators during the period of the provincial codes in the 13th and the 14th century, but ancient figures found in either the Icelandic sagas of Snorri Sturluson (1179-1241) or in the forewords to the medieval codes. The Swedes were especially fond of Snorri's claim that Oden had been a king who came with his entourage from far away and, after travelling through the Nordic countries, decided to settle down in Sweden, where he probably became the first legislator. This story became commonplace in the literature on Swedish legal history, except for a few critical voices concerning the laws of Oden – no one doubted his existence as a historical person. The most remarkable dissident was Olof Rabenius (1730-1772), professor in Uppsala and an admirer of Kofod Ancher. In one of his last studies "De fatis litteraturæ juridicæ in Suecia, commentatio, sect. I" (1770; 1772), an introduction to a history of Swedish legal literature, which never reached historic times, Rabenius expressed serious doubts about the tales of the ancient laws. Rabenius believed neither in the written laws of Oden nor in those of Viger, who was mentioned as a 'lagman' in the foreword to the provincial code Upplandslagen (1296). Rabenius claimed that the first laws were laid down at the earliest during the reign of King St. Eric in the 12th century, because the ancient runic writing had only been used for magical purposes.

The flourishing of Danish legal science in the late 18th century is also manifested in the research on legal history. Kofod Ancher, who was the founder of legal history in Denmark and a well-known authority in Sweden as well as in Finland, published the first comprehensive treatise on the legal history of Denmark, "En Dansk Lov-Historie Fra Kong Harald Blaatands Tid til Kong Christian den Femtes, I-" (1769; 1776), which also became very famous in Germany, and which has subsequently been called 'the most important legal study in Danish in the 18th century'. This treatise was actually advanced for its time in its use of scientific methods, historical criticism and evaluation of sources. The new critical attitude came into view in Kofod Ancher's statement that efforts to find laws 'from the dark ages' brought no glory, because glory based on fables was vain. Thus, Kofod Ancher started his discourse with the reign of King Harald Gormsson ('Bluetooth'), i.e. the beginning of Christianity, 'the dawn of Danish history' according to the author.

In spite of some worthwhile studies, especially those of Kofod Ancher, the research standard was not very high. A weakness in Nordic legal historical research in the 18th and in the early 19th century was the absence of any specialization among scholars. This lack of specialization may explain why a certain superficiality and inability to analyse sources are characteristic of the legal history of that time. The critique of sources developed to some extent, but this critique was mainly reflections based on common sense: supernatural events and obviously incredible stories were abandoned, whereas problems like provenance and tendentiousness of sources did not attract attention. Only Kofod Ancher deserves the title of a professional historian and among the authors of Nordic legal history only he attempted to debate the methodology of historical research.

Kofod Ancher stressed the importance of solid evidence. The best sources were originals and manuscripts contemporaneous with the subject of the research, these sources could nonetheless contain errors 'at least in reading or writing', and a historian was often compelled to use sources that were not completely reliable, rumours, own conclusions and presumptions. A reader therefore had no obligation to take an author at his word. Samuel Pufendorf and others used excellent sources and they had aspired towards the truth, but they would have been more convincing if they had tried to substantiate their claims. Kofod Ancher also discussed the value of conjectures. He himself used educated guesses in the same way as lawyers were forced to fall back on circumstantial evidence when they lacked sufficient proof. What was left of history, if you abandoned all conjectures and conclusions? It was, according to Kofod Ancher, however important that a historian gave a detailed account of the reasons underlying his conjectures in order to let the reader decide their value.

Kofod Ancher's study on King Harald Gormsson's Danish laws illustrates this method. Kofod Ancher's evidence for the existence of these laws, which are nowhere mentioned in the sources, comprises a chain of guesses based on some information derived from much later chronicles. Although Kofod Ancher's methodological deliberations also should invite reflexion in our time, for example, his statement that a similarity of laws is no proof of influence because of the possibility of a simultaneous development, his conjectures are not always convincing. A demand for objectivity became the new ideal of historical research in the 18th century, whereas a demand for truth instead of mere probabilities emerged much later.

Law-giving and Law Traditions

Historical research dealing with questions like "Who was the first Legislator in Sweden/Denmark?", "Who gave the first written laws to the Danes or the Swedes" does not require comparative studies - and besides no one knew the form and content of the allegedly ancient laws, which were lost long ago. The personification of the legislation made the problem of a foreign influence seem ridiculous. It was always the wise king or 'lagman', who observed the needs of his society and by his own efforts found the optimal legal solutions. No one thought of asking if Oden, Skiold, Viger or Lumber had studied Roman law. A comparison with foreign laws and legal systems became first relevant in the early period of scientific historical research focusing on the remaining medieval provincial codes. In the 16th and the 17th century not legal scholars, but certain historians had discussed the foreign influence present in the old Danish laws, and the famous Danish author Arild Huitfeldt (1546-1609) had emphasized the foreign nature of Jyske Lov, the provincial code of Jutland from 1241. It is significant that Stiernhöök, who did not believe in Zamolxis, mentioned in passing the possible foreign influence on Swedish legislation. He claimed that the old Swedish and German laws had had much in common, because Swedes and Germans were originally one people with the same language and the same customs. Furthermore, Swedish lawmakers had borrowed considerably from their neighbours and adjusted it to the needs of their own people, which saw clearly stated by King Birger Magnusson in the foreword to Upplandslagen.

In early Nordic legal science the reception of foreign law, especially Roman law, i.e. primarily that law adopted and amended in Germany, *usus modernus pandectarum,* and, of course, German doctrine was comprehensive. Almost all the textbooks on Swedish and Danish law from the middle of the 17th to the beginning of the 19th century used the structure of the Institutiones in Corpus Iuris Civilis. The adoption of this plan was not the only indication of the massive influence of Roman law although it is more difficult to show to what extent foreign material rules were adopted.

Attitudes towards Roman law were not always positive in Nordic legal science, especially not in the early 18th century. The repudiation of Roman law meant at any rate neither isolation nor an increasing independence of Nordic legal science: Roman law and *usus modernus pandectarum* were temporarily replaced by a doctrine of natural law, which was also of German origin. Already by the middle of the 18th century, Roman law was once again highly esteemed. Kofod Ancher would not accept any conflict between Roman and natural law, and, in his opinion, Roman law was very useful as an example of "Principia Juris privati universalis". In addition, Kofod Ancher also pointed out that jurisprudence without Roman law was impossible.

Needless to say, the Nordic countries had already become a part of the European cultural community under the protection of the Catholic Church during the Middle Ages. Higher education had been possible only at universities abroad, and studies, including legal studies, in foreign countries, especially Germany, were still common after the foundation of the first Nordic universities. It could therefore be supposed that the legal historians in the 18th century would have also been inclined to accept an influence of foreign law on medieval Nordic legislation, especially as they were aware of the contemporaneous dependence on Roman law and German doctrine. Kofod Ancher was probably the first legal historian to debate the foreign influence present in the medieval Danish provincial codes. In his whole production he asserted on several occasions that medieval legislation in Denmark had been entirely independent and national, and one chapter in his 'Law history' was devoted to demonstrating that the old Danish Laws were by no means based on "Sachsenspiegel". According to the author, medieval Danish society had been suspicious of everything of foreign origin, so why should they have used foreign laws, which had been made for other reasons. Not persons with foreign legal education, but righteous men with knowledge of local customs had, according to Kofod Ancher, contributed to the lawmaking. He also claimed that the younger Danish-Norwegian laws, including the codes of King Christian V from the late 17th century, were 'domestic fruits, born among us and growing out of our own soil'.

A modern reader may regard Kofod Ancher's point of view as an example of narrow-minded patriotism. The research of later Danish historians, starting already with Johan Frederik Wilhelm Schlegel (1765-1836), approved of Huitfeldt's opinion and provided evidence of the remarkable international background of Danish legislation in the Middle Ages. Kofod Ancher's opinion was not an incontrovertible truth even in the 18th century. His contemporary, Christian Ditlev Hedegaard (1700-1781), who, like Kofod Ancher, disliked the idea of a reception of foreign law, admitted that 'with the conversion to Christianity, many foreign principles, Canon as well as Roman, had gained influence, although this had been an impairment rather than an improvement'. Anders Sandøe Ørsted (1778-1860) accused Kofod Ancher of 'exaggerated patriotism' and of denying the powerful Roman influence on Danish law.

Why did Kofod Ancher, in many respects the first modern Nordic legal historian, stubbornly deny the reception of German and Roman law in the Middle Ages? At least in the 1770s Kofod Ancher adopted a national political attitude, dedicating the second part of his 'Law History' to Queen

Juliane Marie and Prince Frederic, the royal guarantors of Ove Høegh Guldberg's Danish-national regime after the fall and execution of the German minister Johann Friedrich Struensee in 1772. Kofod Ancher's attempt at developing a scientific critique of the sources did not even in this case prevent him from committing 'patriotic' errors; as mentioned above, his weak point was a strong tendency to succumb to conjecture.

Conclusion

As so many times before, in Kofod Ancher's production as well, medieval legal history and contemporaneous political aims were intertwined. In the research on legal history the answers to the problem concerning the Nordic nature of these laws and its antipode the foreign influence on the old Nordic laws have thus differed much during the centuries: from an early complete negligence of the whole question in the 17th century to a denial in the 18th and finally to a reluctant acceptance of a considerable influence of foreign legal systems in the 19th century. Some historians in the late 20th century have gone a step further and categorically denied any national particularity at all in the medieval Nordic codes - but that is the subject of another story.

POPE ALEXANDER III
AND DANISH LAWS OF INHERITANCE

Michael H. Gelting

– Ole Fenger in memoriam

Introduction

Since his monumental thesis of 1971 on feud and wergeld,[1] the late professor Ole Fenger's work has had a seminal influence on well-nigh every study that has been written on Danish society in the high Middle Ages. In the present article, I wish to develop some possible implications of an idea which Fenger propounded in his contribution to the 750 years' jubilee volume in honour of the Law of Jutland (*Jyske Lov*), concerning the origins of the earliest of the medieval Danish law books, the 'Book of Inheritance and Heinous Crimes' (*Arvebog og Orbodemål*).[2] Fenger proposed to connect this text with the 'giving' or 'publication' of 'laws of the Danes' in 1170, mentioned by one medieval Danish annals,[3] thereby reviving an old

---

1. Ole Fenger: *Fejde og mandebod: Studier over slægtsansvaret i germansk og gammeldansk ret*, Copenhagen, Juristforbundets Forlag, 1971 (German summary p. 547-556).
2. The standard edition of the Danish law books from the twelfth and thirteenth centuries is *Danmarks gamle Landskabslove med Kirkelovene [DGL]*, general eds. Johs. Brøndum-Nielsen and Poul Johs. Jørgensen, 8 vols. + supplement to vol. 4, Copenhagen, Gyldendal, 1932-1961. The Book of Inheritance and Heinous Crimes is edited in *DGL*, vol. 7, *Valdemars sjællandske Lov: Arvebog og Orbodemål*, ed. Erik Kroman, 1942.
3. Ole Fenger: "Jydske Lov og de øvrige danske landskabslove," in *Jydske Lov 750 år*, eds. Ole Fenger and Chr. R. Jansen, Viborg, Udgiverselskabet ved Landsarkivet for Nørrejylland, 1991, p. 37-50, at p. 47. See further below, at n. 28.

hypothesis that had been abandoned in the nineteenth century.[4] This means addressing the question of how the medieval Danish law books came into existence. Contrary to the situation in Norwegian and Swedish research,[5] this question has not attracted much attention among Danish medievalists. Ironically, this absence may also reflect Fenger's influence to some extent: in part because Fenger's work on feud and wergeld has often – to his own dismay – been misused to buttress an illusion of the Scandinavian distinctiveness of Danish society in its first Christian centuries; but in part also because Fenger himself seems to have remained reluctant to abandon the idea that part of the contents of the medieval law books might reflect ancient custom rather than recent innovations.[6]

The possibility of such customary survivals cannot be ruled out; but by demonstrating the extent to which the Danish law books reflect the influence of learned law and contemporary trends in European jurisprudence,[7] Fenger shifted the burden of proof from those who claim to detect innovations in the law books onto the shoulders of those who wish to use these texts as pathways to an earlier, distinctively Danish, Scandinavian or even Germanic social order.[8] This applies particularly to the earliest, less comprehensive texts, for I take it as a truism that the most likely reason for writing such laws was a desire for change or reform, not a conservative striving to uphold existing rules. Writing down uncontroversial points of customary law is likely to have belonged to a later phase, in the context of creating a comprehensive code of law.

In accordance with this view, the hypothesis that I intend to argue in the present article is that the Book of Inheritance did not represent existing customary law, but that it constituted a wholesale and quite radical transformation of Danish rules of inheritance, although with some

---

4. Henning Matzen: *Forelæsninger over den danske Retshistorie: Indledning. Retskilder*, Copenhagen, Schultz, 1897, p. 175-176; cf. Chr. L. E. Stemann: *Den danske Retshistorie indtil Christian V.'s Lov*, Copenhagen, Gyldendal, 1871, p. 21.
5. For Sweden e.g. the controversial book by Elsa Sjöholm: *Sveriges medeltidslagar: Europeisk rättstradition i politisk omvandling* (Skrifter utgivna av Institutet för rättshistorisk forskning, ser. 1, Rättshistoriskt bibliotek, vol. 41), Lund (Stockholm), Nordiska bokhandeln, 1988; see in general Per Norseng: "Lovmaterialet som kilde til tidlig nordisk middelalder," in *Kilderne til den tidlige middelalders historie: Rapporter fra den XX nordiske historikerkongres,* Reykjavík 1987, vol. 1 (Ritsafn Sagnfræðistofnunar, 18), Reykjavík, Sagnfræðistofnun Háskóla Íslands, 1987, p. 48-77.
6. Esp. Ole Fenger: *Gammeldansk ret: Dansk rets historie i oldtid og middelalder*, Viborg, Centrum, 1983, p. 62-63, 96-100.
7. Cf. Ole Fenger: *Romerret i Norden*, Copenhagen, Berlingske Forlag, 1977, p. 50-115.
8. Cf. Ditlev Tamm: *Dansk & Europæisk retshistorie: Studieudgave*, Copenhagen, Jurist- og Økonomforbundets Forlag, 2001, p. 22.

concessions to customary attitudes. Moreover, this reform was the only purpose of the legislation of 1170: Fenger's date of 1170 only applies to the Book of Inheritance properly speaking, i.e. the first book of the law as it has been transmitted to us, while the peace legislation in the rest of the law – the Heinous Crimes part – originated in a parliament in 1184. The Book of Inheritance was transmitted as an independent text, being augmented at the end with new articles based on court decisions, until it was amalgamated with the peace legislation of 1184 into the revised text known as King Valdemar's Law for Sealand in the 1220s or 1230s.

Accepting Fenger's date of 1170 for the Book of Inheritance places it in a quite particular political context. It means that the law was contemporary with momentous shifts in Danish politics: King Valdemar I's (1154/57-1182) shift of allegiance from the German king and emperor Frederick Barbarossa to Pope Alexander III, and the ideological and political founding of a new Danish dynastic royalty. I will further argue that a letter from Alexander III to Sweden from the early 1170s indicates that the enactment of the Book of Inheritance may have been connected with the negotiations that preceded Valdemar I's switch of allegiance. The relevance of this letter in the context of Danish as well as Swedish rules of inheritance has long been noticed,[9] but I believe that its possible implications for our understanding of the origins and political significance of the Danish law have not been sufficiently recognised.

The Book of Inheritance and Heinous Crimes

From the late thirteenth century onwards,[10] the Book of Inheritance and Heinous Crimes, under the name of 'Valdemar's Law for Sealand' (*Valdemars Sjællandske Lov*), was used as one of the two law books in force in the province of Sealand, consisting of the main island of that name with adjacent minor islands.[11] The other law book for this province was the much more bulky and comprehensive so-called 'Eric's Law for Sealand' (*Eriks Sjællandske Lov*), roughly datable to the 1240s.[12] The two texts are

---

9. See below, n. 90.
10. See below, at n. 35.
11. The law of Sealand was extended to the southern islands of Lolland, Falster and Møn by King Eric V in 1284: *Den danske rigslovgivning indtil 1400 [DRL]*, ed. Erik Kroman, Copenhagen, Munksgaard, 1971, no. 16, 1284 May 26, art. 16, p. 143. The two former and larger of these islands belonged to the diocese of Odense in the island of Funen, which used the Law of Jutland.
12. *DGL*, vol. 5, *Eriks sjællandske Lov: Text 1-2*, ed. Peter Skautrup, 1936. For the date of the law, see e.g. Erik Kroman: "Danmarks gamle Love: Deres Alder og indbyrdes Slægtskab," in *Acta philologica Scandinavica*, 29, 1971-1973, p. 111-

usually transmitted together in the manuscripts, being obviously considered to be mutually complementary: the first two books of Eric's Law follow the structure of Valdemar's Law, but their articles supplement rather than replace the provisions of the earlier compilation.[13] However, the manuscripts of Valdemar's Law from the province of Sealand contain a revised text.[14] The most important changes introduced by this revision were the replacement of trial by ordeal with verdict by jury, and the adoption of a number of articles from the Law of Scania (*Skånske Lov*). Both elements indicate that the revision cannot be earlier than the 1220s.[15] While the Valdemar whose name is associated with the law may originally have been Valdemar I,[16] it is obvious that by the late thirteenth century its name was understood to refer to King Valdemar II (1202-1241),[17] who had by then

---

126 (English summary p. 125-126), at p. 121-122. Annette Hoff: *Lov og landskab: Landskabslovenes bidrag til forståelsen af landbrugs- og landskabsudviklingen i Danmark ca. 900-1250*, Århus, Aarhus Universitetsforlag, 1997, p. 22, considers the law to be contemporary with the Law of Jutland of 1241 or possibly slightly later (c. 1250). Fenger thought that the text had been compiled somewhat earlier, but that it did not come into widespread use until the reign of King Eric IV (1241-1250); Fenger: "Jydske Lov," p. 43. Recently Helle Vogt has argued cogently for dating Eric's Law to shortly before 1248; Helle Vogt, *The Function of Kinship in Nordic Medieval Legislation*, Brill 2010, p. 68-71.

13. Erik Kroman and Stig Iuul: *Danmarks gamle Love paa Nutidsdansk*; 3 vols., Copenhagen, Gad, 1945-1948, vol. 1, p. X; Erik Kroman: "Eriks sjællandske lov," in *Kulturhistorisk leksikon for nordisk middelalder [KLNM]*, Copenhagen, Rosenkilde & Bagger, 1956-1978, vol. 4, col. 34-36, at col. 34.
14. The revised text exists in two different versions, traditionally called the Earlier redaction (*Ældre redaktion*) and the Later redaction (*Yngre redaktion*), although there is no convincing evidence for determining the chronological priority of either of them. Edition: *DGL*, vol. 8, *Valdemars sjællandske lov: Ældre og yngre redaktion samt Sjællandske kirkelov*, ed. Erik Kroman, 1941.
15. This date is based upon my revision of the traditionally admitted dates for the Law of Scania from [1200/02 × 1216] to c. 1220, and of King Valdemar II's ordinance on ordeals from [1216 or shortly afterwards] to 1222/23. See Michael H. Gelting: "Skånske Lov og Jyske Lov: Danmarks første kommissionsbetænkning og Danmarks første retsplejelov", in *Jura & Historie: Festskrift til Inger Dübeck som forsker*, ed. Finn Taksøe-Jensen, Copenhagen, Jurist- og Økonomforbundets Forlag, 2003, p. 43-80, at p. 71-76.
16. Fenger: *Gammeldansk ret*, p. 96; *idem*, "Jydske Lov," p. 43.
17. Several manuscripts explicitly designate Valdemar's Law (also in its Scanian transmission, cf. below) as 'Valdemar's new law' or 'Valdemar's second law', implying that there was a previous law issued by the same king; *DGL*, vol. 7, p. 3; vol. 8, p. 3. This must mean the Law of Scania, although in all probability that law was never formally enacted (Gelting: 'Skånske Lov og Jyske Lov,' p. 77-80).

acquired a quasi-canonical status as the founding father of Danish law.[18] The earliest extant manuscript is datable to the late thirteenth century.[19] In the early fifteenth century Valdemar's Law was adopted in the neighbouring province of Scania (now the southernmost part of Sweden) as a supplement to the Law of Scania from c. 1220, which itself was in part based upon the original text of 'Valdemar's Law'.[20] Interestingly, the fifteenth-century Scanian transmission of the text[21] must have been based upon a very old manuscript that pre-dated the thirteenth-century revision of Valdemar's Law. It contains numerous linguistic archaisms,[22] and it retains the extensive use of trial by ordeal. Yet it is probably not a totally faithful rendering of the ancient text. One article seems to be a later addition,[23] and some of the textual variants compared with the Sealandian version may be

---

18. Cf. the epithet 'Legislator' (*leges regis Woldemari legis latoris bone memorie*; *konyng Woldemars loghførræs loghær* in a near-contemporary Danish translation) given him in the election charter of King Oluf in 1376; *DRL*, no. 31, 280, 287. The somewhat deceptive epithet 'Sejr' ('Victory') under which he is now known is a later invention.
19. University of Copenhagen, Arnamagnaean Institute, ms. AM 24, 4°: fragment of the Earlier redaction containing the first 50 chapters, dated late thirteenth century *DGL*, vol. 7, p. VIII and IL (but c. 1300 p. XLVIII). The oldest manuscripts of the Later redaction are not much later: AM 455, 12° (c. 1300); Stockholm, Royal Library, C 39, 4° (early fourteenth century), and C 63, 4° (early fourteenth century/c. 1325): *ibid.*, p. X, XXIV-XXV, L-LII.
20. Kroman: 'Danmarks gamle Love,' p. 112. Kroman is inclined to think that the earlier text had been in continuous use alongside the Law of Scania ever since the writing of the latter, but its absence from any manuscript of the Law of Scania earlier than the mid-fifteenth century speaks against this hypothesis. Cf. the following note.
21. The oldest extant manuscripts are from the mid-fifteenth century, but the so-called Rantzovian manuscript Copenhagen, Royal Library, E don. var. 136, 4°, dated 1472, has a colophon stating that it was copied from a manuscript written in the borough of Væ in Scania in 1430: *DGL*, vol. 7, p. XII, cf. p. XLIV, LVI-LVII.
22. E.g. Johs. Brøndum-Nielsen: "Om Sprogformen i de sjællandske Love," in *Acta philologica Scandinavica*, 29, 1971-1973, p. 81-110 (English summary p. 109-110).
23. Bk. 1, art. 11. The provision concerns procedures in case of doubt as to the validity of a gift from a grandfather to the children of a predeceased child. It refers to testimony from the public court (*tingsvidne*), which did not become essential for property transactions until the Law of Jutland in 1241; and in striving to follow the archaic style of the text, the writer seems to have misunderstood the warning *se the fore guthi hwat the swæriæ* ('what they swear, let it be sworn for God'); on the latter point, see Kroman and Iuul: *Danmarks gamle Love*, vol. 3, p. 68. The article is absent from both redactions of the revised text in Valdemar's Law. It would thus seem to be a late addition, possibly as late as the 'revival' of the law in Scania in the fifteenth century.

the outcome of some reworking of the Scanian text.[24] Moreover, the old manuscript upon which the entire Scanian tradition of the text was based seems to have contained a couple of glaring omissions that were faithfully copied in all the manuscripts descended from it.[25] In the present state of research, it does not seem possible to reconstruct an exact original text from the different versions, but we can be reasonably certain about the substance of its contents.

In the Scanian transmission, the law was of course not called a law for Sealand, and it is this version that is usually known as the *Book of Inheritance and Heinous Crimes*. This title reflects the dual nature of the law book. Its first part is solely concerned with rules of inheritance, while the rest of the law deals with breaches of the peace. Philologists have pointed out that there are some linguistic differences between the two parts in the Scanian version. It has been suggested that the Book of Inheritance was originally written in the dialect of the western Danish province of Jutland,[26] but most philologists now seem inclined to think that the difference rather reflects different dates of composition,[27] the Book of Inheritance being the earlier of the two, probably from the third quarter of the twelfth century, while the rest of the law book is slightly later.

It is the result of these philological studies that opens up the possibility that the law book should be identified with two otherwise unknown legal texts whose promulgation is mentioned in medieval Danish sources. Under the year 1170, the late thirteenth-century annals of the Cistercian abbey of Ryd note that "the laws of the Danes were promulgated" (*Leges Danorum edite sunt*).[28] Like a number of other thirteenth-century Danish annals, the Annals of Ryd drew upon the annalistic tradition of the archiepiscopal see of Lund,[29] which does not seem to have had this piece of information.[30]

---

24. E.g. bk. 1, art. 67, where the Scanian text has eliminated the original reference to property transfers according to Jutish custom which is transmitted by some manuscripts of the Earlier redaction of Valdemar's Law (art. 13). Cf. below, at n. 60-61.
25. Bk. 1, art. 27 (*DGL*, vol. 7, p. 20); art. 47 (Kroman and Iuul: *Danmarks gamle Love*, vol. 3, p. 71).
26. Brøndum-Nielsen: "Om Sprogformen," p. 102-108.
27. Following the meticulous study by Gerd Wellejus: *Jysk, sjællandsk eller skånsk? En undersøgelse af kriterierne for jysk dialekt, baseret på det gammeldanske lovsprog* (Københavns Universitet, Institut for nordisk filologi, Studier, 2), Copenhagen, Universitetsforlaget, 1972.
28. *Danmarks middelalderlige annaler*, ed. Erik Kroman, Copenhagen, Selskabet for udgivelse af kilder til dansk historie, 1980, p. 166.
29. Graphically shown by the synoptic printing of the Annals of Lund, Ryd, Sorø, the two Annals of Næstved and the so-called 'Valdemar Annals' in *Annales Danici medii ævi*, ed. Ellen Jørgensen, Copenhagen, Gad, 1920, p. 72-129 (the year 1170 at p. 84-85). Cf. *ibid.*, p. 16; *Danmarks middelalderlige annaler*, p. 149.

However, the Annals of Ryd also drew upon other, partly unknown sources, and although the legislative act of 1170 is not found in any other source, there is no serious reason to doubt the veracity of the report. Like some of the other Danish annals, the Annals of Ryd tend to be one year off for the late twelfth century,[31] so the event might have occurred in 1169. Then, in the year 1184, a parliament in the island of Samsø is said to have "improved the secular laws".[32] The assertion is found in the *Gesta Danorum* of Saxo Grammaticus, probably written a couple of decades after the event, and although it is not confirmed by other sources, there is no substantial reason for impugning it. I would suggest that the Book of Inheritance should be dated to 1169/70, and that the peace legislation in the rest of Valdemar's Law originated in the parliament of 1184. Due to the nature of the evidence, no positive proof of this hypothesis may be hoped for, but as I intend to show, it might fit in well with the political situation in Denmark in the late 1160s.

It might arguably be a problem to identify a provincial law for Sealand with legislative initiatives that were explicitly designed for the whole of the realm. This problem, however, seems to have been created by legal and political developments during the thirteenth century. A review of the evidence indicates that all of the Danish legislation until the late thirteenth century was designed to produce a national body of law,[33] although some ordinances seem to have made concessions to regional particularism.[34]

---

30. On the annalistic tradition of Lund, see the fundamental study by Anne K. G. Kristensen: *Danmarks ældste Annalistik: Studier over lundensisk Annalskrivning i 12. og 13. Århundrede* (Skrifter udgivet af det Historiske Institut ved Københavns Universitet, 3), Copenhagen, Gyldendal, 1969.
31. Thus the translation of the relics of St. Canute Duke in 1170 is dated 1171, and the abdication of Archbishop Eskil in 1177 is dated 1178.
32. *Saxonis Gesta Danorum [Saxo]*, eds. J. Olrik and H. Ræder, Copenhagen, Levin & Munksgaard, 1931, bk. 16, ch. 4 ¶ 2, p. 541: *Apud insulam deinde Samsam non solum huius negotii explicandi, sed etiam iuris civilis emendandi gratia ingenti nobilitate contracta, amborum legatos excepit.*
33. I have argued this hypothesis at length in Gelting: "Skånske Lov og Jyske Lov", to which I refer for the rest of the present paragraph.
34. In particular, Valdemar II's ordinance of ordeals, which I propose to date to 1222/23 (*ibid.*, p. 76). Like a couple of other early thirteenth-century ordinances, it has only been preserved in the version issued for the province of Scania; edited in *Diplomatarium Danicum [DD]*, 1st ser. vol. 5, no. 96, p. 137-143 (there dated [1216 or not much later]). Similar ordinances must have been issued for the rest of the Danish provinces, replacing trial by ordeal with trial by jury. In 1228, a royal ordinance for the Diocese of Odense mentions a jury called *veridici*; *DRL*, no. 6, p. 42. This jury would seem to be the same as the "truthful men" (*sandemænd*) of the Law of Jutland of 1241, an institution which never entered Scanian procedure, as the project for a national code of law ultimately failed. It is likely to have been

Actual practice was another matter. Despite several attempts, no comprehensive, national code of law was ever issued in Denmark during the Middle Ages, to the difference of Norway and Sweden. Apart from Valdemar's Law for Sealand, the Danish medieval law books – the Law of Scania of c. 1220, the Law of Jutland from 1241, and Eric's Law of the 1240s – should probably all be understood as drafts for a national code or interim legislation in the expectation of such a code. This ultimately left the individual provinces fairly free to choose those texts which they found most suitable for local conditions. And when King Eric V in 1282 had to give in after a prolonged conflict with aristocratic opposition, it was stated that the kingdom was to be governed according to the laws of King Valdemar.[35] Subsequent practice shows that this meant the law book or law books that each province had chosen among the existing texts. It is not until 1282 that we may properly speak of provincial law books in Denmark.

Nevertheless, the Book of Inheritance had obviously been accepted across the whole realm, for its articles were the foundation of the principles of inheritance in all of the subsequent laws, influencing both the structure of the texts and their wording. Although the manuscript is comparatively late (c. 1400), the title given to Valdemar's Law in Stockholm, Royal Library, ms. C 69, may not only be copied from its exemplar, but also be a correct statement of fact: "Here begins the law which King Valdemar gave to do justice to all Danes in Denmark".[36]

An Analysis of the Book of Inheritance

The study of the medieval Danish law books has been bedevilled right from the outset by the assumption that they mainly represented an essentially coherent body of traditional, customary law. Hence all authors have attempted to conflate the laws into an overarching system.[37] This approach

---

introduced by the version of the ordinance of ordeals that must have been issued for Jutland (the diocese of Odense in Funen followed Jutish law).

35. In the great charter of King Eric V of 1282 July 29, *DRL*, no. 13, art. 5, p. 77: *Ordinamus insuper et firmiter promittimus leges regis Waldemari clare memorie, prout in suis libris legalibus continentur, inuiolabiliter obseruare* (version issued for Jutland and Sealand; identical in the Scanian version, *ibid.*, p. 97).

36. *Hær byriæs thæn logh ær konung waldæmar giorthæ allæ danæ til rætæ .i. danmark*; *DGL*, vol. 8, p. 3. The manuscript is the oldest complete text of the Earlier redaction of Valdemar's Law; cf. *DGL*, vol. 7, p. XLVIII.

37. This was already the approach of the founder of modern Danish legal history, Peder Kofod Ancher (1710-1788); Peder Kofod Ancher: *En Dansk Lov-Historie: Fra Kong Harald Blaatands Tid til Kong Christian den Femtes*, vol. 1, Copenhagen, Godiche, 1769, p. 397-524.

was exacerbated in the early nineteenth century under the influence of the German school of legal history and its Germanistic, national romantic assumptions, which for long discredited the idea that any of the law books could have been the product of royal legislation, except for the Law of Jutland, whose prologue leaves no doubt as to the political context of its enactment.[38] It must be admitted that in recent years, Ole Fenger's work has contributed to preserving this approach: in his desire to counter twentieth-century Danish medievalists' penchant for depicting the kingship of the Valdemarians (1157-1241) as a quasi-absolutist regime,[39] he too categorically dismissed the idea that the kings of that era had the power to initiate legislation. In Fenger's interpretation of medieval culture, law was considered to be immanent and pre-existing; hence law could only be 'found', not 'created'.[40] Even an enacted law had to refer to some set of pre-existing rules, and innovation could happen only by adaptation in practice or by referring to a competing legal system, i.e. canon law or Roman law.

While there is no doubt a good deal of truth to Fenger's picture of the ideological assumptions behind the writing of law texts in the high Middle Ages, it does not preclude that changes in the law might happen at royal initiative, nor that the result might functionally be new legislation. But by insisting on traditional conceptions of law as the foundation of the medieval Danish law books, Fenger's work has discouraged studies of the political context and import of the individual law books. It may be added that the exalted status of the Law of Jutland in the national conscience of many Danes, due to its high-principled prologue, has tended to draw attention away from the other law books.[41]

---

38. Cf. Poul Johs. Jørgensen: *Dansk Retshistorie: Retskildernes og Forfatningsrettens Historie indtil sidste Halvdel af det 17. Aarhundrede*, 2nd ed., Copenhagen, Gad, 1947, p. 2.

39. Notably in Aksel E. Christensen: *Kongemagt og aristokrati: Epoker i middelalderlig dansk statsopfattelse indtil Unionstiden*, 2nd ed., Copenhagen, Munksgaard, 1968 (1st ed. 1945), ch. 3, p. 40-67. "The strong kingship of the Valdemarians" (p. 40) is characterized as a "monarchic-autocratic system that otherwise was foreign to the medieval monarchy" (p. 61). The book as a whole constituted a landmark in Danish historiography on the political structures of the Middle Ages, and it remained authoritative for generations of history students.

40. Fenger: *Gammeldansk ret*, esp. p. 83-86; cf. idem, *"Kirker rejses alle vegne": 1050-1250* (Gyldendal og Politikens Danmarkshistorie, ed. Olaf Olsen, vol. 4), Copenhagen, Gyldendal and Politiken, 1989, p. 87-97.

41. The Law of Jutland was twice honoured by a *Festschrift*, on its seventh centenary in 1941 and for its 750 years in 1991. *Med Lov skal Land bygges*, ed. Erik Reitzel-Nielsen, Copenhagen, Nyt Nordisk Forlag Arnold Busck, 1941; *Jydske Lov 750 år*, eds. Fenger and Jansen. Incidentally, the much vaunted prologue is almost entirely composed of translated excerpts from the Decretum Gratiani; Ludvig Holberg: *Leges Waldemari regis: Kong Valdemars Lov. Et Bidrag til Oplysning om*

One of the net results of all these circumstances is that next to no attention has been paid to the structure of each individual law book, despite the fact that such studies are essential for interpreting their purpose and the circumstances of their creation. In a previous study I have analyzed the structure of the Law of Jutland and the precise nature of its relationship to the Law of Scania. This enabled me to propose the hypothesis that the Law of Jutland was intended as an interim law covering the most pressing needs, especially in the field of legal procedure, until a comprehensive law code could be issued, and that its last 31 articles did not belong to the text that was enacted in 1241, but were later additions from the period 1241-1276/82.[42] It may be hoped that a similar analysis of the structure of the Book of Inheritance may produce clues to its purpose and the circumstances of its creation.

The study of the structure of the Book of Inheritance is complicated by the fact that in all probability none of the manuscripts in the complex transmission of the text faithfully reproduces the chapter division of the original law of 1169/70. However, the succession of the items was stable in all branches of the transmission, so that it remains possible to discern the logic of the law's structure.

The Book of Inheritance is a remarkably stringent and systematic piece of legislation, demonstrating quite a high level of abstraction in defining the basic principles that should govern the practice of inheritance and the community of the household that was inextricably bound up with it.[43] The basic principles are set out in its first three articles:[44]

1. Son and daughter are father's and mother's next heirs. Son takes a full lot, daughter takes half a lot. If a son or a daughter is married out of the household community, he or she takes out his or her lot in all of the possessions of the community except for the parents' paternal landed

---

Danmarks Statsret i det 13de Aarhundrede, Copenhagen, Gad, 1886, p. 80-86; idem, *Dansk og fremmed Ret: Retshistoriske Afhandlinger*, Copenhagen, Gad, 1891, p. 37ff.

42. Gelting: "Skånske Lov og Jyske Lov," p. 52-71.
43. The fundamental study of these questions is Stig Iuul: *Fællig og Hovedlod: Studier over Formueforholdet mellem Ægtefæller i Tiden før Christian V's Danske Lov*, Copenhagen, Nyt Nordisk Forlag Arnold Busck, 1940. Like all other Danish legal historians, however, Iuul attempted to conflate and harmonize the law books into a coherent system, although with full awareness of the possibility of regional and chronological variations. See now also Inger Dübeck,: *Kvinder, familie og formue: Studier i dansk og europæisk retshistorie*, Copenhagen, Museum Tusculanum, 2003, p. 13-171.
44. The numbers of the articles refer to the first book of the Book of Inheritance and Heinous Crimes, which is the Book of Inheritance properly speaking.

inheritance and such inheritances as either parent had received after their wedding.

2. The parents' paternal inheritance is all the land that either spouse owned before their wedding.

3. No outsider inherits from a child that dies within the household community.

The remainder of the law is essentially an application of these basic principles to a great variety of possible situations. It will be noted that the definition of the rule concerning children who leave the household community is held in abstract terms. It is assumed that the usual reason for leaving the community would be the child's marriage, but implicitly the rule would apply to a child leaving the community for any reason. This dispensed the law from laying down specific rules concerning dowry or other property transfers in connection with marriage such as the 'morning gift' from the bridegroom to the bride.[45] This feature was repeated in all of the subsequent Danish law books, much to the surprise of modern legal historians.[46] However, it simply reflects the level of abstraction in the earliest of the laws, in which dowry was assimilated to any other form of taking out the child's part of the household community's chattels upon his or her leaving the community.[47]

Having thus posited the basic principles, the authors of the law proceeded to treat the problems of inheritance connected with children who predeceased their parents after having left the household community, according to the following possible situations:

4. The predeceased child had no offspring.

5. The predeceased child had offspring, and their grandfather or their uncles and aunts claim that the children of the deceased have got more than their share in the household community's chattels.

6. The predeceased child had offspring, and they claim that they have not got their full share of the household community's chattels.

Logically, the next articles deal with grandchildren in other respects:

7. A predeceased child had remained within the household community, and after his or her death, his or her children leave the community.

8. Grandparents wish to bestow a gift upon the children of a predeceased child. The gift is limited to the size of the portion that the predeceased child would have inherited if it had lived.

This article shows beyond doubt that art. 1 should be understood restrictively. There was no right of representation, and thus surviving

---

45. Iuul: *Fællig og Hovedlod*, p. 190-196.
46. *Ibid.*, p. 190; Stig Iuul in Lizzie Carlsson, Rigmor Frimannslund, E. A. Virtanen and Stig Iuul: 'Medgift,' in *KLNM*, 11, col. 517-523, at col. 523.
47. Cf. Dübeck: *Kvinder, familie og formue*, p. 96-97.

children excluded grandchildren by a predeceased child, provided the latter had left the household community.⁴⁸

9. If the grandchildren have enjoyed possession of their grandparents' gift for six weeks before the latter's death, they have the right to defend their case.

Determining which of the parties to a lawsuit who had the right to defend his case was a crucial step in the procedures of the medieval Danish law books.⁴⁹ The defence in the Book of Inheritance was almost invariably twelve men's oath (or a multiple thereof) and, in most cases, two witnesses. The formal nature of the defence made it essential to determine who had the right to defend his case.⁵⁰

10. The preceding articles apply to maternal as well as to paternal grandparents.

[11. If the grandparents die before the grandchildren have enjoyed possession of their gift for six weeks, their uncles and aunts have the right to defend their case.] This article seems to be a later interpolation.⁵¹ Presumably the authors of the law expected this to be obvious.

12. In the absence of surviving children, grandchildren inherit.

13. In the absence of surviving children *and* grandchildren, great-grandchildren inherit, because inheritance always descends as long as there are descendants. But great-grandchildren share equally irrespective of sex, because such inheritance is *gangæ arf* – a strange word that may mean something like 'wandering inheritance'; it could hardly have been coined by the authors of the law, but was rather taken over from current usage.

Art. 13 brings two other statements of principle: that inheritage always descends, and that inheritance beyond the grandchildren does not follow the unequal division according to sex that obtains in the case of children and grandchildren. The first of these statements is interesting in comparison with Norwegian and Swedish law, to which I shall return later.⁵² The second

---

48. Stig Iuul in Stig Iuul and Kauko Pirinen: 'Arveret,' in *KLNM*, vol. 1, col. 258-267, at col. 260. If the deceased child remained within the community, his or her children shared the lot of the deceased according to the usual division, full lot to sons and half lots to daughters; art. 7.
49. Cf. Henning Matzen: *Forelæsninger over den danske Retshistorie: Offentlig Ret*, 2, *Proces*, Copenhagen, Schultz, 1894, p. 44-46.
50. For a rare but telling instance of contemporary practice, see King Valdemar I's sentence in *DD*, 1st ser. vol. 3, no. 103 (1182), p. 166: in a dispute between the local peasantry and the Cistercian abbey of Esrom concerning a forest in Halland, the king ruled that the abbey was entitled to defend its case. After the old king's death, the monks duly produced the required defence and secured a sentence in their favour from Valdemar's son and successor Cnut VI.
51. Above, n. 23.
52. Below, at n. 71.

statement is remarkable in showing that the unequal division between male and female children and grandchildren did not spring from systematic discrimination against female property holding, but that it must have had other reasons. It points to the same conclusion that in every applicable case, the mother was entitled to a full lot like the father and the sons. The law itself does not provide any clue to the reasons for the inequality affecting daughters and granddaughters. It is tempting to assume that it reflected traditional norms for the size of brides' dowries: while the household head would normally arrange the marriage of his daughters and might do so for orphaned granddaughters, this was extremely unlikely to happen in the case of great-granddaughters. Obviously it would not apply to collateral inheritance either, which according to art. 80 was also considered as *gangæ arf*.[53] However, the logic of such a reasoning is not particularly compelling. Perhaps the rules simply reflect a compromise between two mutually incompatible opinions: on the one hand the view that even though women might inherit, male heirs ought to be preferred; and on the other hand the position of Roman and canon law, that full partible inheritance should obtain irrespective of sex.[54]

Without going into similar detail, it can be stated that the subsequent segments of the law are equally systematic, logical and thorough in their treatment of the questions involved.

Art. 14-26 deal with the household community, especially the numerous problems involved in the case of the surviving parent's remarriage after the decease of his or her first spouse.

Art. 27-33 state the rules for the curious phenomenon of 'biting' inheritances: if either spouse receives an inheritance after the wedding, it remains his or her separate property, just as the paternal inheritance. But if the other spouse subsequently recieves an inheritance, that inheritance is said to 'bite' (*bidæ/bitæ*) the first spouse's inheritance, so that all the inheritances of both become the common property of the household community (the Law of Scania and the Law of Jutland use the verb *betæ*, i.e. to 'hunt' or to 'catch').[55] This only applies in the immediate; if one of the spouses receives a new inheritance later on, that inheritance remains separate property unless the other spouse receives a new inheritance too. Another way of including the separate inheritance of the wife in the household community is by right of childbirth (*barnmynding*): if the wife bears a child to her husband after having received an inheritance, that inheritance becomes common property. However, in this case the logic does

---

53. Cf. below, at n. 65.
54. Iuul: *Fællig og Hovedlod*, p. 75-76. Cf. below, at n. 82-83.
55. Kroman and Iuul: *Danmarks gamle Love*, vol. 3, p. 68-69; Iuul, *Fællig og Hovedlod*, p. 186.

not operate *vice versa*: bearing a child to the husband does not give the wife part in his separate inheritance. This last rule breaks with the complete reciprocity between spouses that otherwise dictates the inheritance system of the Book of Inheritance; it is not found in this segment, where one would expect it, but at the end of art. 47, concerning the division of a deceased wife's property between the widowed husband and the children. It may be a later interpolation. Under certain circumstances, 'biting' inheritance may also apply to inheritances received by children of a previous marriage who have remained within the household community.

The rather complicated rules concerning the 'biting' of inheritances look suspiciously like a compromise between mutually incompatible principles:[56] on the one hand a point of view that maintained that all inheritance, whenever received, must be treated like the paternal inheritance, i.e. remain the separate property of each spouse; on the other hand the opinion that inheritances received after the wedding should be considered as acquisitions and thus be included in the household community.

The next articles, art. 34-38, detail the rules applying to in-marrying daughters-in-law and sons-in-law, i.e. the option that a child does not leave the household community upon marriage, but instead brings his or her spouse into the community. This includes disputes between the household head and the offspring of such marriages concerning their inheritance from their in-marrying parent.

Art. 39-42 pick up the thread from art. 17, which stated the options open to a widowed spouse upon remarriage concerning the inclusion in or exclusion from the new household community of his or her children by the previous marriage. They make detailed regulations for the resolution of the disputes that might arise from one of the options, namely that of including the children by the previous marriage by formal contract.

Art. 43-45 treat the rules applying to the dissolution of the household community in case of separation or divorce.

Art. 46-47 state the main rules on inheritance in the case of dissolution of the household community by the wife's death.

Art. 48-52 concern the household head's entry into religion or pious gifts. Since entry into religion presupposes that the estate is divided with his heirs, this includes a provision concerning acquisitions that the household head might make after the division has been completed. It has been suggested that all of these articles together with the first part of art. 53 are a later interpolation, since the discussion in art. 46-47 of inheritance upon the dissolution of the household community by one spouse's death is continued

---

56. Cf. Iuul: *Fællig og Hovedlod*, p. 186, where it is considered as a stage in an evolutionary process.

in the last part of art. 53 with the inverse case: that the husband dies first, leaving a widow.[57] However, the rule stated in art. 47 is that if the wife dies leaving offspring, her husband and each son each take a full lot and each daughter half a lot. The subsequent rules on pious gifts all concern what the father is allowed to do with his lot: if he is in good health, he may enter a religious house with his whole lot, but under no other circumstances may he deprive his heirs of more than half his lot. It thus belongs logically in the context of art. 47, and there is no reason to suppose an interpolation, least of all on such a crucial matter. It is more likely that the beginning of art. 53[58] is an interpolation, as it seems a little out of place here. It states that no heathen child is entitled to inherit, i.e. that a child who dies before baptism does not count in the succession. However, this problem would only arise if one of the parents died before the infant child, so perhaps the article was included in the original text in connection with the articles concerning the widow's household community.

As mentioned, the last part of art. 53 picks up from art. 47 by treating the division of the inheritance between mother and children after the father's death, and art. 54-60 continue quite logically with the rules applying to the household community between the widow and her children. They include a peculiar expression, *nokka kunar*, for a household consisting solely of a widow and her daughters. Its etymology seems doubtful, and like *gangæ arf* it was probably taken from current usage. It should be added that in such an all-female household, all members inherit equal shares; but it takes no more than the daughters having another guardian than their mother's to make this rule inapplicable.

Art. 61-66 treat various cases of disputes between the household head and outsiders who raise claims upon the household community's property.

Art. 67-68 state the conditions applying to alienation of land by widows or minors. In the case of minors, it is quite simple: their land cannot be alienated under any circumstances. In the case of a widow it is possible, but she may only alienate land if the transaction is performed by an adult son or brother, or in the absence of such persons, by a guardian who has to be her closest adult kinsman; her role is to stand by and hold on and approve.[59] This is where the Scanian manuscript tradition has eliminated a curious reference to Jutish law that is found in some manuscripts of the Later redaction of Valdemar's Law: if the widow has conveyed the land

---

57. Kroman and Iuul: *Danmarks gamle Love*, vol. 3, p. 71.
58. It is only in part of the manuscript tradition of the Book of Inheritance that this provision is conflated with the first provision in the following segment. The D group of manuscripts as well as the two redactions of the Sealandian Valdemar's Law distinguish between the two parts of this conflated article; *DGL*, vol. 7, p. 39.
59. *DGL*, vol. 7, art. 67, p. 49: *han skøde oc hun stande hoos oc halde a oc gewe ia til*.

according to Jutish law, she will not have to pay compensation if the conveyance is not respected.[60] The provision seems soon to have become incomprehensible and has been eliminated or modified in various ways in the different branches of the textual transmission.[61] The only reasonable explanation of this mysterious provision seems to be that before 1169/70, a widow was entitled to convey land by herself in Jutland, but not in the eastern Danish provinces. It is also noteworthy that the law does not tell anything about land conveyances by the household head. If the eventuality of alienation of land by widows and minors had to be regulated, alienations by adult male household heads are likely to have been a fairly common event.[62] Obviously the rules pertaining to that situation were not within the lawmakers' purview.

Thus far, the law is structured according to a strict and logical plan, systematically and stringently setting out the consequences of the initially stated principles as they apply to the many different situations that might arise during the life course of a household. In contrast, its last articles, art. 69-82, are a veritable miscellany, treating highly disparate matters that would naturally belong in one or other of the previously treated contexts: a son enters into religion against his father's will (art. 69); a dispute between stepfather and stepchildren as to what property belongs to the stepchildren's paternal inheritance and what belongs to their mother, the stepfather's present wife (art. 70-71); a father and a son who has children of his own go abroad and both die without the heirs having any means to determine which of them died first (art. 72);[63] any sibling may question the justness of the division of the inheritance of his or her parents as long as he or she lives, thereby obliging all siblings to equalise their lots, irrespective of whether some of them might have alienated part of their inheritance in the meantime (art. 73-74); the same applies if one sibling claims to have been disadvantaged upon leaving the community of the household compared to other siblings who have done likewise (art. 75); a man goes abroad, leaving a half-brother at home as his only heir, and the half-brother at home dies; he has two heirs, the half-brother abroad and a half-brother to the other side, and no news can be had whether the half-brother abroad is alive (art. 76-77); some of the heirs are abroad when the inheritance is about to be divided (art. 78-79).

---

60. Art. 13b: *æn thot hun scøtæ at iuzk logh a hun æy at bøtæ for hennæ scøtninge en thot hun halds ey*; *DGL*, vol. 8, p. 272.
61. *Ibid.*, apparatus to line 10; *ibid.*, p. 32 (Valdemar's Law, Earlier redaction, art. 65); vol. 7, p. 50.
62. Cf. art. 73-74 below.
63. Generously, the law allowed the children of the deceased son to defend their case, thereby ensuring them the right to inherit from their grandfather. Cf. above, n. 48.

All of these articles look very much like court decisions in individual cases that have subsequently been expanded into rules of general import. This is especially obvious in art. 71 and 72, which end by explaining how the decision applies to other, analogous cases. All of them may therefore safely be assumed to be later additions to the law. The additions must have been made before the Book of Inheritance was amalgamated with the text that I assume to be the peace legislation of 1184 – the Heinous Crimes part – into the Book of Inheritance and Heinous Crimes; this need not have happened before the revision of the texts in Valdemar's Law in the 1220s or 1230s.[64]

The final articles, art. 80-82, are more problematic. They seem to be quite essential to the questions of inheritance addressed by the law. Art. 80 states that if a man or a woman die without legitimate offspring, their father and mother, brothers and sisters are their next heirs, father, mother and brothers to full lots and sisters to half lots. If none of these are alive, the next heirs are grandparents, nephews and nieces. In the latter case, the inheritance is divided equally irrespective of sex, and the same goes for more distant heirs, because such inheritance is *gangu arf*.[65] Art. 81 states that if no closer heir is to be found, the inheritance may reach until the 'seventh man' (*siwnde man*). This is an obvious reference to the canonical prohibition against incestuous marriages in the form it had until the Fourth Lateran Council in 1215, which means that these articles must in any case be dated to the time before the decisions of that council were incorporated into Danish law, i.e. before c. 1220/22.[66] Finally, art. 82 treats the case where an inheritance falls to so distant kin that dispute may arise as to who is or is not entitled to inherit.

Prima facie one would think that such provisions must have been part of the original text of the law. However, by being placed at the very end of the Book of Inheritance, after a series of articles that are most likely to be later additions, it seems that they too must be the product of a later court decision. One feature that might be an indication that this is so is art. 80's precision in saying that it treats the case where a man or a woman dies without *legitimate* offspring (*rettan afkommande*). In previous articles, the law simply says 'without offspring' (*far vdan affkømd*).[67] This calls attention to the peculiar circumstance that the law contains no provisions whatsoever concerning illegitimate offspring, even though the Danish aristocracy at the time seems to have been surrounded by a plethora of

---

64. A possible occasion for the decision in art. 72 might have been the ill-fated attempt of a number of Danish aristocrats to join the Third Crusade, recounted in the little chronicle *De profectione Danorum in Hierosolymam*; *Scriptores minores historiæ Danicæ*, ed. M. Cl. Gertz, vol. 2, Copenhagen, Gad, 1918-1922, p. 443-492.
65. Cf. above, art. 13, at n. 53.
66. Gelting: "Skånske Lov og Jyske Lov," p. 73-76.
67. E.g. art. 4.

bastards. In this it differs from the later law books, including the revised texts of Valdemar's Law, which all contain detailed rules for a father who should wish to advantage an illegitimate child.[68] It looks as if the authors of the Book of Inheritance had decided simply to ignore the very possibility of the existence of illegitimate children, and the implicit reference to the problem in art. 80 suggests that this article, and by implication the connected articles 81-82, are not contemporaneous with the main text.

It is hardly likely that the authors of the law should have considered the case of inheritance outside the household community or the direct descendance to have been covered by the general principles stated in the first articles. Rather, this peculiar absence would be an indication that this extremely systematic and thorough piece of legislation was intended to regulate only those matters where the law was to be changed, and that this desire for reform did not apply to collateral inheritance. Existing rules or customs regulating collateral inheritance – *gangæ arf* – were simply not affected by the law. But as the law gradually became the standard reference in disputes over inheritance, the need was felt for fleshing it out with a statement of the principles applying in such cases. As a consequence, art. 80-82 were added. As they are the last in line, this may have happened as late as the beginning of the thirteenth century.

Recognising art. 69-82 as later additions means that the Book of Inheritance was originally transmitted as an independent text. In all likelihood it was not until the elaboration of the revised version in Valdemar's Law, in the 1220s or 1230s, that it was united with the peace legislation of 1184 to form one single law book.

A close reading of the Book of Inheritance thus yields the result that in its original form, it was an extremely thorough working out of the application of a few basic principles to an essential but limited part of Danish inheritance customs. It is utterly unlikely that such a text should be the product of a legal practitioner writing down what he knew about traditional customary law, as the established opinion has been for centuries. It must have been the result of a conscious and determined will to reform the law. In support of such a view, one may adduce the opinion of the eminent legal historian Stig Iuul, who reached the conclusion that the household community as it is found in the medieval Danish law books must have been a legal institute of quite recent origin, although he interpreted it as a stage in an organic evolutionary process.[69] In a recent book his successor in the field, Inger Dübeck, has expressed doubts about Iuul's

---

68. See e.g. Henning Matzen: *Forelæsninger over den danske Retshistorie: Privatret*, pt. 1, *Personret. Familieret. Arveret*, Copenhagen, Schultz, 1895, p. 92-96.
69. Iuul: *Fællig og Hovedlod*, esp. p. 182; *idem*, 'Formuefællesskab,' in *KLNM*, vol. 4, col. 487-491, esp. col. 487-488.

interpretation of the household community as a recent innovation, but she still concludes that it was shaped by the immediate circumstances of the late twelfth and early thirteenth centuries, notably the problem of protecting family property against encroachment by the Church.[70] There is probably some measure of truth to this interpretation, but the story behind the Book of Inheritance may have been rather different from the narrative of a traditional Danish society struggling to fend off a greedy Church that has dominated Danish medieval history for generations.

The Transformation of Danish Rules of Inheritance

If the purpose of the Book of Inheritance was to operate a major reform in Danish inheritance customs in so far as they applied to the married couple and its descendance, the next question must be what the customs were that it replaced, apparently successfully. We know precious little about Danish inheritance law before 1169/70, but a comparison with the rest of Scandinavia may enable us to propose some hypotheses.

The Swedish historian Birgit Sawyer has pointed out that in matters of inheritance, the Scandinavian law books fall into two distinct groups according to which basic principle of inheritance they applied.[71] The Norwegian and most of the Swedish laws apply a principle of inheritance according to degree of kinship ('gradual system' in Sawyer's terminology). According to this principle, a close collateral might exclude a more distant descendant from inheriting. In contrast, all of the Danish laws and two of the youngest Swedish provincial laws (the laws of Uppland, dated 1296, and of Hälsingland, which is partly dependent on the former and dates from the early fourteenth century[72]) apply the lineal system that is stated so clearly in the Book of Inheritance, art. 13: that inheritance always descends as long as there are descendants (*arf a e fram at ganga mæthin af kymmandi ær til*). Furthermore, while all the laws that apply the parentelic principle accord sisters rights of inheritance on a par with brothers, if only to half lots compared to the brothers' full lots, the laws applying the 'gradual system' mostly disadvantage female heirs to a greater or lesser degree. Moreover, the earliest laws have the most systematic postponement of female heirs: the Norwegian Gulating's Law and Frostating's Law, both of them probably

---

70. Dübeck: *Kvinder, familie og formue*, p. 79-87. Her conclusions p. 85-87 modify the views of Helge Paludan: *Familia og familie: To europæiske kulturelementers møde i højmiddelalderens Danmark*, Århus, Aarhus Universitetsforlag, 1995, p. 115-123, but without questioning the basic assumptions of his interpretation.
71. Birgit Sawyer: *The Viking-Age Rune-Stones: Custom and Commemoration in Early Medieval Scandinavia*, Oxford, Oxford University Press, 2000, p. 84-86.
72. Gerhard Hafström: „Hälsingelagen" in *KLNM*, vol. 7, col. 233-235.

written no later than the mid-twelfth century and possibly earlier, and the Elder Västgöta Law, the earliest (fragmentary) manuscript of which dates from the mid-thirteenth century.

Birgit Sawyer has interpreted these differences in the context of a study of patterns revealed by the rune-stones of the late Viking age (tenth and eleventh centuries). As she points out, there is a remarkable difference in sponsorship patterns between eastern Sweden and the rest of Scandinavia. While stones in eastern Sweden tended to be raised by several close kinsmen and kinswomen of the deceased, western Swedish, Danish and Norwegian stones were mainly raised by a single person, and the proportion of female sponsors was significantly higher in eastern Sweden than in the rest of Scandinavia.[73] She interprets the vast majority of the rune-stones as claims or statements of inheritance, thus inferring that they may reveal inheritance rules antedating the law books by a couple of centuries. While this is probably exaggerated, there can be no doubt that the patterns of rune-stone sponsorship that she has revealed must be significant, and that the most likely explanation for them is that the sponsors of rune-stones usually were the commemorated person's heirs.[74]

In the Danish case, Birgit Sawyer concludes that "Danish inheritance rules were changed between the rune-stone period and the time of the written laws".[75] The change would have been based on two principles: the replacement of the 'gradual system' with parentelic rules of inheritance, and the admission of sisters to share in the inheritance on a par with their brothers. This is exactly what the Book of Inheritance was about. In a pithy, adage-like turn of phrase, its art. 13 states the parentelic rule that inheritance always descends; and every time it is applicable, the rule of division between brothers and sisters is hammered out: brothers take full lots, sisters half lots. Danish inheritance rules were not changed between the rune-stone period and the time of the written laws. They were changed by the first of those laws, the Book of Inheritance of 1169/70.

However, such a momentous change can hardly be expected to have been carried out without encountering some resistance. The law must have been prepared by a commission of experienced men. This is probably reflected in the use of first person plural in some articles in all of the branches of the transmission,[76] although its replacement by first person singular in many articles in the two redactions of Valdemar's Law and by

---

73. Sawyer: *The Viking-Age Rune-Stones*, p. 71-91.
74. Michael H. Gelting: "Predatory Kinship Revisited," in *Anglo-Norman Studies*, 25, ed. John Gillingham, Woodbridge, Boydell, 2003, p. 107-119, at p. 110-112.
75. Sawyer: *The Viking-Age Rune-Stones*, p. 87.
76. E.g. Book of Inheritance, art. 25 = Valdemar's Law Earlier redaction, art. 22 = Valdemar's Law Later redaction, art. 1 ¶ 17: "But we wish you to know (etc.)" (*En thz williwm wi atj witæ / Æn thæt uilia wi at .i. witæ. / Æn thæt wilæ wi at i wittæ*).

impersonal expressions in some articles in the Book of Inheritance has given occasion to many speculations.[77] It is likely that the commission was composed of ecclesiastical as well as lay experts,[78] of conservatives as well as reformers. This would be a plausible explanation for the compromises that seem to permeate the entire text, despite its clear statements of principle. As mentioned above, the unequal division between brothers and sisters in the first and second generation of descendance, but neither beyond nor in collateral inheritance, looks like a somewhat muddled compromise between tenants of full partible inheritance and adherents of a principle favouring male heirs. If the 'gradual system' with postponement of female heirs was the set of inheritance rules that was replaced by the Book of Inheritance, as Birgit Sawyer's study suggests, this was exactly the kind of compromise that might make the reform palatable to conservative aristocrats.

Seen in this light, a similar compromise may have hatched the absence of a right of representation in favour of grandchildren by predeceased children who had left the household community. The rule is illogical from the point of view of the parentelic system and may thus be interpreted as a concession to conservatives who clung to the principles of the 'gradual system'. Birgit Sawyer assumes that the compromise arose because the two principles coexisted before the writing of the law.[79] However, that hypothesis is predicated upon the traditional assumption that the laws were the product of an organic evolutionary growth. If the Book of Inheritance was a piece of conscious, wholesale legal reform, as it seems to have been, there is no need for such a hypothesis.

The character of a compromise also affects the complicated rules concerning the household community. This has already been suggested above in connection with the peculiar system of 'biting' inheritances.[80] Actually the whole phenomenon of the household community looks rather like a compromise. On the one hand, the paternal landed inheritance of each spouse remains separate property; on the other hand, the household head has full control of all the property of every member of the household. This seems to be the most reasonable explanation of the rules concerning

---

77. Kroman: 'Danmarks gamle Love,' p. 115-116.
78. Cf. the important role that Bishop Gunner of Viborg had in the preparation of the Law of Jutland in 1241, the only case where we have a narrative source giving some idea of the process; Michael H. Gelting: "Odelsrett – lovbydelse – bördsrätt – retrait lignager: Kindred and Land in the Nordic Countries in the Twelfth and Thirteenth Centuries," in *Family, Marriage and Property Devolution in the Middle Ages*, ed. Lars Ivar Hansen, Tromsø, Department of History of the University of Tromsø, 2000, p. 133-165, at p. 154-155, n. 30.
79. Sawyer: *The Viking-Age Rune-Stones*, p. 87.
80. Above, at n. 56.

property that is brought into the community by in-marrying daughters-in-law and sons-in-law. Art. 38 of the Book of Inheritance gives the household head two options in case of dispute with his grandchildren over the inheritance of a predeceased in-marrying daughter-in-law or son-in-law: he may deny that anything is the grandchildren's separate inheritance – the problematic nature of such a claim is shown by the qualified defence required in that case, a triple twelve men's oath; or he may admit that they have the right to some inheritance, the size of which he may then defend by the normal proof of twelve men's oath and two witnesses (quite logically witnesses are not required for denying that any inheritance had been brought in by the in-marrying person: it is impossible to witness nothing!). Such disputes could hardly arise unless the property of all members of the household was effectively merged under the sole administration of the household head.

It is reasonable to surmise that the rules protecting the separate property rights of each member of the household were connected to the introduction of the parentelic system, while the powers of the household head over the entire property reflected an earlier form of household community where the household head had full and unlimited powers over the entire wealth of the household. This may have extended to appointing a principal or even a sole heir. Birgit Sawyer suggests that the rune-stone evidence points to unigeniture having been practiced to some extent.[81] The compromise that was worked out in the Book of Inheritance meant that the household head's authority within the household was formally maintained, but concerning alienations of inherited property it was severely curtailed. Even after his wife's death, if the paternal and maternal inheritance was divided with his children, the father did not have a free right of alienation over the full lot that became his separate property – his 'capital portion' (*hovedlod*).[82] Only if he decided to become a monk while in good health

---

81. Sawyer: *The Viking-Age Rune-Stones*, p. 73, 76, 83, 152-154. Cf. the assertion in the Chronicle of the Bishops of Ribe that Bishop Odinkar († c. 1043) left all of his considerable wealth to his see on condition that the bishopric should always remain with his descendants; Ellen Jørgensen: "Ribe Bispekrønike," in *Kirkehistoriske Samlinger*, 6th ser. vol. 1, 1933-1935, p. 23-33, at p. 26; cf. e.g. Kristian Sindballe: *Af Testamentarvens Historie i dansk Ret*, Copenhagen, Schultz, 1915, p. 40. On the probability that there may be some truth to this statement, see Michael H. Gelting: "Elusive Bishops: Remembering, Forgetting, and Remaking the History of the Early Danish Church," in *The Bishop: Power and Piety at the First Millennium*, ed. Sean Gilsdorf (Neue Aspekte der europäischen Mittelalterforschung, vol. 4), Münster, Lit, 2004 p. 169-200, at p. 184.
82. The expression 'capital portion' might also be used for any of the other heirs' lot. It was i.a. a common measure for fines in serious criminal cases; Iuul: *Fællig og Hovedlod*, p. 87-101.

was he allowed to bring his entire capital portion with him to the monastery. If he made his monastic profession while being ill, or if he wanted to make *post mortem* bequests to a church or to anybody else, ecclesiastical or lay, he was not entitled to alienate more than half his capital portion. The same applied to the mother if she survived her husband.[83]

I would suggest that, few as they are, these restrictive rules concerning the household head's powers of alienation were not only a wholesale innovation, but that they even were at the core of the entire legal reform. The clue to such an interpretation may be found in a letter sent by Pope Alexander III to the Swedish king, church and people a few years after the enactment of the Book of Inheritance in Denmark.

Eterna et Incommutabilis

The decretal *Eterna et incommutabilis*, like so many other of Alexander III's letters, is difficult to date exactly.[84] It was issued in Tusculum on a July 6, which according to the pope's itinerary would have been possible in the years 1171, 1172 or 1180. The editor O. S. Rydberg's arguments for preferring the earlier dates have generally been accepted, but his further arguments for ruling out 1171 are too hypothetical to carry much conviction.[85]

The decretal was directed to K., king of the *Swei* and *Gothi*, to the bishops and the duke, and to all the clergy and people in *Gothia*. King K. is Cnut Ericsson, king of Sweden from 1167, when he slew King Charles Sverkersson, to his death in 1195/96. King Cnut was titled king both of the Swedes and of the Goths, but the pope's letter was otherwise addressed only to the clergy and people of *Gothia*, i.e. the provinces of Eastern and Western Götaland. It even fails to mention the archbishop of Uppsala, close to the ancient royal centre of the *Swei*, whom Alexander III himself had only recently elevated to the rank of metropolitan of the Swedish church. As Rydberg pointed out, the archbishop was an adherent of the rival royal

---

83. Art. 48-51.
84. JL 13546, dated [1171 × 1180]. Edited in *Svenskt Diplomatarium – Diplomatarium Suecanum [DS]*, vol. 1, ed. Joh. Gust. Liljegren, Stockholm, 1829, no. 41, p. 60-63, and there dated 6 July 1161 (this date is impossible, cf. the following); *Sverges traktater med främmande makter jemte andra dit hörande handlingar*, ed. O. S. Rydberg, vol. 1, Stockholm, 1877, no. 49, p. 94-98, and there dated 6 July 1172 or, less likely, 1180. I refer to the Rydberg edition. A section of it was included in the *Liber Extra* via the *Compilatio secunda*; 2 Comp. 5.21.1 (X 3.45.1).
85. *Sverges traktater*, vol. 1, p. 98 n. 1. Cf. Gelting: "Odelsrett," p. 156-157, n. 40 and 42.

house that King Cnut had overthrown, and he may still have been in exile in Denmark when the letter was written.[86]

The papal letter was impetrated by a Swedish delegation headed by the priest Richard, and it must be understood as an answer to a request for instructions from the bishops and the church of Götaland. The pope treated a number of subjects: the indissolubility of marriage and the prohibition of consanguineous marriages; the inviolability of ecclesiastical persons and property; the obligation to render tithes; pious gifts to churches; the particular problems of marriage law concerning wives whose husbands had been taken captive by the pagans; and a severe condemnation of attempts to venerate as a saint a man who had been murdered at a drunken feast. The last clause may have had considerable political importance, if the assumption is correct that it referred to attempts by the ousted kinsmen of the murdered King Charles Sverkersson to create a dynastic saint in the person of King Charles's brother-in-law, the Danish king Cnut Magnusson, who had been murdered at the 'bloody feast' in Roskilde in 1157.[87]

However, the part of the letter that is important in the present context is the pope's statement concerning pious gifts. It deserves to be quoted in full:

> "Moreover, it has been related to us that there are some among you who leave all their possessions to the churches, disinheriting their legitimate children, which is certainly not permitted by any law; but he who has one son may make Christ his second son, if he wants to, by leaving half his wealth to the Church; he who has two sons may make Christ the third, and so on; because the Church ought not to receive it all, disinheriting the children; but brothers can indisputably do so to the exclusion of their brothers and sisters, so that they who die childless may leave all their wealth to churches."[88]

This statement described an existing state of affairs, and a remedy for it, that might be expected to produce exactly the kind of legal reform that we have seen in the Danish Book of Inheritance of 1169/70: the existing state of affairs gave the household head such wide powers over his possessions that

---

86. *Sverges traktater*, vol. 1, p. 98 n. 1.
87. Peter Sawyer: *När Sverige blev Sverige*, revised translation by Birgit Sawyer (Occasional Papers on Medieval Topics, 5), Alingsås: Viktoria, 1991, p. 59.
88. *Sverges traktater*, vol. 1, no. 49, p. 97: *Ad hec nunciatum nobis est, quod sunt aliqui inter vos, qui, exheredatis legitimis filiis, bona sua omnia ecclesiis derelinquunt, quod quidem nullo iure permittitur; sed qui habet vnum filium, si uult, alterum faciat Christum, dimidiam ecclesie relinquendo; qui habet duos, faciat tercium Christum et sic in ceteris; quoniam ecclesia exheredatis filiis recipere totum non debet; quod nimirum fratres uel sorores, fratribus uel sororibus pretermissis facere possunt, vt sine filiis decedentes totum ecclesiis derelinquant.*

he might in effect disinherit his children by inordinate death-bed gifts to the Church; and the remedy that was proposed was strict partible inheritance, setting aside an extra portion for Christ, i.e. the Church. However, in the case of persons who died without offspring, the pope did not set similar store by protecting the rights of their collateral heirs. His instructions to the Swedish bishops in this whole section of the decretal were based on a text by Saint Augustine in the strict interpretation given of it in the *Decretum Gratiani*.[89]

The Book of Inheritance seems to reflect just such teaching,[90] although with some concessions to traditional sensibilities. It established partible inheritance, although with an unequal division that disadvantaged daughters compared to sons. It enforced this partible inheritance by setting strict limits to the household head's freedom to alienate, yet it did not introduce a pure parentelic system, since there was no right of representation in favour of grandchildren by children who had left the household community; in addition to the portions of the descendants, it accorded a son's lot to the surviving father and mother, which might be used for pious gifts, yet only half of that lot might be alienated unless its owner decided to enter a monastery while in good health; but originally it only included provisions concerning direct descendance and laid down no rules concerning collateral inheritance. On these points, *Eterna et incommutabilis* does indeed look like a blueprint for the Book of Inheritance.

However, Alexander III's decretal to the Swedes was definitely a couple of years later than the Book of Inheritance; it was written to Sweden, not to Denmark; and it seems to have had no immediate effect upon Swedish law, which even later on remained largely refractory to the principles stated by the pope in matters of pious gifts.[91] Is it possible to suggest that there might be any connection between the pope's views as expressed in *Eterna et incommutabilis* and the Danish Book of Inheritance? The answer can only be hypothetical, but I believe that it is possible to suggest a political context for such a connection. In the case of Sweden, Alexander III did not possess much leverage. But precisely in the years immediately preceding and contemporary with the enactment of the Book of Inheritance, his position vis-à-vis the Danish kingdom was remarkably strong.

---

89. Cf. Iuul: *Fællig og Hovedlod*, p. 66-69.
90. The relevance of *Eterna et incommutabilis* in connection with the inheritance rules of the Danish law books has been noticed previously, e.g. by Sindballe: *Af Testamentarvens Historie*, p. 39-40.
91. Cf. above, at n. 71-72, and Jan Liedgren in Herluf Nielsen, Jan Liedgren, Lars Hamre, Stefán Karlsson: "Testamente," in *KLNM*, vol. 18, col. 218-233, at col. 223-224; and see below, at n. 104-109.

Michael H. Gelting

The Political Context of the Book of Inheritance

In 1169, the Danish king, Valdemar I, and his church had only recently returned to the fold of Alexander III. Since the early 1130s, Denmark had been a vassal kingdom under the German kings and emperors, and from 1131 to 1157 the kingdom was in a semi-permanent state of civil war.[92] When Valdemar I finally secured sole mastery of the realm in 1157, Emperor Frederick Barbarossa subjected him to heavy diplomatic pressure in order to secure his continuing loyalty and upon the outbreak of the Victorine schism in 1159, Valdemar had no option but to follow the emperor in recognising Alexander III's rival, Pope Victor IV. Since an important part of the German diplomatic pressure consisted in threatening with reviving the claims of the archbishops of Hamburg-Bremen to ecclesiastical supremacy over Denmark, the Danish archbishop, Eskil of Lund, obviously opted for Alexander III. He soon left the kingdom for a pilgrimage to Jerusalem and did not return, but went to France, associating with the Cistercians and with Alexander III's entourage. King Valdemar remained loyal to Barbarossa for some years, but by the mid-1160s, when the emperor had run into serious difficulties in Italy, the Danish king began maneuvering for a reconciliation with Alexander III and for liberating himself from his bond of fealty to the German king. Denmark may never have officially recognised the next anti-pope, Paschalis III, after the death of Victor IV in 1164, and an understanding with Alexander was soon reached, probably in 1166.[93]

Alexander must evidently have been eager to secure Danish support, but he was also in a position to demand concessions. Archbishop Eskil was to return to his see, and the schismatic bishops who had been instituted

---

92. Most recently treated in Michael H. Gelting: "Da Eskil ville være ærkebiskop af Roskilde: Roskildekrøniken, *Liber daticus Lundensis* og det danske ærkesædes ophævelse 1133-1138," in *Ett annat 1100-tal: Individ, kollektiv och kulturella mönster i medeltidens Danmark*, eds. Peter Carelli, Lars Hermanson and Hanne Sanders, Göteborg/Stockholm, 2004, p. 181-229, at p. 184-202, 214-223, 223; the assumption there that King Eric III (1137-1146) did not consider himself bound by the Concordate of Worms (ibid., p. 215-216) ignores the evidence of that king's decree of 1142, which is dated by reference to the pontificates or reigns of Pope Innocent II, Emperor Conrad III, King Eric III himself, and Archbishop Eskil, thereby confirming Denmark's continuing acknowledgement of German overlordship and, by implication, subjection to the Concordate of Worms; *DD*, 1st ser. vol. 2, no. 84, p. 159-160.
93. On the course of events from 1157 to 1166, see Michael H. Gelting: "Kansleren Radulfs to bispevielser: En undersøgelse af Saxos skildring af ærkebispe- og pavestriden 1159-1162," in *Historisk Tidsskrift*, 80, Copenhagen, 1980, p. 325-336; Carsten Breengaard: *Muren om Israels hus: Regnum og sacerdotium i Danmark 1050-1170*, Copenhagen, Gad, 1982, p. 263-301.

during the preceding years had their consecration declared null and void and were to be re-consecrated by their repatriated metropolitan.[94] This would also have been a unique occasion for urging a thorough reform of Danish law in the interest of the Church, basically on the same lines as those laid down in Alexander III's slightly later letters to Sweden. The claim would probably have been pressed by Archbishop Eskil rather than by the pope, but the latter would certainly have endorsed it. If such an agreement had been reached in 1166, the three or four years separating that date from the legislation of 1169/70 would seem a reasonable time-span for elaborating a legal reform of the complexity and importance of the Book of Inheritance. In return, the pope in 1170 canonized King Valdemar's father, Cnut Lavard (St. Canute Duke), whose murder in 1131 had triggered a quarter-century of civil war. The canonization was the occasion for a grand political event, as Valdemar let the assembled aristocracy acclaim his young son Cnut VI as co-regent and heir to the throne at the same time as the king's father's bones were elevated to the altar.[95] In this interpretation, the Book of Inheritance thus enters as an element in the consolidation of the so-called Valdemarian monarchy in Denmark.

In its turn, this hypothesis provides a possible context for Alexander III's decretal *Eterna et incommutabilis*. Sweden had been part of the ecclesiastical province of Lund from its inception in 1103/04, but during the schism it had been detached as an autonomous province under the archbishop of Uppsala. As a courtesy to the loyal Archbishop Eskil of Lund, the Danish archbishop obtained the status of primate of Sweden and perpetual papal legate, so that communications between Sweden and Rome still had to pass through Lund.[96] Politically, however, Sweden was outside the Danish king's control, even though twelfth-century Danish kings at times seem to have exerted some sort of formal or informal power in the Swedish frontier regions.[97] Archbishop Eskil's long exile had weakened his see's primatial status with respect to the Swedish church, and *Eterna et incommutabilis* shows that the Swedes had not been slow to profit from the occasion by entertaining direct relations with Rome without bothering to pass through their primate in Lund, even after the latter's return from exile. Once the Danish Book of Inheritance had been enacted, it would be a logical move on Archbishop Eskil's part to prompt the Swedes to introduce similar legal reforms. The question about pious gifts that Alexander III answered in *Eterna et incommutabilis* may have been caused by pressure

---

94. Gelting: "Kansleren Radulfs to bispevielser," p. 335.
95. Breengaard: *Muren om Israels hus*, p. 304-310, 318-319.
96. *Ibid.*, p. 252-254.
97. Cf. Sawyer: *När Sverige blev Sverige*, p. 58.

from the primate to that effect. In this matter, evidently, the pope backed the solution reached in the Danish Book of Inheritance.[98]

At about the same time as the Swedish legation that produced *Eterna et incommutabilis*, Archbishop Eskil sought to assert his own authority over the Swedish church by securing a couple of decretals from Alexander III in which the pope roundly condemned a number of Swedish practices and severely upbraided the Swedish bishops for failing to take a stand against the abuses affecting their church.[99] It is unfortunately impossible to tell whether these decretals were issued before or after the Swedish legation to Rome; they may be dated either 1171 or 1172.[100] These decretals do not

---

98. For Alexander's attitude towards Eskil's Swedish primacy, cf. below, n. 103.
99. Esp. *Gravis admodum* (JL 12114), 9 September [1171 × 1172], *DS*, vol. 1, no. 59, 9. 87-88, and *Sverges traktater*, vol. 1, no. 46, p. 84-85; and *Constituti a domino* (JL 12117), 10 September [1171 × 1172], *DS*, vol. 1, no. 54, p. 76-82, and *Sverges traktater*, vol. 1, no. 47, p. 86-93. These letters form part of the group of nine letters from Alexander III to Scandinavian recipients that is known in Scandinavian scholarship as the "September letters"; Lauritz Weibull: "Påven Alexander III:s septemberbrev till Norden: Orientering," in *Scandia*, 13, 1940, p. 90-98.
100. In the most recent contribution to the literature on the subject, Ludwig Falkenstein has dismissed Tore Nyberg's argument that 1171 should be preferred. Nyberg argued that the dates of some of the letters fell on a Sunday in 1172, and the pope would not normally have issued letters on Sundays; according to Falkenstein there is no evidence for that hypothesis; Tore Nyberg: "Deutsche, dänische und schwedische Christianisierungsversuche östlich der Ostsee im Geiste des 2. und 3. Kreuzzuges," in *Die Rolle der Ritterorden in der Christianisierung und Kolonisierung des Ostseegebietes*, ed. Zenon Hubert Nowak (Universitas Nicolai Copernici, Ordines militares, Colloquia Torunensia Historica, 1), Torun, 93-114, at p. 101; Ludwig Falkenstein: „Die Sirmondsche Sammlung der 56 Litterae Alexanders III.," in *Hundert Jahre Papsturkundenforschung: Bilanz – Methoden – Perspektiven. Akten eines Kolloquiums zum hundertjährigen Bestehen der Regesta Pontificum Romanorum vom 9.-11. Oktober 1996 in Göttingen*, ed. Rudolf Hiestand (Abhandlungen der Akademie der Wissenschaften zu Göttingen, Philologisch-Historische Klasse, 3rd ser., vol. 261), Göttingen, Vandenhoeck & Ruprecht, 2003, p. 267-334, at p. 300, n. 161. I wish to thank Dr. Falkenstein for having sent me an offprint of the article before the book became available in Denmark. – In an earlier article I expressed the hypothesis that there was a connection between the ruling on pious gifts in *Eterna et incommutabilis* and Alexander III's statement in *Constituti a domino*, that once they had been given to the Church, pious gifts could not be taken back: *Constituti a domino*, I thought, was an answer to the next question from the Swedish church, namely whether pious gifts in excess of the norm stated by the pope ought to be handed back to the heirs; Gelting: "Odelsrett," p. 138. On closer inspection, however, Alexander III's point in *Constituti a domino* addressed an entirely different point, viz. that the church's demand for tithes made donators or their heirs threaten to take back the land they had offered for supporting the church; *Sverges traktater*, vol. 1, no. 47, p. 91-92.

explicitly mention the duty of the Swedish church to obey their primate, but the fact that they were clearly impetrated by Eskil through Fulco, missionary bishop to the Estonians,[101] implies that he intended to use them in order to reach that goal.[102] The whole complex of letters illustrates that Lund's primacy might open up opportunities for the Swedes for playing pope and primate out against each other.[103]

The codification of Swedish law became a much more protracted process than in Denmark. The earliest codification of which we know, the Elder Västgöta Law, was probably written in the first quarter of the thirteenth century.[104] It applied the same rule as the Danish Book of Inheritance concerning the division of the inheritance upon the household head's decision to become a monk.[105] But on pious gifts *post mortem*, it did not lay down a specific maximum for their size, but simply made the validity of the gifts dependent upon the agreement of the heirs.[106] This rule, which was repeated in later Swedish law books despite vehement criticism from successive popes,[107] is a remarkable case of codification of the practice of *laudatio parentum*, so well studied by Stephen D. White on the basis of French evidence.[108] It codified the state of affairs as it was in Denmark too before the Book of Inheritance, when any pious gift might be contested at any time by any person who could claim that he ought to have given his approbation to the gift.[109]

---

101. Weibull: „Påven Alexander III:s septemberbrev," p. 95-98; Falkenstein: „Die Sirmondsche Sammlung," p. 302-304.
102. Lauritz Weibull: *Skånes kyrka från älsta tid till Jacob Erlandsens död 1274*, Copenhagen, Rosenkilde and Bagger, 1946, p. 110.
103. Alexander III may not have been entirely happy with his predecessor's decision to let the archbishop of Lund be primate of Sweden; Niels Skyum-Nielsen: „Das dänische Erzbistum vor 1250," in *Kirche und Gesellschaft im Ostseeraum und im Norden vor der Mitte des 13. Jahrhunderts*, ed. Sven Ekdahl (Acta Visbyensia, vol. 3, Visby-symposiet för historiska vetenskaper 1967), Visby/Göteborg, Museum Gotlands Fornsal, 1969, p. 113-138, at p. 119-120, 125; cf. Breengaard: *Muren om Israels hus*, p. 253-254.
104. Åke Holmbäck and Elias Wessén: *Svenska landskapslagar tolkade och förklarade för nutidens svenskar*, vol. 5, *Äldre Västgötalagen, Yngre Västgötalagen, Smålandslagens kyrkobalk och Bjärköarätten*, Stockholm/Uppsala, Hugo Gebers Förlag, 1946, p. XIX-XXIII.
105. *Ibid.*, Ärvdabalken art. 9, p. 77, cf. commentary p. 87.
106. *Ibid.*, Ärvdabalken art. 10, p. 77, cf. commentary p. 87-88.
107. *Ibid.*, p. 88.
108. Stephen D. White: *Custom, Kinship, and Gifts to Saints: The Laudatio Parentum in Western France, 1050-1150*, Chapel Hill/London, The University of North Carolina Press, 1988.
109. Kim Esmark: "Godsgaver, *calumniae* og retsantropologi: Esrum kloster og dets naboer, ca. 1150-1250," in *Ett annat 1100-tal*, eds. Carelli, Hermanson and Sanders, p. 143-180, esp. p. 164-173.

What the Church gained by accepting a maximum limit to pious gifts was thus increased security of possession. It gave up the legal possibility of acquiring huge but scandalous gifts from dying aristocrats anguished by the fear of Hell, but in return it obtained clear legal guarantees for pious gifts made according to the provisions of the Book of Inheritance. In the long run, there can be no doubt that this was to the solid advantage of the Church. However, in order to reach that goal, it was necessary to change the Danish rules of inheritance in their entirety. The principle of partible inheritance had to be accepted in order that the Augustinian precept for pious gifts might apply. That the adopted solution was not the only one possible is shown by the Norwegian and most of the later Swedish provincial law books, where the rules governing pious gifts were based on Biblical precepts for the rendering of tithes and hence laid down a limitation to one-tenth of the inherited landed wealth.[110]

Danish laws of inheritance as they are known from the medieval lawbooks were all based on the model introduced by the Book of Inheritance in 1169/70. Thus they should not be seen as the outcome of a more or less organic development from ancestral roots, but as the product of a politically conditioned, momentous reform, spurred by the Danish archbishop with the pope's support, and aimed at reducing an important source of conflict between the Danish church and lay society, in the interest of Danish society at large, but evidently also very much in the interest of the Church itself.

---

110. Jan Liedgren and Lars Hamre in Nielsen et al.: "Testamente," col. 223, 227.

Three Kingdoms, Three Laws, One Ideology
– A Starting Point Revisited

Per Andersen

Introduction

In May 2003, when I gave a paper on the ideological background of the Sicilian Constitutions of Melfi dating from 1231, the Danish Law of Jylland dating from 1241 and the Aragonese Vidal Mayor dating from 1247, I had commenced working on my PhD thesis which contained an investigation and comparison of the legal procedure laid forward in these three laws. In this respect, my paper – which forms the first part (and was the original version) of this article – more or less functioned as an outline and a starting point for the forthcoming research.

The reason for pinpointing ideological similarities between the three laws was – at that time – a widespread tradition in Danish historiography of viewing Danish medieval law as a special way of organizing a 'national' legal system. The central point of this traditional paradigm is that from the oldest times to the High Middle Ages the formation of law took place in people's minds. It was given its external presence through the decisions of the people in the public assemblies and subsequently through the writing down of agreed legal norms of the laws of the single province. Put simply, this idea means that the contents of the Danish provincial laws – of which the Law of Jylland is one – must on one hand be a reflection of special local Danish ways of providing law and on the other hand must have been difficult to alter since they were based on long-lasting perceptions of what was right and proper. The exponents of this tradition presumed that medieval law was based on the idea that old law was good law and therefore they argued that they were a reluctant to create new law, and when – or rather *if* – they compared with non-Danish laws, it usually was with Germanic laws such as the Sachsenspiegel, which were interpreted in the same way by German legal historians.

I wanted to do something else, namely compare the legal procedure in the Law of Jylland with laws that it was not usually compared with. I hoped to find similarities which could connect the contents of the Law of Jylland to contemporary Europe and give these similarities more depth than most other studies which just scratched the surface. Almost a decade later I think, I have succeeded in doing so (although some would probably criticise me for looking too much for similarities). In this revised version of my article published in the proceedings from the first Carlsberg Academy Conferences on Medieval Legal History I will support the original assumption of ideological similarities between the Constitutions of Melfi, the Law of Jylland and Vidal Mayor by summing up the results of the research which followed. In doing so, I want to stress that it sometimes can be very fruitful to see things in a new perspective, to challenge old paradigms and to compare phenomenons no one thought of before. And to follow questions that others have inspired to.

The Secular Legislator

The question 'How Nordic are the Nordic Medieval Laws' can be approached from different angles: One may find some interesting features in the Nordic laws and try to compare these with the Roman law or Canon law of the period; one may search for well-known Roman or Canonical maxims or legal norms in the Nordic laws – or even Germanic aspects. This can be done concerning one single law or all the Nordic laws as such, but typically – whichever angle chosen – legal historians are mainly looking for single Roman or Canonical aspects and elements in the chosen law or laws. Or for Nordic peculiarities. Under the impression of a functional questioning and an evolutionary historiographic tradition, many legal historians do not conceive the single law as a distinct unity nor differentiate between the types of laws in question. This is also the case in two inestimably important works on the medieval legislation.

More than 50 years ago, the late Swedish legal historian, Sten Gagnér convinced most of his colleagues that the concept of positive law, the *ius positivum* or *Gesetzpositivismus*, was not as new an idea as maintained by the majority of the contemporary legal historians. The tradition was that the idea of positive legislation – that legal norms can be set by men to men in a community – was a modern phenomenon in contrast to the eternal norms of natural law, no matter whether the latter was God-given or expressed in the natural rationality of all humans. In his doctoral thesis *Studien zur Ideengeschichte der Gesetzgebung*, Gagnér ascertained that the idea of *ius positivum* was not an exclusively modern one, but that it dated as far back as the High Middle Ages, to the 'Drang zur Kodifikation' of the old laws in the twelfth and thirteenth centuries.[1] Thus Gagnér contested the generally accepted view among legal historians, that the conception of law in the Middle Ages was based on the idea, that the right law was the earliest legal norms to be found, i.e. that the good and right law is identical with the old – the original – law.[2] He demonstrated that the kings of the thirteenth century gave positive laws under the impression of theoretical maxims like *rex imperator in regno suo* by which the king became *legum conditor* instead of – as earlier – merely *rex iustus*.[3] The idea of *rex imperator in regno suo* – saying that the king could do in his kingdom what the emperor did in his empire according to his old Roman privileges – was actually invented by the canonists of the twelfth century as an argument of the Church in its opposition to the emperor. However, during the thirteenth century the kings adopted the idea and initiated a secularization of the legislation, a development which was probably not foreseen by the canonists or the popes. This idea brought the 'Drang zur Kodifikation' a step forward both by indicating a new understanding (or at least expressed concept) of the individual kingdom as a territorial fact *and* by nailing down the concept of *ius positivum* resulting in the kings asserting their sovereign right to legislate for their own kingdoms.[4]

Thirteen years later, the work of Sten Gagnér became the foundation of another important work, Armin Wolf's contribution "Die Gesetzgebung der entstehenden Territorialstaaten" in *Handbuch der Quellen und Literatur der neueren europäischen Privatrechtsgeschichte*.[5] Wolf's aim was to make

---

1. Sten Gagnér, *Studien zur Ideengeschichte der Gesetzgebung* (Uppsala 1960).
2. Cf. the classic interpretation by Fritz Kern, "Recht und Verfassung im Mittelalter", *Historische Zeitschrift* 120 (1919), pp. 1-79, and Gagnérs' predecessor Herman Krause, "Dauer und Vergänglichkeit im mittelalterlichen Recht", *Zeitschrift der Savigny-Stiftung für Rechtsgeschichte*, Germ. Abt. 75 (1958), pp. 206-251.
3. Gagnér, *Studien*, pp. 341-366. Cf. also Herman Krause, *Kaiserrecht und Rezeption* (Heidelberg 1952), pp. 34-38, 145-46.
4. Cf. among others Peter Landau, "Der Einfluss des kanonischen Rechts auf die europäische Rechtskultur", ed. R. Schulze, *Europäische Rechts- und Verfassungsgeschichte. Ergebnisse und Perspektiven der Forschung* (Berlin 1991), pp. 39-57.
5. Armin Wolf, "Die Gesetzgebung der Entstehenden Territorialstaaten", ed. H. Coing, *Handbuch der Quellen und Literatur der neueren europäischen Privatrechtsgeschichte I* (München 1973), pp. 517-800. Later published as an updated monograph in *Gesetzgebung in Europa, 1100-1500. Zur Entstehung der Territorialstaaten* (München 1996 – this edition to be cited in the following). For an account of the results immediately following the 1973-edition, see Reiner

it easier for legal historians to compare the legislation of the developing territorial states of the High and Later Middle Ages, for which reason his work became a summing up of the accessible knowledge of each individual state of these centuries. And as such, his work is still of inestimable importance to legal historians making comparative studies.

However, everything considered, the only conceivable critic of both Gagnér and Wolf is their lack of qualitative precision concerning the types of laws being studied: they have simply not made a thorough qualitative differentiation between the various types of laws mentioned (though Wolf differentiates between two kinds of laws, namely laws of the towns and other laws). This means that a lot of important characteristics and results may not be brought to light in the works of Gagnér and Wolf. In order to illustrate this *and* to propose a new qualitative course of examining the legal material treated by Gagnér and Wolf I intend, in the following to focus on the king's right to make laws and to legislate for his kingdom just as it – for the first time – was asserted in public and realized in the thirteenth century.

The Legislation of the Realm: A Definition

It is not my assertion that the 'legislation of the realm' was a medieval concept, because this is not the case: It is a modern term and concept.[6] However, being a modern concept it can be useful as a tool to make a qualitative analysis of the royal power of the kingdoms of thirteenth century Europe, in order to show where the idea of a state-like central power was accepted or was possible to assert publicly, *and* it may be a tool to qualify the background of the legal communication of the period.

In spite of the missing medieval concept, it is still possible to avoid the danger of anachronism by holding on to the medieval definition of a law: According to the authoritative Gratian (based on Isidore of Seville) a law must be honorable and just, necessary and practicable, it must be subject to God's natural law and in accordance with the practice of the society in question, it must be explicit to avoid abuse and be useful to the whole society.[7] And in order to secure these things it must be written.[8]

This definition involves three important aspects: *Firstly*, a law must be in accordance with the practice of the society in question, which means that

---

Schulze, "Geschichte der neueren vorkonstitutionellen Gesetzgebung, *Zeitschrift der Savigny-Stiftung für Rechtsgeschichte*, Germ. Abt. 98 (1981), pp. 155-235.
6. Johs. Steenstrup, "Valdemar Sejrs Død og de ved Tronskiftet vedtagne Ændringer i Landets Styrelse", *Historisk Tidsskrift* 3 (1934-36), pp. 1-31, esp. 16.
7. *Corpus Iuris Canonici: Editio Lipsiensis I: Decretum megistri Gratiani*, ed. A. Friedberg (Graz 1959), D. 4, c. 2.
8. D. 1, c. 3.

the individual king can legislate for his kingdom as long as it is accepted by the population (at this point Gratian actually puts kings and emperors on equal terms concerning their right to legislate).[9] *Secondly*, a law must be useful to the whole society, which makes Gratian distinguish between a law as *lex generalis* and privileges. Privileges concern private matters, they indicate deviations from normal conditions, that is – like coronation charters or *Landfrieden* – they are special agreements implying negotiations with an opponent. A law *per se* is thus a 'negotiation without an opponent'; it is an explicit setting of norms, which everybody is expected to acknowledge.[10] *Thirdly*, Gratian emphasizes that a law must be in writing and known by everybody subject to it; a law must be a common and *published* norm. At this point he adapts the crucial legal conception of *promulgatio*: A law is institutionalized when it is promulgated, i.e. published, and confirmed by being used.[11] *Promulgatio* expresses the will to publish, to make the resulting norms known to the public, but at the same time the promulgated law obtains public authority (*publica auctoritas*), it receives public legal protection (*publica fides*) by which it becomes the decisive norm in legal matters.[12] Thus a law according to Gratian is a promulgated, written rule regulating one or more topics in a society for everybody's common good. And when speaking of the legislation of the realm, such a law must be given by a central power with the capability of carrying through the rules applying to the entire kingdom.[13]

Based on the idea of *rex imperator in regno suo*, this definition can be used when looking for some of (what I dare call) the most developed or most powerful central or state-like kingly powers of the thirteenth century. In the following I shall give a brief account of the laws that rightly can be characterized as the legislation of the realm, i.e. which is given in public and applies to everybody in the entire territorial realm.

---

9. D. 2, c. 4. Cf. Krause, *Kaiserrecht und Rezeption*, p. 48.
10. D. 3, c. 3. Grethe A. Blom, *Kongemakt og privilegier i Norge inntil 1387* (Oslo 1967), pp. 6-8.
11. D. 4, c. 3.
    12 J. Spiegel, "Promulgatio (Publicatio)", *Lexicon des Mittelalters* VII, p. 249. Elmar Wadle, "Über Entstehung, Funktion und Geltungsgrund normativer Rechtsaufzeichnungen im Mittelalter: Notitzen zu einem Durchblick", pp. 503-518, esp. 512, and Winfried Trusen, "Zur Urkundenlehre der mittelalterlichen Jurisprudenz", pp. 197-219, esp. 204-205, both articles in ed. P. Classen), *Recht und Schrift im Mittelalter*, *Vorträge und Forschungen* 23 (Sigmaringen 1977). Cf. also Heinrich Fichtenau, "Forschungen über Urkundenformeln", *Mitteilungen des Instituts für österreichische Geschichtsforschung* 94 (1986), pp. 285-339, esp. 303.
13. Cf. D. 20, ante c. 1.

The Legislation of the Realm in Thirteenth Century Europe

It is no matter for surprise that the basis of an examination of the declared, kingly given and promulgated legislation of the realm in the thirteenth century is the Constitutions of Melfi by Frederick II, emperor (r. 1220-1250) and at the same time king of Sicily (r. 1198-1250). As King of Sicily Frederick could not assert his authority as emperor. Thus, when the Sicilian law was finished late in the summer of 1231,[14] he pronounced in the *prooemium* that he, the King, had been chosen by God to put the sinful men of his kingdom back on the right track, back to the order of God. According to Frederick the secular kingdom was a God-given institution meaning that if a person wanted to improve in the eyes of God, he had to obey the king's laws.[15] Frederick seems to have regarded himself as a biblical king not being responsible to his people as long as he was governing and legislating reasonably and according to God.[16] At the same time, the Constitutions of Melfi signified a change *from* the ancient principles of personal right, according to which the right of the individual depended on his place of birth, *to* a new territorial principle making all inhabitants of the whole kingdom of Sicily subject to the same law.[17] And in this form the Constitutions actually remained in force in both Sicilian kingdoms after the division in 1282.[18]

In 1241 the Danish King Valdemar II (r. 1202-1241) gave the law which later was designated Law of Jylland. The earlier historiography considered that this law – like the rest of the known Danish law codes of the thirteenth century – was used in only one province, in this case Jylland.[19]

---

14. On the creation and the context, cf. *Die Konstitutionen Friedrichs II. für sein Königreich Sizilien*, ed. Wolfgang Stürner, MGH Const. 2. Supplementum (Hannover 1996), pp. 1-8, and Wolfgang Stürner, *Friedrich II. Teil 2: Der Kaiser 1220-1250* (Darmstadt 2000), pp. 170-194.
15. *Konstitutionen*, pp. 145-148. Wolfgang Stürner, "Rerum necessitas und divina provisio", *Deutsches Archiv für Erforschung des Mittelalters* 39 (1983), pp. 467-554. Also Ernst H. Kantorowicz, *The King's Two Bodies. A Study in Medieval Political Theology* (Princeton 1997), pp. 97-107.
16. Antonio Marougiú, "Ein 'Modelstaat' im italischen Mittelalter: Das normannisch-staufische Reich in Sizilien", ed. G. Wolf, *Stupor Mundi: zur Geschichte Friedrichs II. von Hohenstaufen* (Darmstadt 1966), pp. 750-773.
17. Herman Dilcher, "Einleitung", *Die Konstitutionen Friedrichs II. für sein Königreich Sizilien*, eds T. von der Lieck-Buyken, H. Conrad and W. Wagner (Köln & Wien 1997), pp. XLVI-XLVIII.
18. Wolf, *Gesetzgebung in Europa*, p. 236, n. 27.
19. E.g. J.L.A. Kolderup-Rosenvinge, *Grundrids af den danske Retshistorie* (København 1832), p. 33, 90; J.E. Larsen, *Retshistoriske Afhandlinger og Foredrag. Samlede Skrifter I* (København 1861), pp. 105-108, 116, 205; Henning Matzen, *Forelæsninger over den danske Retshistorie II* (København 1897), pp.

The reason why this legal historiographic tradition has nowhere been questioned by historians may be that it just supported their perception *that the Danish legal order as well as the rest of society was something special,*[20] *that it was bound by the fact that in the preceding centuries the law was applied mainly in Jylland,*[21] and *that even some of the manuscripts of the law mention that this is the Law of Jylland.*[22]

Recent research into this topic has demonstrated that most probably the law was *meant* by King Valdemar to be in force all over his kingdom at its promulgation in 1241.[23] This is indicated by the fact that the provincial affiliation is not mentioned in the oldest manuscript containing the law from c. 1276 or in the manuscript tradition following the oldest manuscript.[24] On the contrary the manuscripts tell – when they mention it – that this is "the law of the Danes". Only a few manuscripts from around 1300 mention an affiliation to Jylland.[25] Recently Michael H. Gelting has argued that the law was actually in force in the whole realm of Denmark: When the sources of the 1250s, 60s, 70s and 80s mention the law, it is "the

---

192-204; Poul Johs. Jørgensen, *Dansk Retshistorie. Retskildernes og Forfatningsrettens Historie indtil sidste Halvdel af det 17. Aarhundrede* (København 1947), pp. 40-43.

20. Helge Paludan, "Vor danske Montesquieu", *Historie* 3 (1980), pp. 1-32, and "Lighedens lov? Træk af dansk historieskrivnings syn på den sociale opbygning af landskabslovenes samfund gennem 200 år", eds O. Fenger and C.R. Jansen, *Jydske Lov 750 år* (Viborg 1991), pp. 51-64.

21. Poul Johs. Jørgensen, "Nogle Træk af Jyske Lovs Historie efter 1241 indtil Danske Lov", ed. E. Reitzel-Nielsen, *Med Lov skal Land bygges* (København 1941), pp. 121-156; Poul E. Olsen, "Jydske Lov efter Danske Lov", eds O. Fenger and C.R. Jansen, *Jydske Lov 750 år* (Viborg 1991), pp. 229-242. Also Ole Fenger, *Gammeldansk ret. Dansk rets historie i oldtid og middelalder* (København 1983), p. 101, 120-121; Ditlev Tamm, "Mæth lagh skal land byggæs. Betrachtungen zur Rechtsauffassung des Mittelalters mit besonderem Hinblick auf nordische und spanische Rechtsquellen", ed. K. Kroeschell, *Festschrift für Hans Thieme* (Sigmaringen 1986), pp. 127-141, esp. 138.

22. *Jyske Lov. Text 1*, ed. P. Skautrup, *Danmarks gamle Landskabslove med Kirkelovene II* (København 1933), p. 3.

23. Ole Fenger, "Jydske Lov og de øvrige danske landskabslove", eds O. Fenger and C.R. Jansen, *Jydske Lov 750 år* (Viborg 1991), pp. 37-50, esp. 47-50. Cautiously supported by Ditlev Tamm, *Dansk og europæisk retshistorie* (København 2002), p. 25. most thoroughly investigated in my published PhD thesis *Lærd ret og verdslig lovgivning. Retlig kommunikation og udvikling i middelalderens Danmark* (København 2006), pp. 279-298.

24. Cf. Andersen, *Lærd ret og verdslig lovgivning*, pp. 200-216. The oldest manuscript is dated convincingly in Thomas Riis, *Les institutiones politiques centrales du Danemark 1100-1332* (Odense 1977), pp. 60-65.

25. Per Andersen, *Rex imperator in regno suo. Dansk kongemagt og rigslovgivning i 1200-tallets Europa* (Odense 2005), p. 63.

Danish law-book" or "the laws of the Danes."[26] However, it was only in force for about four decades until 1282 when the King Erik Klipping (r. 1259-1286) had to give in to the demands of the nobility and recognize provincial and legal plurality.[27] Not untill then did the law apparently get its name: "Law of Jylland".

The prologue of the Law of Jylland states that it was given by King Valdemar II counseled by his three sons, the bishops and a group of unknown men described as "the best men of the Kingdom".[28] But nevertheless, in some of the manuscripts the king seems to be given extensive opportunities to change the law or to give new laws on his own, if the old ones are against "God", which must mean against natural law.[29] Accordingly the prologue admits a small, but very significant possibility for the king to legislate on his own, and this may be taken as a cautious interpretation of the king having his power directly from God, and not from the Church.[30] The Danish king seems thus to have been acquainted with Frederick II's legal ideology (and why should he not?), but in reality he could not make his point as outspoken as the Sicilian king, probably because of the Church as well as (at least part of) the Danish nobility, who after all could not accept a royal absolute power.[31]

Sixteen years after the Constitutions of Melfi and only six years after the Law of Jylland, James I of Aragon (r. 1213-1276) tried to maintain the same kingly ideology as Frederick II. He did so in Vidal Mayor, promulgated in 1247, and often being associated with the so-called Fueros de Aragón. In consequence of a very difficult and almost impenetrable handing down of the manuscripts which exist in several versions in both Old-Aragonese and Latin, it has often been discussed during the last century which version of the *fueros* had to be regarded as the original one, or whether Vidal Mayor was the first edition of a law-book containing

---

26. Cf. Michael H. Gelting, "Skånske Lov og Jyske Lov. Danmarks første kommissionsbetænkning og Danmarks første retsplejelov", eds H. Dam, L. Dybdahl and F. Taksøe-Jensen, *Jura og Historie. Festskrift til Inger Dübeck som forsker* (København 2002), pp. 43-80, for the sources and discussion. Herein Gelting suggests that the Law of Skåne was a draft of a law-book mend for the whole realm.
27. Fenger, "Jydske Lov og de øvrige danske landskabslove", pp. 49-50.
28. *Jyske Lov*, pp. 14-18.
29. Anders Bjerrum, "Utæn han ær opænbarlic gen guth", *Acta Philologica Scandinavia* 22 (1952), pp. 11-32; Niels Skyum-Nielsen, *Kirkekampen i Danmark 1241-1290* (København 1963), pp. 20-23.
30. Cf. Niels Knud Andersen, "Kanonisk Rets Indflydelse på Jyske Lov", ed. E. Reitzel-Nielsen, *Med Lov skal Land bygges* (København 1941), pp. 84-120, esp. 98-99.
31. On the relationship between Valdemar II and the nobility, cf. Andersen, *Lærd ret og verdslig lovgivning*, pp. 271-298.

Aragonese law.³² The discussion has especially focused on the question which prologue was the original one, because in the different versions there is also different prologues asserting differing constitutional principles. As far as I can judge, the first version of the prologues seems to have been written by Vidal de Cañallas, the bishop of Huesca, whom James I according to this prologue elected to compile the old Aragonese *fueros* and arrange them in accordance with Roman principles and Canon law.³³ The second version, which is in Latin and actually only known from a manuscript not containing the law itself, also seems to have been written by Vidal, and in this version it is asserted that the king can legislate on his own in order to maintain the peace for man and his kingdom according to God's will.³⁴ The third version, which is in Aragonese, states that the Fueros de Aragón is given by the king, *but* only after counseling a number of prominent, named persons and delegates from the towns of Aragon, usually represented in the popular assembly of the *Cortes*.³⁵ The two last versions thus assert two very different constitutional principles.

By convincingly arguing that the Latin version asserting the king's sovereignty was the kingly original version, the latest research has solved the many problems concerning the original version and the following development of the law. However, this prologue and the attached version of the *fueros*, i.e. the Vidal Mayor, was *not* accepted by the nobility, who subsequently pressed the king to work out the Aragonese prologue and the version of the law, today known as Fueros de Aragón, laying down a completely different constitutional framework, which was accepted by the *Cortes*. Later on new rules were added to the Fueros de Aragón, and in the fourteenth century it was re-arranged and systematized a-new.³⁶ Thus the Aragonese got a law applying to the whole kingdom, but they would certainly not accept a kingly right to legislate or change the law without public consent. Still, this did not stop James I or his successor Peter III from actually trying to maintain a kingly sovereignty, but in 1283 Peter III had to confirm the constitutional framework laid down in the prologue of the charter known as 'Privilegio Generales'.³⁷

---

32. On the manuscripts, cf. *Fueros de Aragón. Según el manuscito 458 de la Biblioteca Nacional de Madrid*, ed. G. Tilander (Lund 1937), pp. VII-XXVII.
33. Cf. *Fueros*, pp. 3-4. This prologue is known from several versions.
34. Cf. J.L. Lacruz Berdejo, "Dos textos interesantes para la historia de la compilación de Huesca", *Annario de Historica del Derecho Español* 18 (1947), pp. 18-41.
35. Cf. *Vidal Mayor. Traducción aragonesa de la obra 'In excelsis Dei thesauris'* II, ed. G. Tilander (Lund 1956), pp. 7-8.
36. J. Delgado Echeverria, *Los Fueros de Aragón* (Zaragoza 1997), pp. 41-63.
37. Thomas N. Bisson, *The Medieval Crown of Aragon* (Oxford 2000), pp. 58-90. Wolf, *Gesetzgebung in Europa*, pp. 215-217. Cf. *Privilegio Generales* in

The last kingdom to get a law applying to the whole realm in the thirteenth century was Norway, when Magnus the Law-mender (r. 1263-1280) promulgated The National Code (Landsloven) in 1274. The prologue tells that the law is a compilation of four older provincial law-codes, made by the king "taking counsel with the best men".[38] In this case "the best men" did actually not include the clergy, because the prologue asserts that "God has sent the king to take care of secular matters just as He has sent the bishop to take care of the spiritual matters."[39] Therefore Magnus the Law-mender did not consult the Church, and he seems to have been able to promulgate a law supported only by the secular nobility. However, just like James I, he could not change it on his own.

Based on the proposed definition, we find only four laws of the realm in thirteenth century Europe. Also other kings asserted their sovereign right to legislate on the same theoretical background as these four; however, they were declarations of intention rather than laws, e.g. Alfonso X of Castile's Siete Partidas, which was only promulgated in 1348.[40] And though Edward I of England gave a lot of statutes, they were never given in public, but only as instructions to his judges and officials, whom he addressed directly, and therefore the statutes were regarded as unwritten law.[41]

The above only aims to illustrate that expressing an ideology on paper does not mean that the constitutional order actually rests on such an ideology. The crucial thing is whether the constitutional order is just intended to be or actually is – at least to some degree – a reflection of reality.

Sicily, Denmark and Aragon: A New Perspective

Out of the above-mentioned four laws of the realm I intend to bring into focus only the Constitutions of Melfi, the Law of Jylland and Vidal Mayor,

---

Herrschaftsverträge des Spätmittelalters. Quellen zur neueren Geschichte 17, ed. W. Näf (Bern 1975), pp. 17-33.

38. *Magnus Lagabøters Landslov*, ed. A. Taranger (Kristiania 1915), p. 1 (my trans.).
39. *Magnus Lagabøters Landslov*, p. 3 (my trans.). Cf. Knut Helle, *Under kirke og kongemakt 1130-1350. Aschehougs Norgeshistorie 3* (Oslo 1995), pp. 66-69, and Ole G. Moseng, Erik Opsahl, Gunnar I. Pettersen and Erling Sandmo, *Norsk historie I: 750-1537* (Oslo 1999), pp. 210-212.
40. Alfonso Garcio-Gallo, "Nuevas observaciones sobre in la obra legislativa de Alfonso X", *Annario de Historia del Derecho Español* 46 (1976), pp. 649. Wolf, *Gesetzgebung in Europa*, pp. 200-202.
41. T.F.T. Plucknett, *Legislation of Edward I* (Oxford 1949), pp. 11-14. Wolf, *Gesetzgebung in Europa*, p. 344. For a complete comparison of all the European kingdoms, see Andersen, *Rex imperator in regno suo*.

since these three are more or less contemporary: There are only 16 years between Frederick II giving the Constitutions and James I's promulgating the Vidal Mayor, which means that these three laws may reveal something about the necessary power structures for legislating for the whole realm and about legal thinking and communication in the second quarter of the thirteenth century.

Firstly, the theoretical background of the legislation of the realm occurring in the thirteenth century seems to be identified: the ecclesiastically developed idea of *rex imperator in regno suo* was widespread as a result of the clergy forming the backbone of the kingly administrations all over Europe.[42] However – as this is common knowledge – the idea of *rex imperator in regno suo* is not a sufficient basis for maintaining the legislation of the realm. The decisive point was whether the concept actually resulted in a law, a law recognized by the society and applying to the whole kingdom, in other words whether the king could assert the idea *and* at the same time put a law into force. If and where this was possible, it tells us something about the central powers' capability to maintain the constitutional order put forward, and it tells us something about the power structures of the kingdom in question. And, as a matter of fact, it seems – as far as it is possible to conclude from the sources – that the power structures in Sicily, Denmark and Aragon were somewhat identical with a small group of noble men, personal friends and to some extent members of the royal family, supporting the king and having the same interests as him. Against these we see a more or less successful resisting group of other nobles – maybe supported by the towns – aiming at securing their privileges and social status against an expanding royal power. The relationship between these two groups varied depending on the constellation of men, and at the time of the three laws we actually see three different constellations leading to the same result: a law applying to the whole kingdom, yet with three different constitutional results. However, the power structures were crucial for defining the king's limits in the process of legislation, i.e. in the kingdoms, where the king asserted a God-given office, but did not succeed in carrying through legislation for the whole realm, as he simply lacked a sufficiently strong personal network.

Secondly, another way of studying the theoretical and ideological background of this type of law is to look at the legal systematics of the three laws in order to reveal a possible common systematic structure and thus a common learned legal theory. Actually, by comparing the three laws some characteristics are revealed showing great similarity of systematization. All three laws focus on: 1) organization and to some degree establishment of

---

42. Cf. Gagnér, *Studien*, pp. 324-341. Also Ole Fenger, *Notarius Publicus. Le notaire au Moyen Âge latin* (Aarhus 2000).

kingly institutions for the administration of justice; 2) laying down rules of procedure concerning different legal disputes; 3) laying down criminal rules, especially concerning serious criminal acts; and 4) laying down the kingly privileges. Thus, the leading principle of systematization in the Constitutions of Melfi, the Law of Jylland and Vidal Mayor is to lay down the kingly maintained rules of procedure, i.e. how to arrive at the right settlement of any given legal dispute by kingly established and controlled institutions. This is simply indicated by the systematization of the single law studied as a unity. This is only partly the case concerning the other Danish provincial law codes of the twelfth or thirteenth centuries in which the systematization does not indicate the same institutional focus or procedural order.[43]

Thirdly – and maybe most far-reaching – this short survey has also shown that the kind of legislation of the realm pointing towards state-like, central power structures was for the first time seen in the so-called peripheral areas of Europe: In Denmark, Aragon, Norway and (to a lesser degree peripheral) Sicily. This is not to say that we do not see powerful central authorities in other kingdoms, but only in these four kingdoms the central authorities were able to make their stand in public and to some degree 'give' a law for the whole realm. And by doing so, one must question the still widespread historiographical tradition concerning state-like centers and peripheries in Medieval Europe claiming that the geographical central areas of the old Carolingian Empire – France, Germany and Northern Italy – were developing a state-like society at the cultural, constitutional and administrative forefront. Apparently, the so-called peripheral kingdoms of (at least) Denmark, Aragon and Norway in the thirteenth century did not take up a reversed attitude concerning either power structures, legal ideology or the juridical institutional settlement.

From Ideology to *Ius Commune* and Legal Procedure

From the assumption that Denmark in the Middle Ages was an integrated part of Europe, and that Danish society and the Danish legal system was just one of many various ways in which society and law could be constructed, I began a closer study of the legal procedure in the three laws, especially the Law of Jylland. This has meant that from the beginning of my research into the contents of the laws, I have regarded the development of Danish law as

---

43. Cf. Gelting, "Skånske Lov og Jyske Lov", and Per Andersen, "Lovsystematik i 1200-tallet – dispositionsprincip eller systemtænkning?", ed. Jørn Øyrehagen Sunde, *Nordisk mellomalderrett med eit europeisk perspektiv*, Rettshistoriske Skrifter 17 (Oslo 2006), pp. 81-102.

coterminous with the development of Roman-canonical procedure and other European procedural developments, which has led to new insight and approaches to the Danish sources.

First of all, I approached the problem of the possible uniqueness of Danish procedure from the 'outside': before reading the Danish sources. I learned how Roman-canonical procedure functioned and developed from the end of the eleventh century onwards.

Secondly, I focused on how procedures functioned in practice: what were the necessary practical steps for raising a case; presenting a summons; clarifying disagreements, etc. By taking this approach, it has been possible to circumvent the fact that the terminology does not indicate that Danish procedure is influenced by learned law. An approach in which there is less focus on juristic terminology and the difference between learned and secular law, and more attention to the ideological inspiration that could be provided by the learned law. The inspiration behind Danish procedure is not immediately evident if we only investigate similarities in terminology. However, the situation is completely different if we study practical jurisprudence and procedure. The way in which the ideology of the learned law was implemented in practice and found its expression in Danish procedure means that the present study will hopefully encompass more than just procedure. It offers a broader understanding of how ideology could penetrate and change jurisprudence without being immediately obvious to those, who possibly because of tradition, social or political reasons would have opposed an implementation of this nature. Rather than focusing on pure dogmatics, this investigation will also focus on uncovering the ideological character of procedure with regard to how those learned in law and those holding political power thought that – or could agree with other interested parties on how – jurisprudence needed to be constructed in order to ensure that justice was done in medieval Denmark.

This part of my research began with the Fourth Lateran Council in 1215.[44] According to the summons to the council, all those who had been summoned had the right to suggest subjects for discussion and negotiation, and it was Innocent's clear aim to eradicate the abuses and transgressions that he saw amongst the Christian congregation and to reform their customs so peace could be secured within Christendom, and Christians could join together to re-conquer the Holy Land. One of the means to secure internal peace and man's good relations with God was to ensure that the administration of justice took place in such a way that it did not allow for

---

44. This analysis has been published in my *Studier i dansk proceshistorie. Tiden indtil Danske Lov 1683* (København 2010), which has been reworked into an English version in *Legal Procedure and Practice in Medieval Denmark* (Leiden 2011) – the following is thoroughly analyzed in this work.

abuse. Therefore, the attending bishops, who numbered more than 400, and a similar number of other prelates and secular representatives agreed to a number of procedural reforms that in the first instance were to govern the Church but which in the long term were also to influence secular administration of justice.

The changes of procedure were: firstly, the introduction of inquisitorial procedure at ecclesiastical courts (c. 8); secondly, the prohibition against clerics' participation in the so-called Divine Judgment and ordeals (c. 18); and thirdly, the introduction of written records of cases so that when an appeal was made it was possible to evaluate previously produced proof and objections (c. 38). Each of these new changes was the culmination of a long period of development that had started as early as the ninth century, but taken as a whole the three new rules must be characterized as a change of paradigm in ecclesiastical procedural law. They also presaged revolutionary changes in secular procedural law, where they either had been or would be fixed in local, regional or national collections of laws and customs.

The most important development in the new law of procedure was the final prohibition against clerical participation in cases decided by Divine Judgment such as the carrying of hot iron: 'means of proof' that previously had been seen to reveal the will of God. Since the Church rejected the rationality and possibility of Divine Judgment as an expression of God's just sentence, it made it impossible for secular princes to include such means of proof in valid procedural law and therefore the secular sphere had to find alternative ways to determine the most serious legal disputes.

Generally, the need for new means of proof and new institutions to evaluate these proofs seems to have been answered by an increasing use of juries composed of either an ad hoc group of sworn men or a permanent jury, which both represented their local community. These juries, which in some instances can be found as early as the early twelfth century, had an ideological origin in the recently introduced inquisitorial procedure and were charged with finding the truth in any given case by weighing the evidence produced. In this way, the inquisitorial procedure took a decisive step away from the previously dominant form of procedure, i.e. accusatorial procedure in which one private party summoned another private party and the role of the judge or the court was simply to ensure that fixed proof had been produced so that an already decided sanction could be imposed upon the losing party.

Thus inquisitorial procedure took its starting-point with the Church's wish that legal procedure, at least in criminal matters, was to uncover the truth – the judge or the court was no longer just to acknowledge a decision made on the basis of fixed proof. The aim of inquisitorial procedure was thus not just to determine the accusation of one person against another, but to establish whether a crime had been committed at all. While accusatory procedure depended on the judge's or the court's acknowledgement that the two parties had produced their proofs, the new form of procedure within the Church meant that the judge now enjoyed the right to single-handedly initiate a case if he suspected a transgression against the law, and to question involved parties and witnesses in order to establish the truth. The development of the inquisitorial procedure thus coincided with a transfer of the burden of proof to the plaintiff, who was now to produce positive proof that the defendant was guilty. There was an increased emphasis placed on those proofs that concerned the facts of the case and not the trustworthiness of parties. In other words, an increased weight was placed on personal testimony, on written documents which were taken to be irrefutable proof, and on confession. Implicitly, this meant that the legal system increasingly distanced itself from the previously commonly used compurgators, who swore to the trustworthiness of the defendant rather than to the case itself.

It is in this connection that we must see the demand to record the proofs produced and the objections to them because this ensured that future generations could see evidence of the correct decisions in the case, which proofs had been produced by the parties and how the court had made its decision.

In order to determine whether Danish legal procedure of the thirteenth century was a unique Danish way to administer justice or an adaptation of contemporary legal scholarship, I analyzed the provincial laws' normative expressions of the institutions of administration of justice and of procedural law; both were studied as examples of how such the legal order was thought to be possible and of the ideals and principles that were to be the foundation of each province's legal order. As a consequence of these analyses I argue that the Law of Jylland reflects a qualitatively different stage of learned law than other Danish medieval collections of law, and that the Law of Jylland therefore is fundamentally equal to contemporary learned law outside Denmark. This is the case when we analyze 1) the clearly defined fixed institutions for the administration of justice that are indispensible for a properly functioning legal order, and 2) the law of procedure based on a fundamental principle that cases should be heard in public; this was combined with a duty to carry them through with well-defined terms for appearance and objections and an evaluation of presented or produced proofs. The great difference between the Law of Jylland and other contemporary collections of law is clearly defined by how much it in detail corresponds to the Roman-canonical law of procedure. While the Roman-canonical procedure is present at a very sophisticated, technical and conceptual level in many other European kingdoms, especially in Southern Europe, we do not find the Roman-canonical procedure as explicit or in such detail in the Law of Jylland (although it is much more than in other

Danish laws). This fact leads to three more general considerations about how law was communicated and developed in thirteenth-century Denmark.

First of all, we must consider the fact that medieval secular law was to a large extent 'living law', which we must understand as a law under constant development. My analysis of Danish manuscripts and collections of law and the examples quoted of disagreement between individual redactions of law has demonstrated clearly, that there was an extensive consensus to change or supplement the law found in these collections of law when this was necessary; this was probably based on experience and a will to guide development in a particular direction. Previous scholarships' interpretation, that medieval secular law codes reflected a tradition that simply codified existing law, can thus not be sustained, at least not when considering the developments of the thirteenth century.

This also means that oral law is easy to adapt to changed circumstances or wishes, in contrast to changes in written law, which appear more clearly as changes, so that the difference between old and new law is more explicit in written law. This does not mean that the development of law slowed down in the thirteenth and early fourteenth centuries. The material that I have investigated shows that the development did not slow down, both when considering procedural law and institutions of legal administration.

In some contexts, however, the development focused on developing and refining the institutions of legal administration. In a number of southern European collections of law this was clearly a royal initiative, but in Denmark it appears to have been the result of an interaction between royal central power and regional magnates or local communities in individual provinces. In the case of the Law of Jylland, we see an increased emphasis on the power of the local assembly (*ting*) to reject decisions by jurors as from the beginning of the fourteenth century and a more lenient law of procedure and sanctions in many respects than those found in the older redaction. This indicates that there was not a particularly large distance, at the level of the provincial assembly (*landsting*), between royal central power and local or regional magnates in terms of their power politics and their attentiveness to new developments.

In practice, there was a general awareness that old texts were to be interpreted in the light of later changes. Therefore it is entirely acceptable that there should be textual variants in normative texts: Legal texts were not carriers of solutions to a concrete legal problem because these texts had to be interpreted with regard to their tradition, i.e. their relationship to custom, later legislation, and decisions intended to create precedence. Sometimes this awareness is visible in the manuscripts and sometimes it is not.

Secondly, we must conclude that the legislation, that was most likely royally initiated in the thirteenth century, was strongly influenced by learned law, even in Denmark. This does not mean that the kings and their legal advisers simply transplanted legal rules or institutions as they were known in post-Classical Roman or contemporary canon law, and transferred them into their own secular legal order. On the contrary, combining these new developments with a moral Christian ethic and its ideas about what was just, the thirteenth-century Roman-canon law delivered a number of institutional and procedural ideas and tools, that allowed a secular prince to provide a legal order capable of living up to the ideals that had been formulated by learned law, and which might even underpin royal rule. It was, so to speak, a tool box from which the prince and his advisers and supporters could take what they could use, and if necessary, adapt it to fit exactly those local conditions that were already in place.

Secular law was thus both shaped to fit existing frames and meet the law-givers' goals, and to fit the particular learned tools that the law-givers possessed. These tools, which were admirably suited for their purpose in both Northern and Southern Europe, consisted of course of the large collections of Roman law and canon law, which by being written law were more suited for international distribution, since these collections could be the means of communication over large distances and areas, without changing their shape or content because of them being increasingly studied at universities. It is precisely the fact that the learned collections of law could function as communication media over large distances. That means it can be difficult to identify particular legal centers or peripheries in thirteenth-century Europe, at least if we insist on studying the administration and those social groupings that were closely associated with the centralizing royal powers.

If we look at conditions in the Danish kingdom, the situation is different as the central power apparently 'relinquished' or accepted that a part of the substantial private law, or indeed the sentencing function, was to be resident with the local population during the jury institution. The appointed members of such a local jury could probably not understand the technical subtleties of procedural law or the newer learned principles concerning positive proof and majority decisions. Here the difference between a centralized, learned environment around the king and a conversely less learned local environment may be more visible than differences between central powers.

Thirdly, it must be said that the possibility of introducing Roman-canonical procedural law and its legal concepts was not good in Denmark, even if it had been the king's wish to do so. A possible explanation can of course be, that the Danish king was not powerful enough to introduce learned law without major confrontations. Such an explanation, however, is not enough to explain the difference we find between the open use of learned law found in Southern Europe compared with its more subtle use in

Denmark. It is more likely that this was because Southern Europe already shared a linguistic and legal tradition that was familiar to the institutions that were being introduced. During the Antiquity the Romans had ruled in Southern Europe, and in the centuries between the collapse of the Roman Empire and the medieval royal collections of law in general, law had been based on the practice of law that was built on a simplified Roman law. Such a situation could of course not be found in Denmark.

It is with this in mind that we must interpret the lack of an open introduction of Roman-canonical law of procedure in Denmark. Without a legal tradition to support such an implementation and without a sufficient power base that could guarantee this kind of implementation, it was basically impossible for the Danish king and his legal advisers to introduce and make effective the learned law of procedure, that was preferred and promoted by the Christian Church. My analysis of the Law of Jylland and the other Danish provincial laws has shown, that by 1241 the king did have legal advisers who knew and understood the learned law of procedure, but it was not a knowledge that was obvious in the Danish provincial laws. The most basic principles and ideas of the learned administration of justice and the law of procedure were introduced into Danish law to make it more effective, but this was not done openly through the use of Latin legal terms and suchlike.

Before the Fourth Lateran Council, the Danish legal order was based on accusatory procedure, with its fixed proofs and its fundamental use of negative proof, which was particularly symbolized in its most rarified form through the most difficult of proofs, namely the carrying of hot iron. With the Council's final rejection of Divine Judgment, the frequently used carrying of hot irons was made obsolete, and the Danes were now presented with a pressing procedural problem that demanded an answer. This came in the form of juries, which were fundamentally intended to replace negative proofs with a positive evaluation of proofs produced in a case, but in reality the old practice seems to have continued in some cases, i.e. that the law allowed a compurgation to determine matters.

As the learned law of procedure developed the principles of majority, subjective guilt, tighter time limits, and a more extensive use of inquisitorial procedure, it became clear to the king and the Church that the Danish administration of justice had to be made more effective in order to create a legal order, that satisfied the moral-ethical aims of the Church. In addition, this awareness provided the king with a role to play in the local administration of justice, as it was only him, at least formally, who could appoint jurors. For the central power there were three possibilities:

To introduce a law that openly introduced a new legal order based on learned law with the king as the uncontested lawgiver.

To abstain from attempting the implementation of learned law, which would mean losing the provided possibilities to strengthen the king's position, and to carry through the legal ideology of the Church?

Or to transform learned law's fundamental procedural principles so much, that they would appear to be only minor adjustments of the existing administration of justice, while in fact, for those learned in law, they were a revolutionary change of the fundamental principles behind the Danish administration of justice.

Following through the exalted position of the king in the prologue of the Law of Jylland, the third possibility was followed, probably with an underlying idea that this collection of law, or at least its principles, was to be valid for the entire kingdom. It is also very likely that the law in medieval Denmark developed primarily through the borrowings of Danish jurists from learned law, when faced with a local problem of law, which they could not solve based on the existing system of law. Such legal borrowings or 'transfers', the so-called 'legal transplants', were purely practical, voluntary, and the technical solutions of the dogmatic problem that had arisen. And by necessity this was implemented by juristic authorities against the background of the legal tradition in which they had developed.

PROPERTY AND LAND TENANCY IN NORWEGIAN MEDIEVAL LAWS AND THE EUROPEAN LEARNED LAW

Tore Iversen

Introduction

In this presentation I shall be looking into land property and land tenancy in the three Norwegian medieval laws, the Gulathing Law (G), the Frostathing Law (F) and, the *Landslög* (L) from 1274 - which is the national law of King Magnus for the entire kingdom of Norway. Our focus shall be on the development of concepts and legal categories regarding land property and land tenancy. The perspective of my research is focused on the European development of jurisprudence in the high Middle Ages with it's impact on Norwegian medieval laws. As we shall see, this means a focusing on the Roman law jurisprudence. We shall see that the European influence on the making of law in these three laws in Norway, must have been substantial. In this context my contribution is tentatively to concretize this impact through archbishop Eystein. In the following sections I am going to examine the concepts qualitatively and quantitatively, and subsequently the legal forms of land tenancy and the development of these forms. My main thesis is that the tenants´ possession of rented land moved from being a legally insecure land tenancy (G) to a more proprietary, i.e. 'thingly' *(in rem)* protected land tenancy in F, and specially in L. The central concepts and legal forms we will be dealing with, are formal aspects of a wider socio-economic system concerning land tenancy in Norway in relation to landowners, and the King and Church. It is clear that concepts and law forms thus were adapted and was a special working out of a broadly defined West European system which in other contexts can give options for interesting comparisons. What I will deal with in this lecture are central, and in the Norwegian context, little explored aspects of the development of a system of land tenancy during the later part of the high Middle Ages.

Norwegian Laws of the High Middle Ages

From the 1960s onward the studies of Norwegian medieval law got on to new tracks after a lengthy pause, because the laws and the development of law gradually were seen in the light of influence from European Medieval jurisprudence. My claim is that Sten Gagner's dissertation of 1960 creates a crossroad, in that Scandinavia here is seen integrated as an important area in the development of European law making in the high Middle Ages, where the growth of positive law making is the central theme. Among studies of this new pattern just a few names of significance shall be mentioned here. Vegard Skånland (1969) shows that the *Decretum Gratiani* of ca. 1140 was recepted into the Norwegian Church regulations already in 1170s (Peter Landau, in this book). Klaus von See (1964) gives a new review of sentral Nordic law concepts in the light of European law thinking in the high Middle Ages. Ole Fenger (1977) gives an important account of the influence of Roman law on legislation in Scandinavia.[1]

Before dealing concretely with property- and property related concepts in the Norwegian medieval laws, we shall characterise and place this legislation in a European law context. According to Norwegian historians of recent times, this rather unique making of laws which took place in Norway during a period of approximately 150 years, from ca. 1150 to 1300, is happening in the context of "Norway becomes a state", a characterisation which the historian Knut Helle has given to this period in the history of Norway. It is by now quite generally agreed that this development of law making took place with the King and the Church as principal participants, often in close contact with West- and Central-Europe as we shall see.[2] Viewed in a European context, Scandinavia, although geographically on the outskirts, was in no way lagging behind with respect to law making in this period.[3]

---

1. Sten Gagnér: *Studien zur Ideengeschichte der Gezetsgebung*, 1960; Vegard Skånland: *Det eldste norske provinsalinstitutt,* 1969; Klaus v. See: *Altnordische Rechtswörter*, 1964; Ole Fenger: *Romerrett i Norden*, 1977.
2. Knut Helle: *Norge blir en stat 1130-1319*, 1974 passim.
3. Armin Wolf: "Die Gesetzgebung der entstehenden Territorialstaaten", *Handbuch der Quellen und Litteratur der neueren europäischen Privatrechtsgeschichte I (Hrs. Helmut Coing),* 1973, p. 517f.

The Norwegian medieval legislation may be sketched as follows according to historically known redactions and kept manuscripts:[4] The Gulathing Law (G) exists almost entirely preserved in a manuscript from about 1250 (A: "Rantzau book"), and contains two redactions, the Olav text and the Magnus text.[5] A fragment of the Olav text from ca. 1200 or from the end of the 12th century exists as well. The Olav text refers to a redaction of law into a codex which probably was done at the end of the 11th century, for the King Olav Kyrre (1067-97). The new redaction of the law took place under the rule of King Magnus Erlingsson (1161-84), more closely sometime during the decade after 1164. The oldest Olav text has probably also been reworked before the Magnus redaction and is thus not identical with the legislation of early Middle Ages. We can roughly assume that the law is representative of its actual period of redaction as well as of the previous 12th century.

The secular part of the Frostathing Law (F) is based on a manuscript from 1260-69, (A: "The Resens book") as well as on a fragment from 1220-25. The law probably received important parts of its preserved redaction early in the 13th century, as well as one in the 1240s. The law as we know it today had its redaction completed in 1260. The secular F can thus be assumed to be representative of a period before and after the turn of the 13th century.

The Church Law of F (part II-III in the "Resens book"), which builds on text from the first part of the 14th century including a text from ca. 1260, was probably redacted by Archbishop Eystein (1157-88).

The Resens manuscript (A) of F starts with the 'new law' of King Haakon Haakonsson from 1260 (F intr.1-24). The newer law material

---

4. Norwegian laws of the high Middle Ages are collected and edited by R.Keyser, P.A.Munch, G.Storm and E.Hertzberg in *Norges gamle Love* (NgL I-V) (Chra.1846-95). Translations: *Gulatingslovi* by Knut Robberstad (Norrøne bokverk 33) 1969; *Frostatingslova*, transl. by Jan Ragnar Hagland and Jørn Sandnes Oslo 1994; *Magnus Lagabøters landslov* ved A.Taranger (Kra.1915, new print 1964). English translations: *The Older Law of the Gulathing*, Records of Civilization, No.20:35-213. Ed. L.M.Larson. New York 1935. *The Older Law of the Frostathing*, Records of Civilization, No.20:213-409. Ed. L.M.Larson.New York 1935. German translations: *Das Rechtsbuch des Gulathings*, ed. R.Meissner: Germanenrechte 6, Weimar 1935; *Das Rechtsbuch des Frostathings*, ed. R.Meissner: Germanenrechte 4, Weimar 1939. Of secondary literature concerning questions of sources and dates: A.Taranger: "De norske folkelovbøkene (før 1263)", *Tidsskrift for Retsvidenskap 39*, 1926 og 41, 1928; P.Norseng: Lovmaterialet som kilde til tidlig nordisk middelalder, *Rapport til den XX. nordiske historikerkongress b.1*: 48-77, Reykjavik 1987. Further: Hagland & Sandnes: *Frostatingslova*, 1994; Helle: *Gulatingslova*, 2001.
5. This manus is printed in NgL I s.3-110. A new edition is in: B.Eithun, M.Rindal, T.Ulset, *Den eldre Gulatingslova*, Norrøne tekster nr. 6, Riksarkivet, Oslo 1994.

originates from Magnus the Lawmender's new revision of the "Provincials laws" G and F (1267-69) as the first step in his countrywide law making in the 1270s: The *Landslög* (The Law of the Realm) (L) of 1274, the Town law (1276) and *Hirdskrå,* the codex for the King's men (1273-77). In addition there is the Church law of Archbishop Jon in 1281.[6]

My point of view is that the laws are not passively recorded or re-edited. They should sooner be regarded as products of conscious, political efforts.[7] Even when a redaction of the law can be identified and dated, this does not mean that dating of singular regulations are without it's problems. Older regulations could of course be let into new redactions, but then first after a conscious political selection, not as passively recorded customary law which law historians may make direct use of in order to reconstruct society step by step back in time, which is what the older Germanistic view claimed. Making records and new redactions of laws is considered active political enterprise in the views of legal historians Ole Fenger and Armin Wolf.[8] In my research of the Norwegian thraldom in G and in F I found normative representations of that institution with surprising consistency, separately within G and F.[9] Also taking into account the possibility of 'sleeping regulations', I am therefore inclined to think that through new redactions of the laws, older paragraphs were, as a rule, removed from the law if they came to clearly stand in opposition to a consistent representation

---

6. The Resens manuscript was lost in a cityfire in Copenhagen in 1723, but has been preserved in copies. The copies give us of course an uncertainty. Early Norwegian law material is otherwise the two East-Norwegian Church laws of the Eidsivathing Law (E) and the Borgathing Law (B), as well as the Bjarkøy law – fragments of a town law for Trondheim/Nidaros. In this article I do not take these laws into consideration.

7. Elsa Sjöholm: "Rättshistorisk metod och teoribildning", *Scandia 44,* p.229-56; Sjöholm: "Medeltidslagarna som historiska källor", *Kvinnans ekonomiska ställing under nordisk medeltid. Uppsatser framlagda vid et kvinno-historisk symposium i Kungälv* (ed. H.Gunneng), 1981 p. 74-81. For my own part I will underline my fundamantal stand, which is that the law material can tell social history. In order to achieve this, very thorough examination is needed. This way I would like to keep my distance from Sjöholm's extreme diffusionism which disregards the synchronous and diachronic societal context of the law material.

8. The legal historian Ole Fenger has pointed out that the purpose in writing down laws in the medieval period has not been to maintain customary law, but rather to get an overview of it and preserve changes made by church and King. According to Armin Wolf there are in this period three cleared (explained and accepted) ways for law makers to relate to old law by: (1) Writing down existing law which in this way will be ratified formally through laws. (2) Making new laws which supplements old law without repealing it. (3) Lawmaking which consciously puts new law in the place of old law. (see Ivo of Chartes' principle of 1090: *ex necessitate fit mutatio legis*), Fenger 1977 p. 57; Wolf 1996 p. 548-552.

9. Iversen 1997 p. 67-71, 78-81.

in the new redaction. As for the two presentations of thralldom that I found in G and F respectively, it could be stated that they had clear parallel characteristics of law on the status of un-free elsewhere in Europe. However, I am not without hesitation when transferring these findings to other types of themes in the laws.[10]

Law Making and Customary Law in the High Middle Ages – Norway and Europe

Gagnér points out that in this period there was a development from customary law based on tradition and not registered in writing, to a law by legislation which came about helped by Roman law and learned canon law. By the end of that process at the end of the 13th century, the legislative power of the monarchs had become an actual maxim.[11] Gagner emphasizes certain milestones in canonic law towards the great secular phase of law making in the 13th century. The first important one was undoubtedly the *Dectretum* by the monk Gratian around 1140 in Bologna. The 'theoretical' foundation for the systematic codexing by Gratian, was exactly that of customary law in writing. The *Decretum* was followed up with a series of administrative decretals (papal regulations) which gradually led to the development of a complete canon law. Pope Gregor IX's *Liber extra* (1234), where all canon law after Gratian was systemized into a codex, became the high-light in law making by the Church and normative for secular codexing.[12]

In the same manner as secular legislation thus picked up strong impulses from canon law, so did the Church's own concept of law in a similar manner have its obvious background in secular law through the regenerated Justinian Roman law. The study began in Bologna at the end of the 11th century based i.a. on a then recently discovered, complete manuscript of the great *Digesta* in the Justinian law collections. The learned in the Roman law "glossatores" systematized and annotated Justinian law texts. Thus the new law was called "the learned law". It is easy to point out that the formulators of canon law had Roman law as a model, and lived according to it (*ecclesia vivit secundum legem romanam*).[13] Gratian and others, like him learned in Church Law, claimed that Roman law was to be

---

10. Iversen 1997 p. 70.
11. Gagnér 1960 p. 292-295.
12. Gagnér 1960 p. 288-304, 312f., 351f.: On Canonic Law of the period: James A.Brundage: *Medieval Cannon Law,* 1995, espes. pp. 194ff.
13. Hermann Lange: *Römisches Recht: B 1. Die glossatoren*, 1997 p.93-103; A.Erler in HRG I p. 798 (Handwörterbuch zur deutchen Rechtsgeschichte I-IV. Ed. A.Erler, E.Kaufmann, R.Schmidt-Wiegand, W.Stammer, 1974).

followed where church law gave no answer. Furthermore, one sought to harmonize the two types of law and achieved that to a certain point as *ius utrumque*- the two laws.[14] For our purpose it is here important to underline that with respect to concepts and legal forms on property and land lease, canon law followed Justinian's Roman law and its ongoing development through "the learned law".[15]

The glossators introduced, with their analyses, an entirely new and rational-systematic attitude to sources of law and law procedures (*ratio leges*).With regard to interpretation of the text, jurisprudence was now considered part of the discipline of logic, while early the Middle Ages saw law belonging to ethics. The learned studies thus did, gradually, bring forth a "making law a science".[16] The actual founder of the Bologna School of Law and of the scientification process of law was Irnerius (dead after 1125). During the 12th century there was a grand rise in the law studies in Bologna with " four doctores", of whom Bulgarus, "the golden mouth" (*os aureum*) (d. 1141) and Martinus "the richness of the law" (*copia legum*) (d. after 1158) are the better known. The significance of law studies in contemporary Europe is indicated by an estimated number of several thousand jurisprudence students in Bologna in the middle of the 12th century. [17] Among the later *leges doctores* in Bologna, we must mention Johannes Bassianus (d. 1197), Azo (d. 1220) and finally Accursius (1185-1263) as a culmination. The great *Glossa ordinaria* (ca. 1230), a work of annotations by the last mentioned, gradually gained a dominating significance.[18]

The new studies of Roman law gave, undoubtedly, a strong stimulus to law making in the high Middle Ages, both under the auspices of the Church and gradually stronger also of the kingdom, the latter because the Justinian *Digesta* directly connects *iurisdictio* (legislative power) and *imperium* (execution of power) and regards these as mutually dependent dimensions. It is important to underline that iurisdictio was extensive in the areas of both criminal law and civil law.[19] When problems of regional law were to be

---

14. Peter Stein: *Römisches Recht und Europa. Die Geschichte einer Rechtskultur*, 1996, p. 86-95.
15. Klaus Genius: *Der Bestandsschutz des Mietverhältnisse in seiner historischen Entwicklung bis zu den Natur-rechtskodifikationen*, 1972 p. 57-68. The adoption of Roman law by the Church in this matter did of course not mean that the Church didn't have it's own interests in the system of land lease.
16. Kiefner in HRG IV, p. 971.
17. Dilcher, H in HRG I p.1708-12.
18. Stein 1996 p.80-85; A collected, detailed presentation is given in Lange 1997 p. 151-440.
19. Stein 1996 p. 99-102; Perrin, John W (Azo, Roman law and Sovereign European States) i *Studia Gratiana* XV, 1972, p. 89-101. As a basis Ole Fenger's (1977

solved, one looked to Roman law to solve them, because this could offer a superior conceptual clarity and systematic. The actual conceptualization of customary law (*consuetudo*) is in itself a product of "the learned" Roman law iurisprudence of this period. The new *iurisprudence* came, however to have a pragmatic relationship with the different regionally exciting law arrangements.[20]

It is possible to see our three Norwegian medieval laws in the perspective drawn by Gagnér. Customary law has played an important part in the oldest of the laws, the Gulathings Law. In the writing down / redacting of the law they want to get an overview of customary law has probably been active.[21] The role of the King as positive maker of law is in any case clearly present in G, he is, however, not as superior as in the hundred years younger *Landslög* (L).[22] The law formulation "with law shall land be built" (L I 6, *At lögum scal land várt byggja*) can be seen as an expression of the weakened position of customary law in relation to kingly law-making ideology. It has been pointed out that this formular above had Roman law as a model, *civitas fundaretur legibus* (Dig.1,2,4).[23] Nordic and Continental legal historians have emphasized that Magnus Lagabøter's law giving activity is one of the most prominent examples of 'kingly' legislative

---

p.105-6) point of view that medieval Roman law had less influence on areas of civil law (proprietal law and obligation law) must be incorrect.

20. Bulgarus (d. 1166) was of the opinion that e.g. "generally valid law" had precedence over local customary law. However, written law could only cancel earlier law when it was introduced with conscious intent to go against the older law. Bassianus (d. 1197) thought customary law to be valid in as far as it was logic, i.e. as Roman law claimed. Different learned opinions of the relationship between customary law and legislated law gained, however, different footholds in the different parts of Europe; i.e. Roman law gained precedence over customary law in Southern France, while the opposite happened in England (Stein 1996 p. 105-115).

21. In the land tenancy section of G, 6 of 31 regulations point out old custom/consuetute, in F equivalently only 2 of 41, in L 7 of 65. Could one reason for such a high number of the regulations of G's tenancy segment pointing to the validity of old customary practise be that a great deal of other regulations in the same segment were changed or added at the same time?

22. Writing down / redactioning must thus have lead to lawmaking activity like selecting and giving form to law regulations as Helle has showed, simultaneous with new positive regulations pushing through by the Church and by the King. Knut Helle: "Rettsoppfatninger og rettsendringer: Europa og Norge i middelalderen" (*Festskrift til Historisk Institutts 40-årsjubileum* (ed. G-A.Ersland), 1997 p. 41-70; Helle: "Lov og rett i middelalderen- et tilsvar til Kåre Lunden", *Forum Mediaevale* 2/1998 p. 1-16.

23. Knut Robberstad: *Frå gamal og ny rett,* 1950, p. 7ff.; Ditlev Tamm points out that the formular fits into the legislation ideology of the 13th century (D.Tamm: "Mæth logh scal land bygges", *Festschrift für Thieme zu seinem 80. Geburtstag* (Hrs. K.Kroeschell), 1986 p. 127-139.

strength and power in the European high Middle Ages.[24] In L the King is legislator in a law positive and Roman law sense as *(princeps legibus solutus)* it is said, that the King is as judge above the law *(Þuiat hann er ifir login skipaðr)* (L I 11).[25] The King can within a given framework, primarily in co-operation with the Church, use legislation as a tool for social regulations, through e.g. criminal law, but also step into the "civil" sphere as well by e.g. regulating land tenancy relations which shall be the theme in our in our research as follows.

European Legal Studies and Norwegian Students

The Italian legal historian Francesco Calasso has pointed out that Magnus Lagabøter's *Landslög*, which he regards as one of the three great codifications of law of European significance in the high Middle Ages, would not have been possible without being influenced by the new learned legal sciences. He maintains that Norwegian students could find a *iura communia* in the two great centers of European culture at the time, Bologna and Paris.[26] Since Norwegian connections with the *iura communia* were not new in the second half of the 13th century, we shall now attempt to examine a few early connections. Demographic increase and economic development along with urbanization form the backdrop for the rapid intellectual development that took place in Latin Christianity. The rise of the new universities began in the late 11th century, and these took over and renewed much of the scholarly activities that had taken place at monasteries and in cathedral schools. The rise and development of the new learned legal sciences form part of this picture. Growth in Church and later royal power made it possible for younger sons of the nobility to seek carriers within these public institutions.

---

24. Her emphasized: The Italian legal historian Francesco Calasso: *Medio Evo del Diritto I*, 1954 p. 304f, 620-21; Gagnér 1960 p. 321; Tamm 1986 p. 138-9; Wolf 1973 p. 773-780.
25. Presumably meant that he decides where the law does not speak (Knut Helle). The legislation ideology of the King is found presented in *Konungs skuggsjá* (Kongespeilet/ The King's Mirror*)* (1260). The King as *rex iustus* is solely responsible for upholding peace and justice. Here his authorities are nearly that of an absolute monarch, a *vicarius dei*. Cf. Sverre Bagge: *The Political Thought of The King's Mirror*, 1987.
26. The other two being Fredrick II´s *Liber augustalis* og King Alfonso's *Las siete partidas*. Concerning the Landslög (L), Calasso points out that the great undertaking, systematization of materials and not least, the plan for putting it into effect. Calasso 1954 p. 304f, 620-21; Gagnér 1960 p. 321.

Surprisingly, there is a document that may show possible Norwegian and Danish scholarly contacts with Italy at a time when the new legal science (jurisprudence) was in its infancy. In 1078, pope Gregory VII wrote to King Olav Kyrre, requesting that Olav send him a few young men of noble family so that they might receive instruction in "sacred and divine laws" (*sacris ac diuinis legibus*), i.e., canon law.[27] There was supposedly a centre for legal scholarship in Rome until the city was sacked in 1084. This seems subsequently to have been transferred to Bologna.[28] At the same time, in the 1070s, there are extant documents that demonstrate that legal studies were already taking place in Bologna. We do not know what Gregory's letter led to, but there is no reason to believe that contact here was an isolated case, and it must have been common from the middle of the 12th century.[29]

The first significant Norwegian student of law that we know of is the later Archbishop Øystein Erlendsson (1161-1188). Since he was a great legislator, we must examine his role more closely. It is presumed that he was behind Magnus' revision of the Gulathing Law, which probably dates to the decade following 1164. For his own bishopric, he made a separate law book, the Frostathing's Christian Law, comprising chapters II and III of *Resensmanus*. Øystein was also the patron of a collection of church law known as the *Canones nidarosiensis*, dated to 1163/4 (or possibly the 1170s) and already heavily influenced by Gratian (cf. Landau's article).[30]

Øystein probably began his studies abroad after 1140. Whereas the first Icelandic students, and in all probability the Norwegian ones as well, studied in Northwest Germany, cathedrals in Northern France and eventually Paris became their goal in the beginning of the 12th century. Scholarly contacts with England, whence Norway received fundamental impulses for her early Christianity and church organization, must have been a possibility throughout this period. We assume that Øystein studied at the Augustine monastery of St. Victor in Paris, where Hugo of St. Victor taught until 1141. In England, Lincoln was a probable goal for him as well as for other Norwegian and Icelandic students. In the 1140s and 50s, leading prelates in England began employing legal scholars from Italy; Vacarius, Ambrosius (St. Alban) and Peter de Melide (Lincoln).

---

27. DN VI nr.1 (Diplomatarium Norvegicum 1-21, 1847-1970); RN I nr.50 (Regesta Norvegica 1-6, 1989-1993); E.Vandvik, Latinske dokument til norsk historie fram til 1204, 1959, p. 32-3.
28. Åke Sällström: *Bologna och Norden intill Avignonpåvedömmets tid*, 1957, p. 1-5.
29. The more substantial Icelandic material shows that bishop Isleifur (d.1080) and Gissur (d.1118) studied in Germany. Bishop Jon (d. 1121) in France and Italy, Thorlok at St.Victor in Paris (1153-59), cf. Bagge: "Nordic Students at Foreign Universties", *Scandinavian Journal of History 9*, 1984 p. 4.
30. Skånland 1969 p. 176f; Gunnes 1996 especially p. 99-172; Helle 1974 p. 57-69.

We know that Øystein stayed at St. Victor in 1160-61 when he went to Italy for his ordination.[31] He may have received instruction there from the canonical scholar Stephan of Tournai.[32] Canonical studies formed the foundation for the special connection that St. Victor had with Norwegian students until the early 13th century.[33] Øystein probably resumed old contacts during his period of exile in Lincoln and East Anglia in 1180-83.[34] The diocese of Lincoln included Oxford and Northampton and was the seat of one of the most active learned cathedral schools of the 12th century. In 1153, the bishop commissioned an improved copy of the Digest under the supervision the legal scholar *magister* Ambrosius from St. Alban in East Anglia. Besides the important books of Roman law, Lincoln also offered studies in canon law. Lincoln was indeed one of the most important scholarly centres in England in the latter half of the 12th century. A charter confirms that Vacarius, who introduced Roman law to England, was also associated with Lincoln.

The young Vacarius was brought to England from Bologna in 1143 by archbishop Theobald. He taught Roman law and published the *Liber Pauperum*, a manual containing excerpts from the Justinian's Codex and Digesta for students of small means. Later on, Vacarius also served under archbishop Roger of York. Scholars have previously believed that he founded the law school at Oxford and published his *Liber Pauperum* there in the 1150s, but recent scholarship has shown that this is less likely. The legal historian Peter Stein maintains that the *Liber Pauperum* should rather be dated to the 1170s. Stein further believes that Lincoln is one of the three places where Vacarius may have published the *Liber Pauperum*, the alternatives being Oxford and Northampton. This publication became immensely popular, and the study of Roman law flourished in England towards the end of the 12th century.[35]

---

31. Mary Cheney: "Possessio/proprietas' in ecclesiastical courts in mid-twelfth-century England", *Law and Gover-ment in Medieval England and Normandy* (ed. J.Hudson), 1994 p. 245-255; Erik Gunnes: "Erkebiskop Øystein. Statsmann og kirkebygger", 1996 p. 26-31, 35-48.
32. Iversen 1997 p. 199-204. My hypothesis in this case is that Øystein stands behind the formulation in G 63, concerning marriage among unfree, influenced by Stephan av Tournai's teachings on this subject. In that case, a meeting between the two may have taken place at St.Victor.
33. A.O.Johnsen: "Om St. Viktorklosteret og nordmennene", *NHT (Norsk Historisk Tidsskrift) 33* p. 405-31.
34. Gunnes 1996 p. 32-35.
35. Peter Stein: Vacarius and the civil law in England, *The teaching of Roman law in England around 1200 (*eds. F.de Zulueta & P.Stein) 1990 p. xxii-xxxviii; esp. xxxv-xxxvii; idem. "Vacarius and the civil law", *Church and Government in the Middle Ages (*eds. Brooker, Luscombe, Martin and Owen) p. 119-137; R.V.Turner:

Øystein was not the only visitor to Lincoln, as it fell natural for Norwegians to go there. York, the former focal point for Scandinavian interests, had been the primary objective of Harald Hardrada's invasion in 1066. After his demise, however, Lincoln further to the south became more important. We find many Scandinavian names there, and with the ports Grimsby and Boston, Lincoln became the main centre for the expanding trade with Norway in the 12th century. Crafts also appear to have fostered close contacts, as the same stonemasons' marks have been found in the cathedrals of Lincoln and Nidaros (Trondheim), where Øystein incidentally initiated the first great building projects. These two cathedrals also display similarities in style. In the spiritual realm, East Anglian monasteries (such as St. Alban and St. Edmund) played an important role as recruiting grounds for Nidarholm, Selje and Munkeliv, the first monastic establishments in Norway. The monks in these new foundations maintained contacts with their parent monasteries. In the mid-12th century, the Cistercians were particularly active. Their first two monasteries, founded in 1146 and 1147, had East English parent monasteries in Yorkshire and Kirkstead in Lincoln.[36]

We may assume that a cleric with significant interest in legal matters, such as Øystein, was aware of Vacarius and his writings, as well as other imported legal scholars, such as Peter and Ambrosius, mentioned above. Furthermore, during Øystein's period in exile (1880-83), the first to reach out a helping hand was probably Ranulf Glanville, Chief Justice to King Henry. Ranulf later published (probably in 1188) a judicial *Tractatus*, which became the first authoritative text concerning English common law. This treatise contains a good deal of material influenced by Roman law.[37] We do not know whether they discussed legal matters during their interaction. After Øystein had held the abbacy at St. Edmund, he resided in the see of Lincoln while it was vacant until the spring of 1183. In conclusion, there is no doubt that Øystein interacted with the foremost circles of legal scholars during his period of exile and possibly while studying in England in his youth. While in exile in Lincoln, he had the opportunity to study the fundamental texts of Roman law. Even at home in Norway, Øystein would have been able to stay up to date on scholarly opinions and their development within *ius utrumque*, both laws.[38] The fact that Øystein was

---

"Roman Law in England Before the Time of Bracton", *The Journal of British Studies, Vol.15.1* 1975 p. 1-25; Cheney 1996 p. 252 n. 25.

36. Gunnes 1996 p. 32-35; Helle 2000 p. 26,43-5.
37. Gunnes 1996 p. 251; H.Peter i *HRG I* p. 1692-3; *The Dictionary of National Biography:VII:* Ranulf Glanville (1917); *Encyclopedia Britanica V* (1994) p. 295.
38. Recent research has further demonstrated that the new legal sciences in Europe primarily spread through personal contacts, especially in the early period, Otto

the patron of the provincial statute *Canones nidarosiensis* (1163/4 or the 1170s), which is strongly influenced by Gratian's *Decretum* (1140), obviously strengthens the conclusion that Øystein and his circle were updated with respect to contemporary jurisprudence.[39]

Occasionally, the Norwegian church welcomed visiting scholars. For example, the English Augustinian Nicolaus Breakspear (later pope Hadrian IV) was responsible as papal legate for establishing the archbishopric at Nidaros in 1152/3.[40] Individuals like cardinal Nicolaus and archbishop Øystein belonged to a common European legal culture that flourished in the latter half of the 12th century. A person with legal education was by definition trained in canon as well as Roman law. In the 13th century, Bologna was the leading centre in Europe for both Roman and canon law, while Paris was of equal standing in the latter. There is hardly any doubt that leading circles within the Church, and eventually around the Norwegian King, kept informed about leading scholarly opinion concerning jurisprudence, even though we have little evidence for the early 13th century.[41] We know, however, that Jon Raude, archbishop from 1268, and Tore Håkonsson Biskopsson, Magnus Lagabøter's chancellor, probably studied in Bologna in the 1260s. The diplomat Audun Hugleiksson, also a man of law, must also receive mention. Several of these scholars among Magnus Lagabøter's circle of advisors were involved in his national legal reforms in the 1270s. In this connection, we must also mention Bjarne Lodinsson. Bjarne was an advanced student of Roman law at Bologna, since he held the title *iuris civilis professor*.[42]

Although most of those with a university degree went for a carrier in the Church, royal service was also significant, especially in Norway where the aristocracy depended on it. The student lists from Bologna shows that two out of six Norwegian students had secular posts in the royal service, whereas all the Danish and Swedish students were attached to the clergy. The Norwegian King Hákon V also appears to have promoted university

---

O.Clavadetscher: "Wandung der Rechtssprache im 13. Jahrhundert", *Festschrift Karl Siegfried Bader (*Hrs. F.Elsener, W.H.Ruoff)1965, p. 90.

39. Skånland 1969 p. 176f; Gunnes 1996 p. 13,135f, 250-255. *Canones* along with other legal documents were probably left behind by Øystein during his exile and found by the canon scholar Walther Holzmann in English archives in 1938 (Steinar Imsen, Nidarosprovinsen, *Ecclesia nidrosiensis* 1153-1537 (red. S.Imsen) 2003 p. 30f.

40. Nicolaus Breakspear completed his studies in Roman law at the school of law in Die in southern France (Stein 1996, p. 96-97).

41. Student lists from the University of Bologna are only extant from the late 13th century (Sällström 1957 p. 151f).

42. Knut Helle: *Konge og gode menn i norsk riksstyring,* 1972, p. 578-81, 583-84; Sällström 1957 p. 231-55, 270-4.

studies actively by assigning 300 silver marks to such pursuits. Neither the Danish nor the Swedish kings had any similar recruitment policy for providing administrative personnel with university degrees.[43]

Concepts of Land Property and Land Tenancy in the Laws of G, F and L

In dealing concretely with qualitative and quantitative use of terms on land property- and land lease conditions in the Gulathing Law (G), in the Frostathing Law (F) and in the *Landslög (L)*, my focus will be on changes in the use of terms and concepts during the approximately hundred years between the last redaction of G and the passing of L.[44] Thus the main theme is to see the changes in a European legal history context together with further insights into medieval society this can give. This last and larger perspective will, however, not be of major concern in this presentation. The three laws to be examined here, do not share exactly the same basis for quantitative comparisons, however, their differences will at any rate be manageable.[45] I will underline the following outcome of my examination of the laws found in G compared with F and L:

Firstly, I found a striking difference between G and the two later laws with respect to the concept of property concerning land. G barely operates

---

43. Sverre Bagge has found 81 Norwegians who studied abroad in the period 1200-1350, 43 of these before 1300. Most of them were attached to the (domkapitlene), mostly as canons. There is information that 17 canons held the Master's degree in period 1300-1350. When it is estimated that 5-12% of all students completed this degree, this may mean that somewhere from 140 to 340 Norwegians studied abroad in the period 1300-1350. (Bagge 1984 p. 1-13).
44. For a more extensive presentation of this theme I refer to my article: "Jordeie og jordleie – Eiendomsbegrepet i norske middelalderlover", *Collegium Medievale V.14*, 2001 p. 79-114.
45. The relative size of the three laws must be taken into account when one compares the number of occurences of terms for land ownership and land leasing. We get an impression of this by the standardized pages of print of the editions of NgL I og II, where G makes up all together 115 pages, F 137 pages and L 171 pages. The frequency of certain words in a regulation of the law is counted just once, even if this word may occur more than once in the regulation. All in all G has 320 regulations, F has 475, whereas L contains only 227 regulations. In G and F there is, however, a big difference in the size of the regulations, while the fewer regulations in L are more equal in size. Thus the three laws do not entirely have same basis for quantative comparisons, but the differences can still be handled. The fact that L is considerably larger than G, is e.g. partly countered by G containing more articles. The segment on land lease, i.e. the part of the law where most of the regulations are gathered, contains however far more regulations in L (65) than in F (34) and esp. G (10).

with an overall, substantive concept of land property. In F and L, however, the name *eign* has come through as a general term for land property.[46] However, in G, one can several times, especially in the Church law segment, find the use of another combined concept *landeign* - more precisely *landeigns konongs* - of the king's areas of power and control. *Eign* in these regulations does not represent property in the narrowly private interpretation of the word, rather power and control. Here the control over an area is not distinct from the property rights to the same area. The European parallel to *landeign konongs* seems to be *dominium regis* which is used in texts from early Middle Ages until the 12th century[47]: Legal historians have further pointed to the use of *dominium* in a very broad sense in the language of law throughout the period before the 12th century about control and conditions of power, including control over things. Property *(dominium)* in a later more narrow sense, domination over things, exists just as a lesser part of the understanding of the comprehensive concept of control, *dominium,* of early Middle Ages.[48] There was a gradual change in use of concepts in the sources of law. This became very clear from the end of the 12th century. The concept *dominium* is from now on in use in German sources increasingly as a term for immobilia.[49] This is the actual period when learned Roman law thought began to have its marked influence, and the dominium term that gained terrain was just the Roman "thingly" law

---

46. In G 265 and 266 only does <u>eign</u> indicate land property, in a juxtaposition which is either a tautology or a specification, *at eign oc at oðrle* (til eige og odel). With this it seems obvious to understand <u>oðrle</u> in G 265 and 266 as a specification of <u>eign</u>. Knut Helle and Per Norseng are of the opinion that allodial rights is a rather new institution which came about as a defense against selling and buying land became increasingly common into the Middle Ages. (Helle 1974, p. 154-5; d.s. 1995, p. 118; Per Norseng: "Kommentar til Christer Winberg", *NHT 2/*1991 p. 273-81, spec. p. 278. Allodial right is thus to be seen as a pre-emptive right on buying land and a right of land repurchase, on the continent also known in the early Middle Ages as *laudatio parentum*. Norseng does not preclude though that an allodial right may have been in existence in an older sense where family/kin and the right to land were tied together (cf. the concept *haugoðal* in L VI 16). This concept of property cannot in this case have been a "thingly" property concept.
47. *Dominium regis*- is offen used in the texts from the early Middle Ages and up in the 12th century. The Church might had been the prim motor. In the sources the names *dominium episcopi* and *dominium patris* also used. *Dominium regis* is also used by Adam of Bremen [Gesta Hammaburgiensis ecclesiae Pontificum, MG (Monumenta Germaniae) SS. rer. Germ. (ed B. Schmeidler) p. 225]; Dietmar Willoweit, Dominium und Proprietas, *Historisches Jahrbuch 1974,* p. 133-34.
48. Gerhard Köbler: *Das Recht im frühen Mittelalter,* 1971, p. 43f, 49; Karl Kroeschell: *Haus und Herrschaft im frühen deutchen Recht,* 1968, p. 45f; Willoweit 1974 p. 135.
49. Willoweit 1974, p. 136, fn 20. In such a way the term was used i.a. by Otto von Freising, Gesta Frederici.

property concept. There is incidentally a well known anecdote which can illustrate the understanding of property in this period: Emperor Fredric Barbarossa supposedly asked the two famous Bologna doctors, Bulgarus and Martinus, if, in their opinion, he was *dominus mundi*. Bulgarus denied this in his answer. Martinus on the other hand gave a confirmative answer and was given a horse from the emperor as his reward. This shows that a considerable ambivalence had occurred in the latter part of the 12th century. The confirmative answer of Martinus had its background in the previous lack of separation between 'lord' and 'owner'. Bulgarus's denying answer expressed that the Roman law 'thingly' property concept from a private sphere had begun to spread.[50]

Dominium, with the basic meaning "power and control/ domination", had not until the 13th century the proprietal, "thingly" law meaning "control over things" in European language of law.[51] Another important concept from the learned law is *proprietas,* "have, possess, have something especially, have something for oneself", and more simply be translated with the Norse *eign.* The legel historian Dietmat Willoweit underlines that the area of meaning of *proprietas* had nothing to do with a "thingly" property concept of early Middle Ages. The meaning gave merely in one form or another relation between a subject and another object or condition. The type or degree of disposal in the arrangement is then not mentioned, and it may exist within very heterogenous law conditions. Willowweit's thinking is that it is incorrect to understand a concept here of property in our sense, until well into the 13th century. The formular *dominium proprietas* which sometimes is used during the 12th century as well can underline this view.[52] This makes it evident then that *proprietas* as a 'relation' between the subject and an object shall also include dominium, "power and control ". We can probably find this formular again expressed in *eiga at eign (oc at orðle)* (have / own for property) in the Gulathing Law (G 265, 266).

My research has also involved the occurrence of the verb *eiga.* This verb carries a very wide and many sided use of meaning, from "having", "presiding/ruling over" land and other objects and persons (among others matrimonial partner, children, slaves), to "being entitled to", "obligated to", "indebted to", "receiving the fines paid", to "having judicial power over", and other additional rights. Comparing the usage of the verb *eiga* in the three laws, there does not seem to be any great difference between the laws

---

50. V.Savigny 1850 p. 180f., jfr Stein 1996 p. 103.
51. The first definition of property in Roman law stems in fact from the 14th century Roman jurisprudence prof. Bartolus: *Est ius de re corporali perfecte disponendi, nisi lege prohibitur.*
52. Willoweit 1974, p. 137-9.

concerning "having objects, land and persons (matrimonial partner, children, slaves)".

The Gulathing Law, however, appears to make more frequent use of the verb *eiga* than F and L where the meaning exceeds that of ownership over things (in G 38, F 18, L 14 times).[53] These aspects not relating to "objects, land and persons" may be dealing with "being entitled to, obligated to" "having rights to being restored", "rights to legal demands, legal position", that is to "own" various kinds of authority, rights/entitlements, claims etc. The fact that the same verb *eiga* is used to indicate, on the one hand, that land and objects "belong" to a person and on the other hand that authority, rights and claims "belong" to that person, must mean that the Gulathing Law to a lesser degree regards two such spheres as separate ones.

The absence of a clearly perceived separation between two such spheres can be traced in a wider European context: The historian Susan Reynolds states thus that property (rights) was not clearly separated from the authority to rule, firsts and foremost due to the fact that there was no distinct division between a private and a public sphere, especially not in the early Middle Ages.[54] In line with Reynolds the legal historian Damian Hecker points to a fundamental unity in medieval sense of property – a unity between "property" and "domination". On the one hand there was no abstract, general governmental power domination, definitely not in the early Middle Ages, merely a dominating control concerning concrete rights and areas of power of authorization with respect to taxes, judicial power e. a. On the other hand there was no form either of "pure" thingly property conception, since "domination" and "property" was so strongly entangled.[55] It is this wide, relational and entangled use of "eiga/owning" the historian Gudmund Sandvik establishes as well regarding the local Church's land-property in medieval Norway.[56] Owning rights could include mass for the

---

53. For details in this research, see my article, Tore Iversen: "Jordeie og jordleie – Eiendomsbegrepet i norske middelalderlover", *Collegium Medievale* V. 14 2001 p. 94-99.
54. Susan Reynolds: *Fiefs and Vassals. The medieval Evidence Reinterpreted*, 1994 p. 48-53.
55. Acc. to Hecker there was no form conceived for "abstracted" domination/ control in the Middle Ages. Domination was always seen as reletional, i.e. concretely in relation to something, be it the power of the lord, the Church, or the King etc., areas of power which all could take different shapes (Damian Hecker: *Eigentum als Sachenherrschaft. Zur Genese und Kritik eines besonderen Herrschaftans pruchs*, 1990, p. 32-6).
56. Gudmund Sandvik: *Prestegard og prestelønn*, 1965, p. 98. Sandvik concludes this way primarily based on the Diplom sources.

soul, possession and land rent etc., in such a manner that there could be several and crossing owner conditions in one relation.[57]

The broad spectrum of concrete part-relations to owning is most prominent in the Gulathing Law as we have seen, because G does not have a fixed conceptual separation of land property *(eign)* and other object-property, and that G most frequently has occurrences indicating non-object property connotations of *"eiga/* to own". The aforementioned *landeigns konongs* of the Gulathing Law is precisely an expression of the fact that the power and domination of the King in an early phase combine governmental authority and property.

So far the research has enabled us to state that the Gulathing Law had not yet, in the latter half of the 12th century, made use of any fixed concept of land property. According to legal historians it is only in the 13th century that the tendency to make use of a thingly, superior land property concept breaks through in West European sources of law. In line with this a specific contrasting concept relating to land tenancy and feudal land developed. The new, abstracted property concept came to take the place of vague concepts of "owning" with its many interpretations.[58] Beyond doubt, it is the influence from the new 'learned law' of the period, the studies of Roman law, which gave shape to the new making of judicial language in this area. Roman law could offer a property law related, 'thing-like' view with a more limited and precise structure of concepts than local-regional customary law made use of. This does not in any way exclude a dynamic specific to development of law, contingent on the 'inner' judicial problems in the old law and of course, not the least, external conditions of society in West-Europe.[59]

---

57. A comparative analysis of the legal language in medieval Germany may be relevant. The legal historian Dieter Schwab emphasizes firstly that *eigen* could have very different content. (In German legal language *eigen* corresponds to the Norse *eiga.)* Conscerning owning-relations connected to land, the meaning could change from that of owning "full"- property (allod) to that of "owning" use-and lease-rights and all types of owning-relations. Among others, possesson for life could be indicating an owning –relation to "eigen" (lat.: proprietas ad dies vitae). "Eigen" could also be used of a relation where the owner (of the right-of-use) had a fixed obligation to pay rent. Thus excisting rights could be attatched to an object and shared between more than one owner. Schwab thus wants to underline that the concept "eigen" did not have a permanent, fixed content in the earliest part of the high Middle Ages, and not in relation to land either (D. Schwab, Eigentum, *Geschichtliche Grundbegriffe* (Hrs. O. Brunner, W. Conze, R. Koselleck). B 2 1975, p. 66-9).
58. Schwab 1975 sp. 66-69.
59. Dietmar Willoweit, Gelehrtes Rechtsdenkens in Urkunden des 13. Jh., *Studiea Gratiana 1996* p. 590-1 Willoweit calls this early phase of influence from Roman law a "Frürezeption", a reception that had an impact only in certain areas.

In the Norwegian laws I have further in my research found a great difference between the Gulathing Law and the two later laws with regard to land property/land owner and land tenancy/land tenant: The nouns *eigandi, landsdróttinn* about land owner, and *leiglendingr (leidurliðr, landbui)* about land tenant, are found in total merely in three regulations in G compared to in 36 and in 57 regulations in F and L.[60] The technical term for land rent, *land-skyld* does not exist at all in the Gulathing Law.

There is also a considerable difference between the Gulathing Law and the two later laws when it comes to stating contrasts between *landsdróttinn, landskyld* (landlord, land rent) and *leiglendingr* (land tenant). G has here only one regulation having contrasting. F and L, on the other hand, contrast the nouns in most circumstances: In F *landsdróttinn* (landlord) has one or two contrasting concepts in 10 out of 16 regulations, *leiglendingr* (land tenant) in 8 out of 9, *landskyld* (land rent) in 5 out of 7 regulations. Accordingly, L has contrastings in 16 out of 24 regulations, in 19 out of 20 and in 9 out of 11 regulations.[61] There is not such a distinct division between G and the other two laws when we examine contrastings of the verbs '*eiga*' (to own) and '*leiga*' (to rent) with each other or with opposing nouns. All in all there is, however, far fewer contrasting in G.[62]

Subsequently, there is a marked increase in the use of contrasting concepts about land owning- and tenancy relationship from G to the later laws. The conclusion is that the two later laws to a higher degree and in a clearer sense seem to relate land property to land rent, and landlord to land tenant. The relationship between land property and land tenancy appears to have been vaguer, that is, viewed in a less limited and less structured way in the Gulathing Law than in the Frostathing Law and the *Landslög* (L). Land property is, further, much more separated out from other types of property in the two later laws than in G. In F and in L *eign* has become a term for land property. Oppositely in these two laws *lausafé* has become the term for mobilia. This latter term is not found in G. Additionally, in the two later laws land rent is separated out with its term, *landskyld,* a technical term which is not found either in G.

In addition several other circumstances point in the same direction when it comes to difference between the Gulathing Law and the two later laws: Contrary to in G, technical terms for contract of land tenancy are found in the two later laws, and then contrasted with other concepts within a system of land tenancy. The term *máli (leigumáli)* is found in this manner just twice in G and only once connected to tenant (G 72), while it in F and in L, with the addition of *tekja*, has become a technical term for lease

---

60. For details, see Iversen 2001, p. 100.
61. Iversen 2001 s. 101.
62. Iversen 2001 p. 102.

contract within a tenancy system in both of these laws. The verb *byggja*, which in F and L is a special term for 'leasing out land', is not found in the Gulathing Law. G uses just *leiga* (to rent) with regard to land tenancy, and also, however, about renting in general. Conceptually there is, then, no separation in the Gulathing Law between leasing out land and renting out mobilia (cows, slaves). Further: If we take a closer look into ' to have', 'to possess' the land compared to the right to own land (property rights), (Latin: *possessio/proprietas*), the verb *hafa* (meaning 'having', 'possessing', 'making use of') is put to use without exception when it comes to the right of use in F and L. Oppositely, however, in the Gulathing Law the meaning of *hafa* seems, in connection with land, to carry an ambivalent and not fixed meaning.

My examining of the laws so far show a clear disparity between the law from the 12th century and the two later laws from the 13th century concerning clarifications of concepts, systematizing and structuring. On a general level we must state that there is influence from the learned law of the period, which gave shape to the formulation of legal language in F and L. The language of law in G is at the onset of a development which came through fully in the 13th century. We have seen that some concepts and contrasting about land owning/land lease-conditions, which came to dominate the law scene in the two later taws, already, are in use a few times in G (the concepts *eign* about land property twice; the *landsdróttinn*, later the spesific term for land owner three times; the *leigulidi*, about tenant is used twice. Some contrastings used in G are: *Leiguliði/ eiga* (G 72) and *leigulið/ landsdróttinn/eiga* (G 75), and the verbs *eiga* and *leiga* about land are contrasted six times. In G 72 alone the term *leigumáli* about tenancy contract is related to contrasting concepts concerning land lease *(leigumála/leiga/leiguliði/eiga)*, as it also most frequently appears as a technical term in F and in L. Beyond doubt, the "learned law" of the time with it's firmer categories and relationes has thus started impacting on the Gulathing Law. The development in Norway seems here to be totally in accordance with what Sten Gagnér points out as an important phase in putting the secular laws into writing from the beginning of the 13th century.[63] Concerning social history we may assume that the new formulations are expressing a transition to a more formally structured system of Land Tenancy which is a system not expressed in the Gulathing Law.

---

63. Gagnér 1960 p. 288-307.

Tore Iversen

The Legal Forms of Land Tenancy – *Ususfructus*

In the Gulathing Law we find uncertainnes regarding the conditions of land tenancy if we in addition look into the content of the legal forms, i.e. institutes, of land tenancy. In spite of lacking a fixed use of *concepts* with contrasting terms, we actually find a rather distinct influence from medieval Roman law in the regulations of the land tenancy section in G. During the high Middle Ages, however, the Glossatores further developed the legal forms of land lease.[64] I the following we shall see how the development has left traces in our three laws. Starting with reception of the "learned law", our focus shall be development of the law scenario regarding land lease from the Gulathing Law to the Frostathing Law and the *Landslög* (L). While land lease forms in the "pure" Justinian Roman law were "obligatory", i.e. simply contractual with limited duties between to parties, the Glossatores moved the land lease towards a "thingly" right, i.e. forms of rule over the land itself *(ius in re)* which i.a. implied protection against a third party.[65]

The paragraph on land lease in the Gulathing law opens with the preliminary G 72 announcing that a man who rents land according to rightful lease contract shall have the land and live on that land for one year

---

64. Genius 1972 p. 46-68; Eltjo J.H.Schrage: *Non quia romanum sed quia ius. Das Entstehen eines europäischen Rechtsbewusstseins im Mittelalter*, 1996 p. 17-55.
65. Roman law makes a sharp division between <u>obligation</u> law (contract law, claims/debt law) and proprietary/ 'thingly' law (the law on things versus law on persons). The forms of tenancy in the Justinian Roman law belong above all to obligation law, i.e. they deal merely with certain and limited claims, demands of contributions between two parties agreed upon by concentual contract. (Concensus did *not* require equality in status). *Locatio conductio* was the most important form of contract used with tenancy; it was a loose and rather compounded law institute. Just one singular type of land lease, *emphyteusis,* long-term leaseholding of land property, poss. with a hereditary right of succession-lease, gives a "thingly"/property right *(ius in re)*, because it concerns rule over the thing per se and gives rights to the tenant, i.a. pertaining to legal protection of the lease (actio in rem) which is reminding of a landowner's *dominium*. Allthough the Roman property concept had an absolute and protected character, it still acknowledged limitations in the owner's right to rule over the thing through a special institute, the servitude, i.e. a right in a thing (ius in re aliena) of which another person had *dominium*. In connection with land tenancy is the special *ususfructus*-institute (a right to the fruits of something one did not own oneself, an alien thing) which is close up to the servitudes, in Justinian law *u.f.* belongs to personal servitudes acc. to Grosso (see next f.n.). What is special with *u.f.* then is the fact that it is a *personal* 'thingly' (proprietary) right, but in an *alien* thing. Introduction to classic Roman law, esp. law on things and on obligation: Max Kaser: *Das Römische Privatrecht, Handbuch der Altertumswissenschaft X.3.3.1,2*,B I 1971,B II 1975*;* Theo Mayer-Maly: *Römisches Recht*, 1999 p. 91-161; Ditlev Tamm: *Retshistorie bd. 2: Romerret og europeisk retsudvikling*, 1991 p. 51-160.

and answer to the owner the rent that they agreed upon. The entire last section of the regulation puts emphasis on subletting being prohibited, with the exception that the tenant had subletting as his requirement. The Roman law institute which primarily sticks out for us is that of ususfructus. This is a limited right to use an alien 'thing' *(ius in re aliena)* in order to obtain the fruits of it, but in such a manner that the substance of the 'thing' *(nuda proprietas)* remains unharmed for the owner (Inst.2.4.3).[66] In a few cases ususfructus may have been combined with the contract-form *locatio conductio* which is a loosely worked out and legally little protected consensus-contract used for land leasing in Roman law. The background for supposing such combining is primarily the very short formal leasing period in G, while *ususfructus* usually had a longer duration (cf also interpretation of G 78 below).[67]

G 72 forbids then subletting of the land, due to the fact that *ususfructus*, according to the model, is a highly person-connected right, i.e. closely tied to one or more persons, and can subsequently not be transferred to others (Inst.2.4.3) (also here, see below G 79).[68] Because the right of *ususfructus* is concerned merely with acquiring the fruits, the right falls away in the case of the land not being cultivated (Dig.7.1.9pr. and 7.4.20). In line with this, the regulation G 76 addresses the case of the tenant not wanting to take over the leased land. The owner then sows the land, makes use of it and may also fetch the rent from the person who leased it (about the last passus, cf. Dig.19.2.61.1).[69]

---

66. The best edition of Justinian Roman law is: Th.Mommsens Digesta edition 1868-70 (Dig), P.Krüger's Codex edition 1887 (Cod). New print 1962-63. The short textbook Institutiones (Inst) is published, text with German transl., O. Behrends/R.Knütel/B.Kupish/H.H.Seiler, UTB-Serie, 1993. The definition of *ususfructus* according to Justinian law: Usus fructus est ius alienis rebus utendi fruendi salva rerum substantia (Inst.2.4 pr). Most important literature on *ususfructus* is: Giuseppe Grosso, Usufrutto e figure affini nel diritto romano (1958); Gunther Wesener: "Usus fructus",*Paulus Realencyclopädie der classischen Altertumwissenschaft, 2.Reihe,*17. (1961) p.1137-1176.
67. The longest duration for a person is for life (Wesener 1961 p.1138-9), see f.n. 94f. The understanding of G 78 as well may indicate a combination of *u.f.* and *locatio conductio* (on "buying breaks lease", see below).
68. Allthough *ususfructus* is connected to a person, it is possible to share. (Dig. 7.5). The background for it being person connected, and a socalled person-servitude, and not transferrable, was that the institute generally was used in the context of family responsibility. (Kaser I p. 448, II p. 303, Wesener p. 1138). Wesener calls attention to *ususfructus* being an original creation in Roman jurisprudence, and that the need for support of dependents through the institute came about in a period where the strong Roman family ties where loosened with emancipation (p. 1139).
69. The first important legist in Bologna who was concerned with lease issues, Irnerius (d. ca.1125), brought this up (Dig.19.2.61) in a preserved Distinctio ('Discussion

The regulation G 73 deals first with maintaining the houses on the leased land, in the same manner this is treated in Dig. 7.1.7.2-3. G 73 then deals further with houses build on the leased land (cf here Dig. 6.1.38). Here we notice that G 73 in the use of examples presupposes the Roman law principle *superficies solo credit,* " constructions belong to the grounds", which in the examples of G 73 are not obvious conditions.[70] This principle is shown, among others, in Inst.2.1.30 (cf 2.1.29) and Dig.43.17.3.7.

Further then, the detailed G 75 deals with what a land tenant legally may bring with him when the lease period is ended, as this is treated in Dig. 19.2.55.1. Additionally, G 75 brings up the issue of what the tenant is entitled to of developed products *(averk)*, however, just up to the worth of ½ mark, if he informs the landowner. In Dig.7.1.9.7 it says further that the tenant may make use of wood material *(silva caedua),* but is not allowed to sell this. G 75 moves on to say that the tenant shall have any hawks in the outfields unless the landlord made a certain reservation. Birds and the proceeds of hunting and of fishing going to the tenant, is dealt with in Dig. 7.1.9.5.[71] The same regulation G 75 brings up also the limited forest material the tenant may leave to a third person (cf. Dig.7.1.12.5.) If the tenant sows winter rye in a field, he shall not have any after the lease is over (cf. Dig.7.4.13). However, when he has cleared a new field in the outfield, he who sowed shall share the yield with "him who comes to the land" *(sa er til fer iarðar).* This last passage, which does not seem to have any direct Justinian model, encourages the tenant to clear new fields.

Based on the study of the regulations so far, a Justinian model appears on the whole to have been present, allthough it seems to have been readjusted or further formulated in line with the law-makers wants and the conditions in society. My assumption that *ususfructus* appears to have been the main regulation model used in the land lease section of G, can probably be substantiated by other use of that institute elsewhere in G as well. According to the Justinian law then, the institute is not applied with the right of use to land fields only – allthough this application is the most important - but hence applying right of use to other kinds of areas as well,

---

      on one theme') cited by Lenhard Teigelac Locatio conductio, 1996 p.20-2: *Si vero steterit per conductorumvel casum fortuitum contingentum ex parte ipius, quominus re locata utatur, solidam pensionem praestare cogitur* (Wenn es aber am Mieter oder an einem von ihm zu vertreten Zufall liegt, dass er die gemietete Sache nicht benutzen kann, bleibt er zur Zahlung des Mietzinses verpflichtet).

70.   This is empasized by Professor Alfons Bürge. I am greatly indebted to Bürge for elucidating the abovementioned regulations in G and their relation to *ususfructus, superficies solo credit etc*. Alfons Bürge is professor in Roman Law at the Faculty of Law, University of Münich.

71.   The tenant (usufructarius) may also make use of bees (Dig. 7.1.9.1) quarries, chalk and sand (Dig. 7.1.9.2).

primarily slaves *(servus fructarius)* and cattle. The work force (man power) is here regarded as fruits.[72] The responsibility for leased thrall and leased cattle is dealt with in G 69 and G 41 with the same base theme as in the land tenancy regulation.[73] Of our three laws it is the Gulathing Law only that contains regulations about lease thrall and lease cattle. And thus displays the *ususfructus* – institute in full scope.

Finally, in connection with the institute of *ususfructus*, we shall look more closely into G 79: Should one of the parties in the lease contract die, either owner or tenant, the contract is cancelled. This is in line with *ususfructus* to a high degree being a person connected right. It may not be transferred to others or inherited, as showed in Inst. 2.4.3. The tenant and his inheritors have no legal protection, according to G 79, should the landowner die.

Land Tenancy from the Gulathing Law to the Frostathing Law and the Landslög

We may modify the fragility inherent in the land tenancy in the Gulathing Law by comparing with the later laws: F XI 15 states that if the landlord or his bailiff dies, the tenant is entitled to continue the lease for one or two years. If the tenant dies, his heir shall hold the lease for a harvest year. When the rent has been paid in advance, it is valid until it expires (F XIII 3). According to L VII 1, the agreement shall last another harvest year if the landlord or the tenant dies, regardless how long the original lease is for. Beyond the fact that land tenancy in G is intended to be attached to specific individuals, we may relate the fragility in the leasing relationship with the very brief leasing agreement that G formally utilizes – one year (G 72). (Of course, this formula does not exclude renewal of the agreement every year. Concerning long-term leases in F and L, see below).

---

72. Wesener 1961 p. 1156-7; Grosso 1958 p. 201-211; W.W.Buckland: *The Roman Law of Slavery*, 1908 p. 356-369. In addition to *servus fructarius* there is *ususfructus* to buildings, ships.
73. In G it is said that the owner may let a man make use of the work capacity of his thrall, the tenant shall then have full responsibility for the lease thrall, he must i.a. not lead him on to dangerous places (bear caves, ice, cliffs or sea). Dig.7.1.15.1-2 says that the tenant must not put the lease thrall to dange<rous and unsuitable work. (As an example of dangerous work is gladiator fight (!) is mentioned in a fragment (Fragmenta Vaticana: V.Fr.72), cf. Buckland 1908 p. 358). Like G 69 seeks to protect the lease thrall as the property of the owner, Inst.4.4.5. (Dig.47.10.15. 45-48) says that abuse of the lease thrall is directed done to the owner.

Thus, in the Gulathing Law, the death of one of the parties terminates the lease agreement. How do the laws deal with the sale of already leased land? The Frostathing Law and the Landslög (L) treat leasing land and sale of land as two different kinds of transactions and explicitly states that a sale shall not terminate an existing leasing agreement (F XIII 2, L VII 1). We shall discuss this problem since it also looms quite large in medieval jurisprudence.[74] The statute in G, which addresses this most explicitly, is § 78 ("if someone dispose of a piece of land to two men"), which concerns double lease or double sale. In case of sale or lease, respectively, the agreement made first is valid.[75] As opposed to F (XIII 2) and L (VII 1), rather conspicuously, G 78 does not address what happens if already leased land is sold. Nor does G make any reference to this issue anywhere else.[76] Lack of an overall systematic organization may explain the law's silence on this matter, as the owner actually *can* sell and pawn land limited by *ususfructus*, according to Cod.3.33.2. However, the fact that G stipulates the shortest possible time for leasing land, one year, could mean that the institution of *ususfructus* was intended to be combined with the *locatio conductio* type of contract, which provided extremely limited legal protection (see above). According to this "mandatory" type of contract, found in Cod.4.65.9, the leaser has no protection if the owner decides to sell.[77] The glossator's main interpretation of Cod.4.65.9 was indeed that "purchase terminates lease".

74. Schrage 1996 p. 39-57.
75. Fr.Brandt: *Forelæsninger over den norske Retshistorie I-II,* 1880, I p. 203. G 78 states: *Nu selr maðr eina iorð tveim monnum. sa scal hava er fyrri toc. oc hverhvítna þess er maðr selr tveim monnom hit sama. Þa scal hava er fyrri kaupir. æða leigir* (If a man conveys the same land to two men, the one who leased it first shall have it. And in every case when a man conveys the same thing to two men, the one who bought or rented it first shall have it).
76. We may disregard the interpretation of G 78, that when the lease has been made first; no sale should take place, because G 78 has been taken over by L almost verbatim (VII 6). L VII 6 is concerned only with double lease or double sale, as is evident from both L (VII 1) and F's (XIII 2) treatment of the relationship between lease and sale of land in separately in new regulations. Thus, the conclusion must be that G 78 does not give the leasing agreement any explicit protection against the landlord later selling the land. G 78's non-regulation of the relationship between lease and later sale is also noted by Karl v. Amira, *Nordgermanisches Obligationsrecht II* 1892 p. 760-1; A.Taranger: *Den norske besiddelsesret,* 1897 p. 94-6, cf. idem. *Ábuð jarðar heimlar tekju, Sproglig-historiske Studier tilegnede Professor C.R.Unger,* 1896 p. 108-24; Mons Nygard: *Eigedomsavhending i norsk rettshistorie,* 1972 p. 123-4.
77. The text of Cod.4.65.9 is: *Emptorem quidem fundi necesse non est stare colono cui prior dominus locavit, nisi ea lege emit. Verum si probetur aliquo pacto consensisse ut in eadem conductione maneat, quamvis sine scripto, bonae fidei iudicio ei quod placuit parere cogitur,* cf. Schrage 1996 p. 40-41. Cod.4.65.9

The transition from G to the later F and L appears parallel with the development of European scholarly law on this point. From the main interpretation of Cod.4.65.9, which meant that the buyer of a piece of land could evict anyone leasing it, the glossators sought to find as many exceptions from the main rule in accordance with contemporary social conditions. The exceptions were eventually inherited as well long-term leases (*ad longum tempus*). Partial lease (*colonia partiaria*) also became an important exception. In these leasing conditions, the leasing party had a proprietary, or "thingly", right (*ius in rem*) because of the length of the leasing period, or that owner and leaser were proprietally or "thingly" entitled to each their share of the harvest, as in the partial lease. Eventually, the main rule in reality became "purchase does not terminate lease".[78] This new glossators' rule thus found its way into F XIII 2 and L VII 1. (I shall return to thingly or proprietary law (*ius in rem*), long-term tenancy and partial tenancy).

The beginning of G 79 addresses the case when a leasing agreement has been made but the owner will not allow the tenant to take over the land after all. If the leaser brings suit with witness, there must be a *skiladómr*, i.e. the tenant has the right to sue, or more precisely, submit with witnesses a claim to leased land. The same theme (the owner keeping the tenant from taking over the land) is also treated later in the Landslög (L) (VII 5). The novelty here is that the leaser, before suing, shall establish by law (*logfesta*) the land he believes he has properly leased. This was a solemnly proclaimed ban, which put an item, particularly real estate, under legal bonds. Anyone who breached this ban, including the owner, had to pay double *landnám* (see below) as well as a fine ("ransbot") to the King, as stated by F XIII 23.[79] The process involving *logfesta* (lit. "law-fixing") seems to parallel the *interdictio* (court order protecting possession of property) in Roman law. According to Roman law, regular tenants were not entitled to protection through interdict, but one who held an inherited lease did (*emphyteusis*).[80] It is obvious that land tenancy agreements were far more secure in the Landslög (L) than in the Gulathing Law as a result of "law-fixing" along

---

somewhat ambiguous, and in the Middle Ages several interpretations were possible (Schrage 1996 p. 41). It might be of interest that the old school of Germanist legal historians believed that the principle of "purchase does not terminate lease" expressed an ancient "Germanic legal understanding". This was subsequently believed to have been replaced by the principle that "purchase terminates lease" (correspondence with Professor Peter Landau).

78. Schrage 1996 p. 39-55.
79. Concerning *logfesta*: Brandt 1880 II p. 375-381; Lars Hamre in *KLNM (Kulturhistorisk leksikon for nordisk middelalder) 21* p. 171-175; Hagland & Sandnes 1994 p. 231.
80. Mayer-Maly 1999 p. 52f, 55f, 101.

with *landnám*-fines in case the ban was violated. We can probably interpret such protection in L in light of the long-term lease (*ad longum tempus*).[81]

Landnám – Protecting Landed Property and Land Tenancy

In order to gain further insight into the development of land tenancy in relation to property rights from G to the two later laws, we will discuss the *landnám*, i.e. the fine imposed for damage and illegal use of land and what was considered to belong to the land in the three laws. The fine was paid to the owner when something was "taken" from his property; e.g. when land was used, but not properly rented, when someone gathered wood from the farm's forest, hunted, slaughtered beached whales unlawfully, caught seal etc.[82] Indeed, *landnám* is seen as the very acknowledgement of property rights. Its development can however provide valuable insight into the tenant's right to his leased land. Through the *landnám* fine the possession of land is minutely intertwined with a person's *réttr* or social rank in all three laws (G 91, F XIII 15 and L VII 20).[83] The strictly ranked fines of the *landnám* have no parallel in Roman law. We may still fit the *landnám* within the larger framework of the Roman concept of *iniuria*, though we do not find a completely parallel recepted institute.[84]

We shall focus on the right to receive a *landnám* fine when a third party causes the damage. According to the Gulathing Law, it is clear that the owner is to receive the fine not only when the tenant causes damage to his property but also when the third party causes such damage.[85] There is only one exception, in G 101, which is concerned with royal land distributed to notables (*veizlu iorð*). The King and his men shall, according to this

---

81. Brandt (1880 p. 380) understands L VII 5 differently, as the law-fixing applied to a new tenant who moved the farm, i.e. not with respect to the landowner. The text does not support this interpretation. (*Nu sælr maðr iorð a leigu oc vil eigi lata þann hafa er tok. þa skal sa logfesta iorð er leigði*). Most likely, Brandt could not imagine that the tenant had such strong rights in face of the landowner. Only property rights were thus protected, as Brandt (1878 p. 76; 1880 I p. 205) observes "that the ancient Norwegians recognized property rights in the widest sense".
82. Robberstad in *KLNM 10* (1965) p. 210-1.
83. Brandt has described the minutely formulated right to *landnám* as "a fine which thus takes the character of a sign of recognition of ownership rights, as a compensation for a violation thereof" (1880 II p. 128).
84. The wide Roman term of *iniuria* includes all attacks on the legally recognized person. Furthermore, Roman law's iniuriedelikter normally prescribed a fine as compensation. (R.Lieberwirth i *HRG I* p. 357-358). Concerning fines, *iniuria, damnum iniuria datum* og *actio iniuriarum*: Kaser I p. 623f.; E.Kaufmann i *HRG* I p. 575-577.
85. This is elaborated in G 81, 85, 89, 91, 93, 95, 149, 150.

paragraph, have equal shares of the *landnám*. Also in the Frostathing Law, the owner is entitled to the *landnám* fine; including those cases where a third party may be involved.[86] Yet there are several cases in the land tenancy section of the Frostathing Law where the landlord is not mentioned, and there may be doubts as to whether the owner or the tenant is to benefit from the fine: XIII 13, concerning men who burn someone's harvest; F XIII 20, concerning men living (i.e. are tenants) on the same farm when one lets his cattle ruin the other's grain. A similar case is found in F XIII 19, concerning neighbours' grazing rights.[87] F XIV 1 states that landowners absent from their county shall have a bailiff (*omboðsmaðr*), who is entitled to half of the *landnám* fine. The bailiff can also rent out the owner's land. He thus has the right to dispose over the owner's property protected with the *landnám* fine in several important matters, but this is clearly limited to three years.

In the Landslög (L), it appears that the *landnám* fine should go to the tenant in several cases: The tenancy section (VII) 30, concerning gate-keeping obligations, and VII 42, concerning cattle damage, specifies that the *landnám* fine should be paid to whoever owns grain or grass (*korn eða gras a*). Since it does not mention the landowner, it naturally implies that the tenant receive the *landnám* fine. L VII 49 (concerning damage while fishing) clarifies the distribution of the *landnám* in the following manner: "But the *landnám* and damage compensation are divided between landlord and tenant according to the law book's previous statement concerning tenancy" (*En landnam oc ausla bot skipizt meðal landzdrottins oc leigu liða eptir þui sem logbok vattar aðr i landa byggingum*). Perhaps this provision refers to the division of the *landnám* fine between owner and bailiff in L VII 26 (cf. F XIV 1).[88] It may also be the case that L VII 49 refers to an implied provision in L VII 30 and 42, which states that the tenant who owns grain and grass is the recipient of the *landnám* fine.[89] If the *landnám* fine is interpreted as a marker of land ownership, we must conclude that the tenant

---

86. F XIII 21, XIV 11, XV 5, XVI 1.
87. Concerning the tenant's proprietary right to the harvest, in cases of *separatio* versus *perceptio*, cf. n. 114. The fact that tenants could also receive *landnám* i F, can probably be supported by the issue we have touched upon previously, that F, as opposed to G, has its own technical terms concerning proprietal possession. In F XIII 23 and 25 *hafnarvitni*, testmonies of proprietal possession of land, is set up against *óðalsvitni*, testimony of ownership.
88. In addition, L VII 26 is interesting because it must be interpreted so that the landowner's bailiff can also rent out the owner's land to a new bailiff. Neither does the regulation set an upper limit as to how many years a bailiff holds his office.
89. In this connection, the tenants right to half a mark in compensation for grass may be relevant in this connection, cf. L VII 40. Concerning the tenant who owns the harvest at *separatio*, cf. n. 114.

has proprietal possession of it.[90] The development of this type of possession, with features of regular ownership, means that the tenant's rights may be based in the land itself, besides the agreement with the landowner. In the terminology of Roman law, this means that the tenant has received a proprietal, or "thingly" right on his (leased) possession, an *ius in rem*. Thus, it is primarily in the Landslög (L) that proprietal possession is expressed along with regular ownership. In G, the tenant only has right to an alien property, *ius in re aliena*, attached to certain individuals with features of obligation law based on the shortest possible leasing period. Thus, leases in G were fragile arrangements and had little protection.

Long Term Tenancy and Proprietary Rights

According to the Justinian Roman law, the tenant did not normally have proprietary rights, that is, he had no specific right to protect the leased land *qua* possession of property (*agere in rem*). The Roman law scholar Azo (d. 1220), however, ascribed a tenant "for a long period of time" (*ad longum tempus*) such a proprietary right, as opposed to cases of short-term tenancy. The exact meaning of the term "for a long period of time" is uncertain, but ten years seems to have been the lower limit. Accursius (1185-1263) maintained that the long-term tenant had a *dominium utile*, proprietal possession, which entailed *actio utilis*, the right to sue as the proprietor of the land, just as *dominium eminens (directum)*, direct ownership.

We must see the development of the tenant's right to *landnám* from G to F and L in light of the evolution of medieval learned, or Roman, law. We can observe that an extended proprietary right to rented land conforms to the topography of the country, the single farm settlements of the high Middle Ages, and a more extensive structure of scattered estates. Could the legal premise of *ad longum tempus* have been present in F and L? The Frostathing Law states that the owner's bailiff can only rent out the land for three years (F XIV 2), but does not impose any such limit on the owner. F

---

90. Taranger notes in his translation of L VII 49 (p. 145): "There is no such rule in L". Brandt 1880 (II p. 129): "(VII 49) must result from a mistake; as the regulation referred to does not exist." One could ask whether the end of L VII 49 points to a specific regulation. In any circumstances, it must be wrong to call the end of VII 49 a mistake. Brandt's statement, as I see it, is an example of the early Norwegian legal historians' obvious tendency to regard the Norwegian medieval laws as one single system void of development. Brandt's statement is furthermore ideologically colored by the view that "the ancient Norwegians recognized property rights in the widest sense and maintained it in all connections, whether it applied to movable or immovable property" (Brandt 1880 I p. 205). In this view there was thus little room for possession as *dominium utile* as we find it in the rest of medieval Europe.

only states that the agreement shall be kept for as long as its validity can be confirmed through witnesses (F XIII 2, cf. also 3). The Landslög (L) (VII 1) also states that the bailiff may rent out the land for only three years, but otherwise accepts tenancy for as long as may be confirmed by witness (*sem uattar hans uitu at hann tok ser arðar mala*). Both L VII 7 and 53 refer indirectly to long-term tenancy. We may also add that F Innl.18 (from 1260) refers to a period of tenancy that would last far longer than six years.[91]

Norwegian medieval laws thus seem to follow a trend that was clear in both the contemporary jurisprudence as well as in the real historical development, at least in Western Europe, that the tenancy period in the tenancy agreements were extended substantially.[92] The preconditions in Roman law's long-term tenancy (*ad longum tempus*) appear to have been present in F and L, and just as the process involving *logfesta* - the parallel to the Roman law *interdiction* - this could be a legal foundation for the proprietal right to possession of land (*ius in rem*). The glossators also found another basis, through the partial tenancy (*colonia partiaria*) of Roman law.[93]

Colonia Partiaria: One Legal Framework for the "Skyldpart" System in Norway?

We shall consider a legal form that also became significant for land tenancy in contemporary jurisprudence, the *colonia partiaria*, translated as "shared land property / tenancy" (German "Teilpacht"). The tenant in this legal form is designated as *colonus partiarius*, the landlord *dominus fundi*.[94] This form of land tenancy has, in the first place, probably contributed to the legal development in Norway of the land ownership and tenancy system which toward the end of the high Middle Ages may be termed as a "skyldpart" system.[95] This system is characterized by a fixed rent for each individual

---

91. L VII 7 states that even if the bailiff is replaced, the leasing agreements shall remain in force. L VII 53, concerning clearing of new land, states that the size of the land rent should be fixed only after three years by qualified individuals, after the first three were free of rent.
92. Phillipe Dollinger: *Der bayerischen Bauerstand vom 9. bis 13. Jahrhunderts,* 1982 p. 373; H.Woptner: „Freie und unfreie Leihen im späten Mittelalter", *Vierteljahrschrift für Sozial- und Wirtschaftsgeschichte III B* 1905 p. 251.
93. Schrage 1996 p. 28.
94. Most scholarly work on colonia partiaria is obsolescent: Max Waaser: *Colonia partiaria* 1885; Franz Kobler: *Der Teilbau im römischen und geltenes italienischen Recht*, 1928; D.Grimm: *Zur Frage über den Begriff der societas im klassischen römischen Recht*, 1933; Schrage's article (1996), p. 17-29 is thus an exception.
95. Andreas Holmsen: "Det norske „skyldeie"", *Norske historikere i utvalg* V (eds. C.Krag, J.Sandnes), 1981 p. 178.

farm unit, which was the basis for shared ownership of the farm, i.e. several landowners owned their separate shares of the farm's fixed rent. Several landlords with "ideal" shares in the rent dealt with one tenant with possession over a single farm. This user of the farm could also own a share of it. Secondly, the legal form *colonia partiaria* may also have been the model for renting out in case of division of a farm unit, i.e. when the farm unit's fields and pastures had been divided up and parceled out. A farm unit owned by one or possibly several individuals, when rented out, could thus be divided between several tenants.

In short, the *colonia partiaria* in Roman law is land rental in return for a fixed share of a variable annual agricultural harvest, and is thus distinct from a regular agreement where they agreed upon the tenant's rent. The characteristic feature of *colonia partiaria* is that this form of tenancy has taken over features from the *societas*, "company" or "partnership", of Roman law.[96] The idea at the base is that the tenant and the owner enter a clearly defined partnership where each receives his share of the income. The owner receives his share because he has waived the natural yield of the land, while the tenant receives his since he does the required labour on it.[97] However, we must keep in mind that *societas* according to Justinian Roman law is quite different from our "partnership", as it is far more fragile – it is dissolved whenever one of the parties withdraws (cf. Inst.3.25.4).[98] We must also remember that con-sensus and the idea of *societas* do not involve any form of equal status between the parties.

Several varieties of *colonia partiaria* tenancy with fixed shares of the yield have been widespread in diverse areas in different periods, e.g. in the eastern Mediterranean under the Roman Empire and in Central Europe from the 12th century. In Central Europe, the extent of this form of tenancy, also called "Teilpacht", was even taken as a part of the agricultural revolution in the high Middle Ages.[99] The pattern provided by the *societas* and *colonia partiaria* thus provides the opportunity for several parties on the owner and/or tenant side in a common enterprise according to the partnership ideal. For example, there can be one tenant and several owners or one owner and several tenants; and the user/tenant may also own a share of the farm. The *colonia partiaria* may in this manner cast light on important aspects of the

---

96. Waaser 1885 p. 42ff.; Kobler 1928 p. 24-29; Schrage 1996 p. 17. Concerning the definition of *colonia partiaria* as a *societas*, the main source is Dig.19.2.1.25.6 (*partiarius colonus quasi societas iure et damnum et lucrum cum domino fundi partitur*). We must emphasize "quasi" (almost) in the text.
97. Kobler 1928 p. 37; Schrage 1996 p. 17-20.
98. Kobler 1928 p. 27. A major difference is that societas is not a cooperative corporation. One cannot sue the corporation as a whole; cases must be presented against the individual members (Kaser I 1971 p. 572ff).
99. Kobler 1928 p. 7-15,59f; Dollinger 1982 p. 131-3.

Norwegian "skyldpart" system, where the property shares are calculated as regular shares of a fixed land rent (*landskyld*). Thus, on this last issue, the "skyldpart" system differed from the *colonia partiaria*. We must emphasize how sparse our knowledge is concerning the early development of this system. So far, what we know is mostly deduced from late medieval and early modern source materials. In addition, I wish to emphasize that the following outline of my investigation of the three laws is highly hypothetical.

There is not much in the three laws that points toward the "skyldpart" system. None of the laws seems to make a direct connection between shared ownership and shared tenancy.[100] However, landowning partnership is addressed in terms of protecting landed property through the mentioned *landnám* fine. G 91 states that all joint owners shall have *landnám* for undivided property according to their *réttr*, or social status. But when the land has been divided, i.e. parceled out *(oðals skipti skipt)* and distributed among the owners, each shall have full *landnám* for his share (*þa tecr fullt landnám hver at sinum luta*). Even though the tenant side is not mention explicitly in this context, the fine must of course also be paid by the owners' own tenants on this land.[101]

F XIII 16 also states that joint owners are entitled to *landnám* according to social status. The novelty here is that only partial owners who did not give permission for someone to use the land shall receive full compensation, according to how great a share he has of the farm (*sem á i eign*). Even though it is not stated, we must assume that the latter applies when the land is not distributed among the owners. The provision in L VII 21 is more specific than F: *Landnám* fines imposed according to the rights of the owner of highest rank shall be distributed among all joint owners according to their share in the farm, also when the land remains undivided. Those who did not consent to use of the land, shall have full *landnám* according to their status.

The arrangement at the base of both F (XIII 16) and L (VII 21), when land was not parceled out and a tenant rented land from the joint owners, we could assume that a shared ownership based on shares of the tenant's pay, *landskyld*, or land rent, i.e. a "skyldpart" system. The legal pattern for a partnership between several landowners and one tenant may very well derive its essential features from the *colonia partiaria*. The Gulathing Law (91) does not say how the *landnám* fine is to be distributed between owners when the land remains undivided, and it is not very likely that we can find

---

100. It appears that renting land for a share of the harvest is only mentioned directly once, very briefly, in F II 19, concerning leasing out the land for a share *(til lutar)* of a product (here: fish)'.
101. On this: Brandt I 1880 p. 226.

any regular arrangement in G based on shares of the land rent. According to this law, the arrangement according to ownership shares is in force only when the land has been parcelled out to the owners.

The last three regulations concentrate on joint ownership, i.e. when several owners are dealing with the tenant in a partnership. In order to explore the reasoning behind partnerships, we shall first deal with two regulations concerning joint tenancy when its users divide a farm unit. The first section of G 81 states that when two tenants live on the same farm and rent from the same man, their parcelling arrangement shall remain in force as long as they live there. But if one of them moves out, the new tenant may demand a new parcelling. The third section of L VII 15 initially says the same, but adds: *En ef einhuer fer af iorðu brott [en annar kemer til. hafi sa [Þa teiga i iorðu oc huss Þau er til kemr sem hinn hafðe er brott for oc niote huer sinnar abuðar* (But if one of them moves off the land, the one who moves in shall have the fields and houses of the one who moved away, and each enjoy their habitation right). L VII 15 concludes that everyone should have parcels of the same width and quality according to land rent.

These two provisions are concerned with two (G) or more (L) tenants who rent part of a farm unit from the same landlord. In the case of G 81, the provision is probably modelled on the practice of *ususfructus*, since this supposed to be attached to specific individuals and not transferred to others, but it may still be *divided* among several users. G 81 may also have been adapted on the pattern of *colonia partiaria* in classical Justinian Roman law. Like *ususfructus*, this was as mentioned a very fragile arrangement and was terminated either by the death of one of the parties or by consensus upon expiration of the stipulated period.[102] After termination, the parties would have to make a new agreement, if so was desired.[103]

In the *Landslög* (L) (VII 15.3), as we have observed, a more nuanced image emerges concerning replacement of joint tenants. If tenant in an established shared tenancy moves out and another one takes his place, he should only take over the part of the tenant that moved out. Contemporary jurisprudence can support this passage, in the same way that glossators used a text from the Justinian law (Dig.17.2.16.2) to support the *colonia partiaria*. Indeed, on this point, there was developed an exception from dissolution of a shared tenancy when a new tenant came in and simply took over the former tenant's share.[104] Tenants thus had a proprietary right to possession, since old shares were transferable to new tenants. The glossator Azo (d.1230) similarly saw a *partiarius colonus* as *possessor suo nomine*, i.e. with a proprietary right to protection for the possessor (*actio in rem*)

---

102. This is apparent from Dig.17.2.65.9f and Dig.17.2.63.10.4, cf. Kaser I 1971 p. 575.
103. Inst.3.25.4-5; Kaser I 1971 p. 572-6, esp. p. 575.
104. Schrage 1996 p. 27-28 and 48.

without having to go through the landlord.[105] As we have seen above, proprietary law (*ius in rem*) is in agreement with the right of the long-term tenant. The Landslög (L) thus provides us with a more stable image of shared tenancy than G (81), in that the arrangement should remain unchanged once it is made, even if tenants are replaced. L VII 15 emphasizes that the extent of land and the size of land rent must correspond in shared tenancy, which is another stabilizing factor.

We may sum up the influence from the practice of *colonia partiaria* by stating that there was probably such a legal pattern based on the idea of partnership behind the provisions from F and L, which we have addressed above: The establishment of regular tenant shares of a farm unit through fixed parcels (L VII 15) is probably based on the glossators' development of the pattern of *colonia partiaria*. The *Landslög* (L) approximates such a pattern closest when it points out (VI 21, cf. F XIII 16) that the size of an ownership share shall determine the size of the fine in case of undistributed land, i.e. when the owner's share is an "ideal" part, probably taken from the land rent. Shared ownership of leased land based on fixed shares of the land rent means that a "skyldpart" arrangement, also known as a system of "skyld" (i.e. rent) ownership, is emerging.[106]

The system of "skyldpart" and "skyld" ownership, as it developed in Norway after 1200 and until the end of the high Middle Ages, obviously took shape according to the country's diverse agrarian topography, where single farms and scattered settlements were significant features. As mentioned, the *colonia partiaria* was the pattern for "Teilpacht" tenancy in central Europe from the 12th century.[107] The important features of this arrangement entailed not only fixed shares of an agricultural product, but also rent which varied according to the size of the annual harvest. It was therefore necessary to control the size of the year's harvest in one way or another. The "skyldpart" system was not based on *colonia partiaria* in this last instance and thus differed from the "Teilpacht". Besides the "Teilpacht" arrangement, however, there was another form of tenancy in Central Europe, which involved completely fixed rents. It was an important milestone for the Norwegian system when the size of the land rent for most of the farms in the country were fixed regularly through some kind of public "matriculation", probably sometime in the 1260s.[108] The land rent was

---

105. Schrage 1996 p. 28.
106. Tore Iversen: "Fremveksten av det norske leilendingsvesenet i middelalderen", *Heimen bd. 32*, 1995 p. 176-8.
107. Dollinger 1982 p. 131-133; K-H. Spiess in *HRG 5* p. 141-3.
108. There has been a great deal of discussion concerning this matriculation, which must have taken place sometime before the Landslög (L) was ratified (cf. L III 6, VII 7). Kåre Lunden, *Norges Landbrukshistorie II*, 2002 p. 45f has believed that the land rent was only a private agreement between the land owner and the tenant.

subsequently based on what each individual farm could normally yield. Norwegian historians have thus assessed the land rent at about just below 1/6 of total yield.[109] Thus, we may characterize the Norwegian "skyldpart" system as unparalleled, as it was formed as an intermediate stage between the central European tenancy arrangements, but including the partnership idea we find in the "Teilpacht".[110]

Proprietary Right and the Tenants' *Leidang*-Tax

In our investigation of recepted forms of law, the main clue has been the development of the tenant's proprietary right from G through F to the *Landslög* (L). We can summarize the results thus: In L the right to a fine for violation of landed property, the *landnám* fine, and the right to establish tenant land by law means that the tenant's rights in the law are centred on the leased land itself, without necessarily going through the landowner. The lessee had also the legal right to *logfesta*, i.e, before suing, lays down a legal bond on the land itself. *Logfesta* was a ban solemnly proclaimed by law, which put an item, particularly real estate, in attachment. Anyone who breached this ban, including the owner, had to pay double *landnám* fine as well as an extra fine to the King. Thus, the proprietal possession is manifested along with regular property rights primarily in the *Landslög* (L). The sections concerned with the length of the lease appears to be another area of the law where proprietal possession is manifested, where the conditions applied to long-term tenancy in learned law (*ad longum tempus*) appears to have been present in F and L. Furthermore, the *Landslög* (L) fixes shares and makes them transferable to new tenants, something that also provides 'thingly' right according to the glossator Azo. Thus, the high medieval glossators developed the tenant's 'thingly' right from the Justinian law, where such rights barely exist in terms of land tenancy.

I shall conclude my investigation by filling in this picture of legal development. We must consider the investigation into proprietary tenancy rights in Norwegian medieval laws by the legal historian Taranger published

---

J.Sandnes maintains that it must have been a public taxation, since both tenant farms and owner-run farms were "bolsatt" (Jørn Sandnes (book review) *Heimen 3/2003* p.221). The obvious question is how such a matriculation was administratively possible. Perhaps the contemporary calculation of the tithe to the church was a possible foundation.

109. H.Bjørkvik in *KLNM X* p. 277-82.
110. The continental Teilpacht-arrangement obviously demanded a degree of control that was not easily attainable considering the topography of Norwegian estates. On control mechanisms in the Teilpacht, cf. K.H.Spiess in *HRG 5* p. 142.

in 1896.¹¹¹ His theme is concerned with F XIII 1 and L VII 1, the introductory provisions in the tenancy sections. Both commence thus:

> Með váttum scal land leiga oc svá leigu giallda. Ábúð iarðar heimlar teciu. En landleiga heimlar lóð oc allan áverca. (One shall rent land and pay rent with witness. The fulfillment of the *ábúð* duties gives the tenant the right to continue as such, but payment of the landskyld gives him the right to the whole harvest and to run the farm.)

The underlined text has long been debated.¹¹² The parallelism in F XIII 1 and L VII 1 consist in the two distinct duties of the tenant leading to two distinct legal consequences: The obligation of *ábúð* (i.e. maintaining farm and house) warrants possession of the land and prevents the landlord from evicting the tenant, while the land rent obligation warrants the tenant's free disposal over the harvest and free use of the farm.¹¹³ The consequence of this text is thus that even if the land rent obligation is neglected, this does not mean that the tenancy agreement (*tekja*) is invalidated and the tenant evicted. This is contrary to the introductory paragraph in the tenancy section of G 72 (cf. G 283), where it says that the tenant loses the right to the land if the rent is not paid. According to Taranger, F and L thus give the tenant far more legal protection than G. He sees F and L's introductory paragraphs in context with F's provision that the tenant has proprietary right, the first Norwegian law to provide this. He also sees this manifested in F XIII 2, where the rule that "purchase does not terminate lease" was in harmony with the glossator's reinterpretation of Justinian law, as we saw above. We may also associate Taranger's interpretation of F XIII 1 and L VI 1 with the issue of long-term tenancy which we have discussed: When these provisions maintain that only neglecting the *ábúð* duty leads to the expulsion of the tenant, and not the rent as in G (72), this is clearly a reflection of long-term tenancy (*ad longum tempus*), which the 13th century glossators ascribed to proprietary right, had become the legal foundation for F and L.

---

111. Taranger 1896, p. 108-24.
112. Taranger (1896) provides an introduction into the discussion. The regulations are also commented upon by Hagland/Sandnes (1994 p. 225), who follow Taranger: In F and L *ábúð* is the technical term for the tenant's duties with respect to the proper administration of the farm, i.e. maintaining road and house. *Tekja*, which does not occur in G, is primarily a technical term for a leasing contract in F og L. *Ábúð* and *tekja* may however have two interpretations that provide very different meanings. *Ábúð* originally meant "living somewhere" (Hagland/Sandnes) and has this meaning in G (283) (Taranger:"brugsbesiddelse af jord" (proprietal possession of land).
113. Taranger classes this parallelism as "nobel jurisprudens" (1996 p. 114).

The passage in F XIII 1 and L VII 1, *landsleiga heimlar loð oc allan áverca* (payment of land rent gives him the right to the whole harvest and to run the farm), thus gives the tenant possession over the whole harvest and the right to keep running the farm if the land rent is paid.[114] Thus may lead us further to an important change in social organization established by the *Landslög* (L), namely that public *leiðangr-* tax has been converted to a land tax with the farm's rent as a basis for calculation (cf. L III 6 and VII 7.3). The *leidang* tax had previously been a poll tax (G and F). The basis for converting it to a land tax in L was the public matriculation in the 1260s of both rented and private property where each farm's fixed land rent was the calculation basis for the tax as well.[115] A change from poll to land tax represents a legal approximation between the right to own property and the right to use it. The tenant is thus responsible to the King for taxes from his rented land, in the same way as the landowner is responsible for his owned property. Basing the state tax on tenancy became a milestone in the development of the tenant's proprietary right to his own rented land (*ius in rem*) during the high Middle Ages. Another side of state tax based on rented land, was the increased protection provided for the tenant's land in the *Landslög* (L).

Summary and Further Implications

The theme of our research has been concepts and legal forms of land owning and land lease and the development of these in the three Norwegian laws of the Middle Ages. Our focus has been important formal aspects of developing systems of controlling land recourses, recourses which in the broadest respect were central for social relations and the execution of power in the high Middle Ages. The other side of executive power was to what extent the peasants had right of disposal. When provisions about property

---

114. When Taranger says concerning F XIII 1 and L VII 1 that the landlord owns all produce until the land rent is paid, this requires further qualification. According to Roman law, the *tenant* is the owner of the harvest by its separation (*separatio*) from the mother object (here the land itself), when there is a proprietal lease, i.e. through inhereted tenancy (amongst other things, cf. Dig.22.1.25.1). Whoever holds the ususfructus and short-term tenancy only attains this by actually acquiring the harvest (through *perceptio*) (Dig.47.2.62.8). *Separatio* and *perceptio* seems to fit well with the difference between F (XIII 1), L (VII 1) and G (72, 283). The fact that the tenant only acquires full possession of the harvest after paying the land rent can be explained by the pawn *(pignus)* that the landowner and tenant have agreed upon to take in the harvest for the rent, cf. Dig.20.2.7pr. Cf. Kaser I p. 427, 465; Landsberg 1883 p. 227-229.
115. Bjørkvik in *KLNM vol.10* p. 432-442.

and land lease showed up in laws, it means that they contribute to limiting and simplifying the control by the landlord. It is the development of this relation between landowner, land tenant and public bodies that concepts and legal forms about land leasing in our three Norwegian medieval laws can give us a view into. This inspection is especially interesting because the century between G's last redaction in the decade after 1164 and the *Landslög* (L) in 1274 is a period of rapid development on most levels of society.

I will sum up as follows: The law making activity of this period, with respect to the legal sphere, has it's background in customary law as well as in positive, i.e. changeable, law. As we have seen, the evolvement in this sphere moved towards greater elements of positive law, firstly by the Church's coordination of customary law and and positive law making (Gratian), and afterwards by the King's "the land shall be built on law" – law making in a Roman law sense. The legislative power of the Norwegian King appears to have been among the most marked in Europe. The perspective in this research has primarily been the influence of the European jurisprudence on owning and leasing land conditions in the three laws, i.e. on a "civil law"-area in society. The examinations carried out appear to show that the influence must have been rather extensive. Undoubtedly, studies are at the back of this influence, studies at centres of learning in monasteries, Episcopal seats, and later in universities on the Continent and in England. More thoroughly we looked into the study travels of the later Archbishop Øystein and his possible contacts with law learned men, primarily in England where Roman law had a rise in his period. Clergymen and other Norwegians had close contacts in East-Anglia and especially with Lincoln which had one of the leading centres of law studies in England. As is well known, Bologna and Paris were the two learning centres most visited by Norwegian students far into the 13th century, for Roman law and canon law respectively.

In the oldest law, the Gulathing Law, we could first of all ascertain that the law hardly at all makes use of the fixed, substantive concept of property, *eign*, which in the later law-codes F and L is a general term for land property. G, however, does make use of a compound word, *landeign*, to define the King's power and area of dominion. Not when it comes to the use of verbs either, does G appear to operate with any clear separation of terminology between having the right to rule and having the right to own. Also in a West-European picture of law an object/ thing linked property concept is not explicitly expressed until in the 13th century when a 'thingly' Roman law property concept breaks through in sources of law (Willoweit, Hecker, Reynolds). In line with this one also developed specific contrasting concepts dealing with leasing- and owning land (owning/leasing, owner/tenant etc.). In my research I found, in this respect as well, a marked disparity between G and the two later laws: In G there are very few contrastings concepts like that, while they are quite common in F and L. Unlike G, the two latest laws operate in addition with technical terms as well for land tenant (*leiglendingr, leigulið, landbui*), land rent (*landskyld*), as well as technical terms for lease contract (*mali, leigumali*) and in connection with leasing land *(byggja)*. We ascertained nevertheless that some of the more fixed terms and relations which became common in F and L, in a few instances are taken into use in G. One can conclude that F and L to a higher degree and more clearly relate land property to land tenancy and land owner to land tenant.

Clarifications of concepts, systematising and structuring can probably be seen in connection with influence from "the learned law" of the 13th century. Land owning/ land tenancy relations seem to have been understood in vaguer, less limited and less structured ways in the law G of the 12th century. Somewhat surprising we all the same find a rather distinct influence from the Roman law of the glossatores concerning legal forms/law institutes on land lease in the Gulathing law. The legal form which first and foremost stands out to us is *ususfructus*. This is the right to crop and yield from the use of alien land (*ius in re aliena*). This right is strongly tied to a person, in that it may not be transferred or forewarded to others. If one of the parties die, either owner or tenant, the lease contract shall immediately be cancelled. The land lease provisions are otherwise given a distinct 'obligatory' character in that the formal period of lease is one year only. The regulations thus present a rather insecure land lease in G. The model seems to be a "pure", i.e. Justinian Roman law in the same way the first Glossatores presented land lease conditions before the later iurisprudens developed the Justinian model in the 13th century. Regulations are, however, written out in accordance with concrete conditions in society.

One problem connected to the formulation of land lease in G is how Roman law institutes and regulations could be taken into the vague and not so limited and structured world of concepts about owning-and renting relationships that we see in the same law, although we did see some tendencies towards a firmer use of concepts also in G. If reception of thought structures happened over a longer period of time, one would still probably expect that terminology and concepts were the first to be given admittance, and that the larger forms of law were entered in the next round. However, could it possibly be that certain legal forms/institutes as such were the first to enter into the law if we assume that they were introduced through a positive law making, implanted in an otherwise vague and quite unprepared conceptual system? It is my opinion that in our case there are certain possibilities for the latter view, due to the fact that there existed paths of transferring knowledge and bodies of power behind positive law decisions. The close contact between Norway and England, especially the

Lincoln-area, may well have played a large part in this. We have seen that mayor prelates of England began importing learned in law from Bologna from the 1140-50s, among others the well known Vacarius who is supposed to have introduced Roman law. The Episcopal seat of Lincoln had the important Roman law texts before 1153. Obviously, the influences can be seen concretely through Øystein or someone in his circle, however, knowledge may also have passed via the monastery connections we mentioned.

The Roman law forms of land lease may very well have been accepted into the law through Magnus' revision of the law in the decade after 1164. A plausible factor here can be that in the introductory regulation of the land tenancy section (G 72) one finds just two words which become fixed terms in F and L: *máli*, land tenancy contract, is found in G here only, and *leigulið*, land tenant, here and in G 75.[116] In all probability it is the Archbishop Øystein who is responsible for this revision of the Gulathing Law. We find, however, clear characteristics in the revision of what could be called a "program of Europeanizing".[117] We can probably take for granted that Øystein in this respect was as up to date as with his *Canones* where Gratian's *Decretum* was recepted 20 or 30 years after its publishing in Bologna. Despite these alleged arguments I will still underline the uncertainty in a hypothesis that places the provenance of the land tenancy forms in G in connection with Øystein and his circle.

We ascertained that in F and L vague concepts of land ownership- and land lease were replaced by new, fixed substantives and structured by contrasting concepts probably under influence from "the learned law" of that period. Concerning the content in legal forms of land lease, it was the glossatores who came to carry out new thinking and further developing the model through their annotations to the Justinian Roman law. In the two 13th century laws F and L we see firstly that the one year contract period of G has become strongly extended. The tenancy contract is not annulled either by the death of one of the parties, which it is in G. The two laws follow in this manner a main tendency in Western Europe with extended time for leasing contracts. Regulations of land tenancy in the two laws demonstrate above all that the right of possession has gained increased importance. Both F and L contain, opposite to G, provisions that explicitly protect the land tenancy/land lease, even if the owner were to sell the land. If a landowner F

---

116. Iversen 2001 p. 100, 103. Further: only in G 72 and 75 is *leigulið* contrasted (with the verb *eiga*=to own). Another element pointing towards additions incerted into the law is that the segment on Land Lease introduced by G 72 does not have the fixed introductory frase *Þat er nu Þvi nest* (It is now next so...), the way all bigger paragraphs in the previous part of the law are introduced. G 72 is just introduced with *nu* (=now) which is the usual in regulations. Taranger 1926 p. 204-211.
117. Helle 1974 p. 63.

and L does not deliver rightfully leased land to the tenant, a judicial restraint shall be put on the leased land before the case is brought to court, i.e. the land is under legal rule/fixed by law *(logfesta)*, which is strongly reminiscent of the Roman law *interdictio*, a legal ban in order to protect land possession. According to Justinian Roman law ordinary land tenants did not have such protection.

Important to the development of the right of possession is the right to *landnám*-compensation. In G there is no *landnám* given to the ordinary tenant. In Landsloven (L), however, the land tenant's right to *landnám* is clearly revealed in several cases, among others when the leased land was legally established and then violated by the owner (cf. *logfesta*). In such cases the land tenant shall receive a double *landnám*, as well as the King receiving compensation. The development of proprietary possession with characteristics similar to those of property, pluss extension of leasing period *(ad longum tempus)*, implies that tenant rights, in addition to the leasing contract, may have a basis in the leased land per se. In terms of Roman law this expresses that the land tenant *(leilendingr)* has been given a 'thingly' right in his *own* possession – a *ius in rem*. It is then first and foremost in L that proprietal possession is shown as parallel to the actual property right. In the Justinian Roman law the land tenant usually had no 'thingly' *(in rem)* right. The glossator Azo (d.1220) did, however, declare such a 'thingly' right to the land tenant "for a longer period" *(ad longum tempus)*, then as an opposite to short term lease.

Emphasizing of proprietary or 'thingly' right to leased land in F, and especially in L, may have had a background in another Roman law institute which probably began to gain importance, that of *colonia partiaria*, shared ownership / lease. The institute was most likely a startingpoint in form for the "skyldpart"-ownership of land rent, a "share-of-rent-property" system which developed in Norway from the 13th century, as well as through dividing farms units into holdings/ separating shares as homesteads out of whole farms. *Colonia partiaria* is part of partnership *(societas)* thinking in Roman law. In the Justinian Roman law, however, partnership according to *colonia partiaria* was a frail relationship which could easily be dissolved and was not even transferrable. In this matter also "the learned law" in the high Middle Ages carry on the "pure" Justinian Law in the direction of a more stabile and transferrable, i.e. 'thingly' *(in rem)* pattern between the parties, something we can find impacts of in L. In this connection it should be underlined that the learned in law first and foremost had specific law regulations in mind. Combinations of institutes formulated in accordance with local conditions are thus frequently used.

I have added a few conditions which further underline the evolvement of proprietary right *(ius in rem)* in F and especially in L. Both laws stress the duty to maintain the land as giving a legal authority for the right to possession of land. Neglecting to pay the land rent *(landskyld)* does not lead to the tenant being expelled. The landlord has anyway security in all crop and yield until this rent is paid. Generally the tenant had the right of disposal of the crop and yield. The tenant is here given a *ius in rem*, a 'thingly' right. Final manifistation of the significance of the right to proprietal possess is found first in L where state tax *(leidangr)* to the King shall be paid by the peasants, whether these are owners or tenants. Land property for use *(dominium utile)* has thus become a basis for public power.

In this research the clue has been the development of the tenant's proprietary, i.e. 'thingly' right *(ius in rem)* from G to L. During the century leading to the *Landslög* (L) of 1274 we are able to point out that there was a growth indeed in the tenant's right to possession of leased land. At the very beginning of the century the vague and barely contrasted use of concepts for owning- and land leasing conditions in G shows that there was no firm and regulated system of land tenancy developed in the law. In the agrarian society it is easy to imagine land tenancy arrangements which could vary from district to district and even within an area conscerning commitment. In this we can probably find formulations according to the pattern of patron-client. However, G does not make any statements about direct non-economic obligations of the land tenant (i.e. services). However this did not imply that un-free persons were nor in a position to have land lease contracts in G and F.[118] A beginning use of more fixed concepts and contrasting combined with the land tenancy form of *ususfructus* can show that structuring in the direction of a more consistent, unified system was in the making. Land tenancy in G, however, is legally insecure, short lasting and not transferrable. Evidently, this must have given the landlord a great right of disposal.

Towards the end of the 13th century the *Landlög* (L) more formalised land tenancy arrangement can show a different picture of society. Through 'thingly' right the tenants' right of possession to leased land has become a more firmly regulated social concern. Land lease and the tenant has through the state tax *(leidangr)* become a direct base for the kingdom and secured through a protected possession. The connection of local and central administration developing next to that of the church is clear here. Simultaneously with the tenant's land lease increasingly turning into a societal concern, it can be said that bigger landlords, as "ideal" owners through a "share-of-rent"-ownership and through geographically spread property as well, distanced themselves from the local community and towards "public" tasks. The law making on land property and land tenancy, especially in L, is one of the King's tools in the shaping of this development, and is thus an expression of the legislative power of the King

---

118. The freedman's *(leysingi)* land tenancy is manifested in F XI 23.

which we brought up initially. The regulations by the King thus encompass all levels of status in the population. The phasing out of thraldom is part of this picture as well. The background of knowledge for the working out of law we can therefore find in an independent relationship to the European "learned law". Continental and English development follow parallel, but far from identical paths in this period.[119]

---

119. To be briefly mentioned here is the English discussion which shows clear parallels to the issues discussed in this article. In several long articles Robert Palmer has claimed that the understanding of property in our sense first appeared around 1200 in England. Before this, land possession was marked by personal relations: "The Origins of Property in England", *Law and History Review III*, 1958 p. 1-50, spes. p. 4-5; Palmer: "The Feudal Framework of English Law", *Michigan Law Review* lxxix, 1985, p. 375-89; Palmer: "The Economic and Cultural Impact of the Origins of Property": 1180-1220, *Law and History Review III*, 1985; "Anglo-Norman land law and the origins of property", *Law and Government in Medieval England and Normandy* (eds. G.Garnett, J.Hudson) 1994 p. 198-221; Mary Cheny 1994 p. 245-253.

THE CONCEPT OF KINSHIP ACCORDING TO THE WEST NORDIC MEDIEVAL LAWS

Lars Ivar Hansen

Introduction

It may seem presumptuous to return once more to the analysis of the wergild systems of medieval Norwegian and Icelandic law - as this has been an ever recurring topic in the study of Nordic medieval law, since the middle of the 19th century. In fact, this very year we might for instance celebrate the 90th anniversary of Bertha Philpotts' outstanding dissertation on *"Kindred & Clan",* published in Cambridge in 1913. Nevertheless, the aim of this paper is to review some features of kinship reckoning in the old provincial laws in the western Nordic area, with particular emphasis on their possible connections to canon law. Such an approach is clearly inspired by the opinion articulated ever more strongly during recent years, whereby the Scandinavian medieval laws to a greater extent are seen as products of processes and actors at the actual time of their coming-into-being, and not so much as a reflection of older, customary principles.[1] For this purpose I have deliberately singled out some of the wergild regulations laid down by these laws, as these regulations often have been held to reflect ancient social principles, stemming from the time prior to ecclesiastical influence. In

---

1. See Sjöholm, Elsa: Sveriges medeltidslagar. Europeisk rättstradition i politisk omvandling. (*Skrifter utgivna af Institutet för rättshistorisk forskning grundat av Gustav och Carin Olin, Serien I*), Lund 1988. cf. discussion by Norseng, Per: "Lovmaterialet som kilde til tidlig nordisk middelalder", in: Kildene til den tidlige middelaldershistorie. *Rapporter til den XX nordiske historikerkongres*, vol. I, Reykjavík 1987, pp. 48 - 77.

particular, I will compare the regulations within the laws of *Gulathing* and *Frostathing* in Norway, as well as the Icelandic *Grágás*. In the first part of my paper, however, I will give an outline of the historiographical background to the study of kinship structures in medieval Nordic society. In addition, I will try to present the main findings in the context of more general changes in legislation during the first part of the high Middle Ages.

Outline of the Historiographical Background

Kinship structures and kinship reckoning as expressed in the old Scandinavian laws have now been a focus of study for more than 150 years. It is well known that the old, Germanistic-influenced school interpreted the very specific normative regulations of the laws as evidence of a very strong position played by the *kinship group* in early Nordic – and early Germanic – society. The kinship group – in the form of the "*ætt*" or "*die Sippe*" – was regarded as attending to and fulfilling basic social functions in a pre-state society characterized by few institutions of public power or authority.[2] Thus, it was conceived as playing a decisive role in the transfer and keeping of *property* and in providing for the individual's needs of *social security*. Seemingly, the latter was partly carried out by safeguarding social peace and regulating social conflict to a certain extent through the framework of the *wergild system*, specifying payments to be paid in case of manslaughter. And partly it was implemented through the obligations laid down on members on the kin for *the sustenance of poor relatives* and those of minor age without means, so-called 'umagi',[3] as well as *guardianship for*

---

2. Kroeschell, Karl. "Die Sippe im germanischen Recht", *Zeitschrift der Savigny-Stiftung für Rechtsgeschichte, Germanische Abteilung*, 77 (1960), pp. 1 - 25; Murray, A. C.: *Germanic Kinship Structure. Studies in Law and Society in Antiquity and the Early Middle Ages* (Pontifical Institute of Mediaeval Studies. Studies and Texts; v. 65), Toronto 1983, pp. 14 - 32; Sørensen, Helle: *Det kanoniske slægtskab. En undersøgelse af kirkerettens betydning for den nordiske landskabslovgivning i det tolvte og trettende århundrede* (Speciale i Historie), Københavns Universitet 2000, pp. 9 - 11; cf. examples cited by Winberg, Chr.: *Grenverket. Studier rörande jord, släktskapssystem och ståndsprivilegier.* (*Skrifter utgivna af Institutet för rättshistorisk forskning grundat av Gustav och Carin Olin, Serien I*), Stockholm 1985, pp. 10 - 14.

3. Cf. Rindal, Magnus: "Úmagi", in: *Kulturhistorisk leksikon for nordisk middelalder*, vol. 19, 1975, cols. 286 - 289; Miller, William Ian: *Bloodtaking and Peacemaking. Feud, Law, and Society in Saga Iceland*. Chicago & London 1990, p. 147; Arnórsdóttir, Agnes S.: *Kvinner og "krigsmenn". Kjønnenes stilling i det islandske samfunnet på 1100- og 1200-tallet.* (hovedoppgave i historie ved Universitetet i Bergen), 1990, pp. 40 - 43.

unmarried women and minors.[4] The role of the kin group in negotiating marriage alliances and in establishing social networks by way of the fostering institution has also been emphasized.[5]

The conception of the "ætt" (die Sippe) as a clear, corporate kinship group, with extensive functions and great internal solidarity, found a ripe and fertile ground for reception in the various historical conceptions which tried to sort out the historical phenomena and processes by ordering them according to models of linear evolution. Disregarding whether these conceptions were inspired by purely evolutionistic lines of reasoning or more specifically by historical materialism – with its notion of historical progress through successive, social transformations - they all encompassed the concept of the "ætt" or "die Sippe" as a useful idea. Having allegedly great integrating capacity, it could be construed as a core institution of Nordic society in its early, pre-state mode.[6] Following this view, the organisation of society according to "ættir" was regarded as being opposite to the ideals and power structures which were promoted by the new aspiring powers, the church and the national monarchies. However, though the kinship group or "ætt" was ascribed a function like some kind of "glue of society" in pre-state times, the notion of what the "ætt" really encompassed, how it functioned in practice and under what circumstances kinship solidarity in fact was materialized, was nevertheless rather vaguely defined. Such vague conceptions of what the "ætt" really amounted to and what kind of norms that ruled the manifestation of kinship solidarity, may still be found in general synthesizing works and textbooks up until the last decade.

However, this does not imply that more analytical and adequate approaches to the concept of "ætt" were completely lacking. Already in 1976, the Norwegian expert of medieval canon and indigenous secular law, *Lars Hamre*, pointed out that the notion of "ætt" was ambiguous both in older and newer Norwegian law, and that at least three meanings might be discerned:

1) "All the people descending from one common male or female ancestor" (a cognatic descent group),

2) "all the people one individual is related to" (a cognatic kindred), or

3) "all the agnatic descendants of one male ancestor" (a patriline).[7]

---

4. Hastrup, Kirsten: *Culture and History in Medieval Iceland. An anthropological analysis of structure and change*, Oxford 1985, p. 93.
5. Hastrup 1985, pp. 98-99; Miller 1990, pp. 122-124, 171-174.
6. The title of a well-known book by the Norwegian historian Arne Odd Johnsen (1948) may be taken as an illuminating example: *Fra ættesamfunn til statssamfunn*, in translation: *From kin group society to state society*. Cf. also Olgeirsson, Einar: *Ættsamfélag og ríkisvald í Þjóðveldi Íslendinga*, Reykjavík 1954 [Norwegian edition: Fra ættesamfunn til klassestat, Oslo 1968.]
7. Hamre, Lars: "Ætt", in: *Kulturhistorisk leksikon for nordisk middelalder*, vol. 20,

New research, carried out during the last two decades, has further substantiated these distinctions and brought forth more nuanced insights into the nature of kinship organisation in early Nordic society – not least inspired by the work, approaches and analytical tools of *social anthropology*. I refer here to the distinctions between alliances and descent relationships, between lineal kinship organisation with the point of departure in a real or presumed pair of ancestors on the one hand, – and ego-centred, bilateral kindred on the other.[8] Likewise, the clear-cut distinctions between agnatic (patrilineal) and cognatic kin on the one hand, and the complementarily of consanguineous and affinals on the other. Important contributions have here been made by Kirsten Hastrup, Christer Winberg, Birgit Sawyer, Agnes S. Arnórsdóttir and others. Thus, it has been established beyond any reasonable doubt that the kinship system prevailing in the Nordic countries so far back as it is discernible, was *basically bilateral* in structure - that is: kinship was traced both along the male and female line – but combined with some patrilineal elements of varying degrees, according to region (country) and period. Kinship was defined on the basis of ego-centred, bilateral kindred. In such a system, all individuals will have separate kindred, only slightly overlapping with each other in the case of relatives. Only in the case of genuine (real) siblings will two persons have exactly the same bilaterally-defined kinship group. Under such conditions the notion of a stable, corporate kin group is very difficult to preserve.

By studying the more actual workings of kinship in early medieval Nordic society these scholars have also come up with more modified conclusions, taking into account the cooperation of two or more contending principles. In an analysis of the old Icelandic kinship system (primarily on the basis of the law material) the social anthropologist *Kirsten Hastrup* (1985) thus concluded that three organizing principles were at work, at different levels: two versions of the cognatic principle, as well as a weak version of the patrilineal. Laterally they defined bilateral kindred, but vertically they made up what she called a 'stock' in English terms, i.e. the descendants of an ancestor couple, but structured from the viewpoint of an individual (ego). The lateral principle played the greatest role in defining the 'social universe' of the old Icelanders - in delineating the extension of one "ætt" in relation to others.

In a dissertation from 1990, *Agnes S. Arnórsdóttir* also reached similar conclusions. Though recognizing the basic bilateral and individual nature of medieval Icelandic kinship, she nevertheless discerned a certain contradiction between patrilineal and cognatic elements. According to her

---

      1976, col. 586.
8.   In the Nordic languages, the concept 'kindred' is usually rendered as 'slektskrets'.

view, obligations always rested on individual relatives – in a sequential order from ego – and not on the kinship group as such. However, certain patrilineal elements may be observed in different sectors, like the favourisation of men and the male line in inheritance, in the wergild system and in a greater obligation laid upon the male line for providing for minor relatives without means. But she also observes a great discrepancy between these patrilineal principles – for instance in inheritance matters – and the actual inheritance practices as they were recorded in the sagas, in particular the Sturlunga-saga. The patrilineal elements were therefore interpreted as *ideological constructs*, aimed at serving the interests of the great chieftains' families during the fierce and protracted struggles for power during the latter part of the 12th and the beginning of the 13th centuries.[9]

Though inheritance practices modelled after kinship relations may have been of great importance to the landowning aristocracy of the Nordic countries, comprehensive studies by *Thyra Nors* and *Lars Hermansson* have demonstrated that the loyalty of the biological kin was no leading principle or guarantee which automatically could be relied on by the Scandinavian dynasties in their struggles for power during the first half of the Middle Ages. Taken in a broader sense, "kinship" could be said to be of importance, but that it was a kind of self-elected, strategically constructed kinship, where relations based on friendship, political alliances and marriage connections supplemented the biological ones. The lack of established norms for kinship solidarity led to a situation where the individual to a certain extent could select his or her alliances.[10] On the whole, one should warn against over focusing "kinship" as such and ascribing it too much significance as an instrument of mobilizing alliances and social resources in Nordic medieval society. As *Jon Viðar Sigurðsson* too has pointed out, other institutions such as *friendship* and *fostering* should be taken into account – along with the social units of the *household* and the '*hreppr*'. Together with kinship affinities they were all part of the social fabric, but to the majority of Icelanders the attachment to a household and the protection offered by the household heads and the chieftains, mattered the most.[11]

---

9. Arnórsdóttir 1990, pp. 25-60.
10. Nors, Thyra: "Ægteskab og politik i Saxos Gesta Danorum", in: [Danish] *Historisk tidsskrift*, vol. 98, 1998, p. 1 – 33, and "Slægsstrategier hos den danske kongeslægt i det 12. århundrede: Svar til Helge Paludan", in: *Historie 1*, 2000, Århus 2000; Hermanson, Lars: *Släkt, vänner och makt. En studie av elitens politiska kultur i 1100-talets Danmark* (Avhandlingar från Historiska institutionen i Göteborg, 24), Göteborg 2000, in particular p. 180 - 184.
11. Sigurðsson, Jón Viðar: "Forholdet mellom frender, hushold og venner på Island i fristatstiden", [Norwegian] *Historisk Tidsskrift*, vol. 74, 1995, pp. 311 - 330. Sigurðsson, Jón Viðar & Teuscher, Simon: "Slektens rolle på Island og i Bern", in:

Regarding the structure of the kinship system as such, the most penetrating analysis so far has been undertaken by the Danish social anthropologist *Torben A. Vestergaard* (1988) on the basis of the oldest versions of the Gulathing and Frostathing's Law books. Vestergaard focuses on the inheritance and wergild sections of the laws, and has been able to throw new light upon the exact way that genealogical distance was computed in these 'gradual' systems.[12] For instance, the priority of patrilineal kinsmen before cognatic is borne out by the fact that kinship mediated through female links is considered as being twice as distant as kinship related through male links.[13] Though the system is conceived as fundamentally *bilateral* and *cognatic*, one of the most interesting aspects of Vestergaard's analysis is his demonstration of a *special patrilineal group*, given a special status in these two laws. This group, which he calls the *"three-generational agnatic group"* or the *"minimal* ætt*"* is defined as "... a group of patrilineal brothers and cousins descending from a common grandfather" or: "male descendants through male links from one and the same grandfather."[14] Laterally this patrilineal descent group comprises male relatives that are three degrees apart, but vertically it can encompass father-son relations in five generations (see sketch, figure 1). This three-linked group of near-agnates is given priority both in the numbering of inheritors and in the wergild systems

---

Sv. Bagge (ed.): *Det europeiske menneske. Individoppfatninger fra middelalderen til i dag*, Oslo 1998, pp. 112 - 117.

12. As i.a. E. Sjöholm (1988, pp. 123ff.) and Sawyer, Birgit: Kvinnor och familj i det forn- och medeltida Skandinavien, *Occasional Papers on Medieval Topics* 6, Viktoria Bokförlag, Skara 1992; 2. utgave: Skriftserie fra Historisk institutt; nr 24 (Historisk institutt, Det historisk-filosofiske fakultet, NTNU) Trondheim, 1998, have demonstrated, the medieval laws of the western Nordic area (the laws of *Gulathing* and *Frostathing*, as well as the *West Göta law*, the law of *Dalarna* and the Icelandic *Grágás*) all implemented a so-called *'gradual'* principle of kinship reckoning, whereby the decreasing kinship affinity from a deceased person or killer was expressed in *grades* of genealogical distance; whereas the laws from eastern Nordic regions based their inheritance regulations on the so-called *'parentela'* principle. According to this principle, kinship is reckoned by parent-couples and their offspring. Thus, the inheritance from an individual will first go to the individual's own children and children's children, and only thereafter - if nobody one from this group is alive - will it pass on to the parents of the deceased and the other descendants stemming from them, i.e. the siblings of the deceased. At the next turn, the grandparents and the cousins of the deceased will come into consideration, if neither the parents nor the siblings are alive.
13. Other structuring principles, according to Vestergaard, are that ascending kinship is regarded as twice as distant as descending, and that relatives forming reciprocal pairs around ego are given equal status, something which breaks fundamentally with a "parentela" way of reckoning kinship.
14. Vestergaard, Torben A.: The system of kinship on early Norwegian law, *Medieval Scandinavia* 12, 1988, p. 175.

(particularly in the Frostathing's Law). Two more distant categories of male relatives, the junior patrilineal cousin once removed ("father's brother's son's son") and the father's patrilineal cousin, are also included, but further out and individually numbered. According to Vestergaard, they are not proper members of the 3-generational agnatic group, but make up intermediate links to *other patrilines*.

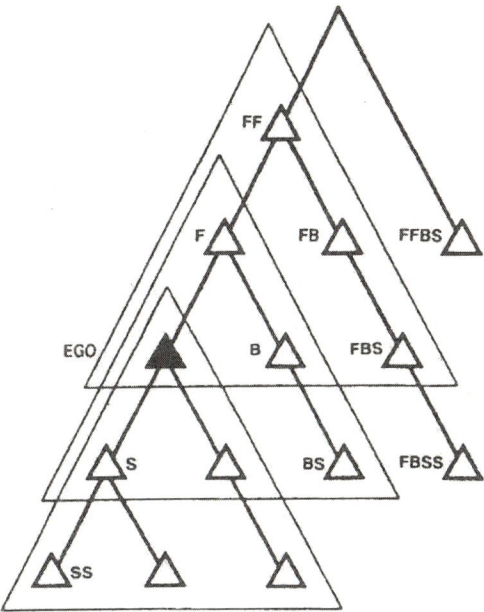

Fig. 1. The near-agnates mentioned among the first 6 categories of heirs and forming a three-generational patrilineage, which Torben Vestergaard defines as "the minimal ætt" ("the minimal kin group"). The figure is reproduced after Vestergaard 1988:176.

It is worth noting that no trace of this 3-generational group of "near-agnates" can be found in the Icelandic material. Thus, it seems to be a purely Norwegian occurrence. This feature has excited attention. How should it be explained? Might it be regarded as an innovation on Norwegian soil, since it was completely absent from the Icelandic law material, which presumably should be an adaptation of the old western Norwegian law? In an article written ten years ago, I reflected around the possible historical contexts which might explain this peculiar status of a clearly defined agnatic group in the Norwegian material, and put forward three alternative hypotheses:

1) The patrilineal elements could have been remnants of an older system, ascribing greater weight to the patrilines, which might have formed

the basic structure of a patrilineally organized society. The constellations documented in the written laws might thus be regarded as expressions of a transition towards a greater degree of bilaterality. This would amount to a rewriting of the traditional historiographical viewpoint, but formulated in more precise kinship terms.

2) The kinship system might have been basically bilateral and cognatic even in older, prehistoric times, and the patrilineal aspects could then be regarded as innovations suited to serve the interests of rival fractions of the landowning aristocracy, who would seek to preserve control over property and power by reserving it for the male line and male members of the kin. In particular, this could be construed as a relevant response to what they viewed as an upcoming threat from the aspiring monarchy and church organisation. This viewpoint might gather support from a parallel shift occurring in central western European countries from the beginning of the 11th century and onwards, whereby control over property and positions by female kin was subjugated to ever increasing restrictions, and lines of succession to an increasing degree defined along the male lines, and by primogeniture.[15] This would also conform with Arnórsdóttir's hypothesis mentioned above, about a strengthening of *patrilineal ideology* in Iceland during the latter 12th and early 13th centuries.

3) The third option would consist of regarding the patrilineal aspects as an *attempt* by the landowning kinship groups to try to set more rigid restrictions, but an attempt which met with obstacles and failed in the long run. Thus, the development might take on a more "wave-like" movement.

Even though the two last options stand in contrast to the old, evolutionary view, they still take as their premise that there should be a fundamental opposition between the kinship solidarity as manifested by the strategies of the landowning aristocracy, and the new policies of the church and the aspiring, realm-building monarchy. In conformity with the traditional viewpoint the new state structures and the policy of the church are regarded as being opposed to the kinship alliances of the aristocracy.

Recently, however, an alternative to this conception has been launched by *Michael H. Gelting*. In two articles, from 1999 and 2000 respectively, he has put forward the contrary hypothesis that it was *the church* that took the lead in promoting kinship solidarity. New modes of "thinking and relating

---

15. Duby, Duby, Georges: *La Société au XIe et XIIe siécles dans la région mâconnaise*, Paris (1953) 1971. [Eng.: "Lineage, nobility and knighthood. The Mâconnais in the twelfth century - a revision", in: Duby, G.: *The Chivalrous Society*, London 1977.]; Bisson, Thomas, N.: "The "feudal revolution", i *Past & Present* No. 142, 1994, pp. 6 - 42. Bois, Guy: *The transformation of the year one thousand. The village of Lournand from antiquity to feudalism*, Manchester & New York 1992. Bonnassie, Pierre: *La Catalogne au milieu du Xe à la fin du XIe siècle: Croissance et mutations d'une société*, 2 vols., Toulouse 1975 – 76, as well as others.

to kinship" – based on the notion of kinship as articulated in the canonical marriage impediments – should supposedly have been launched by the church *in order to promote social peace*. Contrary to what has been surmised by earlier research, the policy of the church should have had as its aim to *strengthen the cohesion by the aristocratic kindreds*, by making their obligation to mutual love and solidarity an absolute one.[16] In the first article, Gelting sought to explain the extreme extension of the incest prohibition in Carolingian times by calling attention to the church's policy aimed at subduing and moderating the intense feuds of the Frankish aristocracy of the time.[17] In the next article, he went on to study the way the "*odelsrett*" ("the allodial right") or "*bördsrett*" ("birth right") was formulated in the Nordic medieval laws.

Provisions relating to this right, or remnants of such regulations, can be traced in all Nordic countries – except Iceland – during medieval times, but Norway is the only country to have retained the full force of this kind of regulation in its legislation down to the present day. The content of these provisions was primarily to secure members of the kindred *the right of pre-emption of landed property that had been alienated from the kin group*. Thus, it served as a measure for regulating the relationships between possible heirs who might be offended by the desire of one individual to sell or donate parts of the inherited property. Thereby, it can be conceived as a procedure for solving the same kind of contradictions that the French institution of 'laudatio parentum' sought to regulate - but in another way. The strength of Gelting's argument lies in a combined discussion of several changes which took place more or less at the same time: the introduction of new inheritance regulations which provided *all siblings with a fixed share of the inheritance*, the ability to *donate 'pious gifts' to church institutions* and the introduction of "odal right" or "bördsrett" in the form of *right to pre-emption*. One major feature pointing at a connection between the canonical view of kinship and "odal right" is that the definition of the group having the right to pre-emption is *coterminous with the group of relatives who were forbidden by canon law to marry each other*, and that changes in the extension of this odal right group followed the changes in the canonical marriage prohibitions issued by the Fourth Lateran Council. Nevertheless, it should be stressed that Gelting also considers it likely that the notion of

---

16. Gelting, Michael: "Odelsrett - lovbydelse - bördsrätt - retrait lignager: Kindred and land in the Nordic countries in the twelfth and thirteenth centuries", in: L.I. Hansen (ed.): *Family, Marriage and Property Devolution in the Middle Ages*, Tromsø 2000, p. 149.
17. Gelting, Michael: "Marriage, Peace and the Canonical Incest Prohibition: Making Sense of an Absurdity?" in: M. Korpiola (ed.): *Nordic Perspectives on Medieval Canon Law*, (Publications of Matthias Calonius Society II), Saarijärvi 1999, pp. 98, 118.

'odel' has deeper roots, and may go back to previous customs and earlier conceptions of what was considered reasonable conduct towards potential heirs who might be excluded from receiving property through the actions of one individual (entitling them to compensation etc.). His point is rather that the precise configuration that these rights to pre-emption had been given in the preserved laws could hardly have been formed before their codification during the 12th and 13th centuries. While kinship ties supposedly could have been conceived more loosely or ad-hoc in earlier times, the exact formulation of the kinship degrees and the rights/obligations pertaining to each of them, presumably may be seen as a reflection of *an ideological change* brought about by the church, in the ways kinship was conceived.

More recently this perspective has been followed up by *Helle Sørensen* (now *Vogt*) in a dissertation discussing what she calls "the canonical kinship".[18] On the one hand, she focuses on *the control over property*, as it is spoken out through the regulations concerning inheritance, wills, donations, pre-emption rights ("odal right") as well as the particular institutions regulating the generational succession of a farm's occupants. On the other hand she studies regulations concerning *the kin's collective control with its members*, in particular in the matters of marriage, manslaughter and the paying of compensating fines ("wergild").

Regarding the wergild payments, she draws particular attention to the obligations assigned to the individual slayer, in comparison with the responsibility ascribed to the whole kin group as such. Through this study, she is able to draw interesting conclusions about the ecclesiastical influence on kinship reckoning, which may have influenced earlier notions of kin relations that were vaguer, and not so clearly defined. The fundamental idea behind the notions promoted by the church was allegedly that one held a moral responsibility for keeping peace with one's relatives within the canonical degrees, because it was God's will.[19] However, her analysis is primarily confined to the Danish and Swedish laws, and does not include the concrete wergild regulations that were developed in Norway and Iceland. Therefore, it would seem appropriate to return once more to those very regulations, bearing the new set of questions in mind.

Analysis of Four Wergild Systems

Consequently, I shall now proceed by analyzing in more detail the wergild provisions and distribution of payments in four known systems.[20] They are:

---

18. Sørensen 2000:4-5, 73-77.
19. Sørensen 2000:73-74.
20. In contrast with kinship studies carried out on the basis of inheritance provisions, a study based on wergild regulations would necessarily have to be confined to *male*

1) The apparently "main wergild scale" of the *Gulathing's Law*.[21]

2) The regulation given in the *Frostathing's Law* in its edition from *c.* 1260, but which may reflect a revision from the first decades of the 13th century.[22]

3) The scale of payments found in the *"Baugatal"* of the Icelandic lawbook *Grágás*.[23]

---

relatives only, since the scales of payments only comprise kinsmen in various distances from the slayer or the slain.

21. In its preserved edition the Gulathing's Law book is nowadays considered to reflect the state of legislation in western Norway during the first half of the 13th century (Helle, Knut: *Gulatinget og Gulatingslova*, 2001.), but it bears the direct and explicit imprint of a revision undertaken on ecclesiastical initiative in the 1160s, when passages ascribed to *Magnus Erlingsson* (1161 - 1184) were incorporated in the text. Furthermore, it is also held to reflect an edition from the earlier part of the 12th century, of which something may go back to the time it was committed to writing, possibly in the middle of the 11th century (Norseng 1987, pp. 51-52; Helle 2001; Rindal, Magnus: "Dei norske mellomalderlovene: Alder, overlevering, utgåver," in: *Skriftlege kjelder til kunnskap om nordisk mellomalder* (ed.: M. Rindal), Noregs forskingsråd, KULTs skriftserie 38, Oslo 1995, pp. 17-20). Obviously, the law book in its latest exemplification may contain *several layers of regulations concerning wergild payments*. The supposedly "primary one" analyzed here is rendered in "Den ældre Gulathings-Lov" [G], chapters 222 - 252, printed in *Norges gamle Love* (NgL), vol. I (1846) pp. 75 - 82; cf. the translation into modern Norwegian by Robberstad, Knut: Gulatingslovi (*Norrøne bokverk* 33), Oslo 1969: 206 - 224.

22. For details of the dating and various presumed editions of the Frostathing's Law, see Taranger, Absalon: "De norske Folkelovbøker (før 1263)", in: *Tidsskrift for Retsvidenskap, ny Række V*, 1926, p. 183 - 211; *ny Række VII*, 1928, p. 2 - 68.; Knudsen, Trygve: "Frostatingsloven", in: *Kulturhistorisk leksikon for nordisk middelalder*, vol. 4, 1959, cols. 656 - 661; Translated into modern Norwegian by Hagland, Jan Ragnar & Sandnes, Jørn (eds.): Frostatingsloven, *Norrøne bokverk*, Oslo 1994, pp. IX-XI, XXX-XXXIII and Iversen, Tore: "Landskapslovene og kanonisk rett", in: A.Dybdahl & J.Sandnes (eds.): *Nordiske middelalderlover. Tekst og kontekst*, Senter for middelalderstudier, Skrifter nr. 5, Trondheim 1997, p. 82. The structure of Frostathing's Law in 16 sections is held to have been modelled after the *Compilatio prima*, assembled and completed by Bernard of Pavia in 1191. It is therefore assumed that a revision must have taken place after this date, possibly between 1200 and 1225. But later revisions, inspired by King Hákon Hákonarson as an effort to prepare realm-encompassing legislation, took place probably in the 1240s and certainly in 1260.

23. *Grágás, Grágás, Islændernes lovbog i fristatens tid (I)*, udgivet efter det kongelige Biblioteks Haandskrift og oversat af Vilhjálmur Finsen, for det nordiske Literatur-Samfund. Konungsbók, I a, Første Del, København 1852: 193 - 207; see *Grágás - Lagasafn íslenska þjóðveldisins*, ed. by G. Karlsson, Kr. Sveinsson & M. Árnason, Reykjavík 1997: 447 - 458, and 514.

4) The wergild scale appended at the end of the Gulathing's Lawbook, attributed to the royal judge ("lagmann") *Bjarni Márdarson* – known to have been active in 1198/99 and at a national assembly meeting in 1223.[24]

In particular, I shall assess the different wergild regulations in relation to the following five points:

a) The extent to which the systems display features of *bilaterality*.

b) More specifically: The relative positions allotted to *agnatic* (patrilineal) and *cognatic* kinsmen respectively.

c) Which system of computation of *genealogical distance* that is being implemented: the Roman or the Canonical?

d) *How far* - in genealogical distance from the slayer or the slain - *the payments extend*?

e) The feature of *reciprocity*; that is to say the grouping of relatives in pairs, related reciprocally to each other, around *Ego* (= the slain or the slayer): To what extent is this principle followed?

However, in order to keep the analysis within the scope of this paper, I have been compelled to exclude one category of relatives mentioned in the wergild regulations: the so-called *"increasers of fines"* or '*sakaukarar*'. This category includes relatives of a particular or exceptional status – if they at all exist – such as illegitimate sons (by thrall-women), half brothers, half brothers of fathers, stepfathers, stepsons and a few affinals ("in-laws"). If existing, various selections of these people were supposed to contribute with minor additions to the payments, thus "increasing" or "augmenting" them.[25]

The Gulathing's Law Book

In the first place, we observe a certain priority given to *the members of the patriline* vis-a-vis the cognates, notably in the fact that some patrilineal relatives are allotted a higher rank than they would otherwise have, following a strict calculation of distance from the slayer/deceased. At the top, the nearest agnates stand out for themselves, as responsible for and partaking in the *"baugr" payments*.[26] These agnates were responsible for these payments, both individually and collectively – *in solidum*. Payments should, for instance, go from brother of the slayer to brother of the deceased, and from male cousin to male cousin (father's brother's son), but

---

24. G, chapters 316 - 319, *NgL* I: 104 - 110; Robberstad 1969: 285 - 299.
25. See for instance G, chapters 236, 239; Ftl. VI, 21.
26. "Baugr" means literally "ring", in particular a ring of gold or silver used as means of payment in the Viking period /early Middle Ages. From this basis a more specific meaning evolved, namely payment, contribution fixed by law or regulations, thus also "fines", "compensatory payments". See "Glossarium" in *NgL* V, 1895.

if anyone of these did not exist, the slayer nevertheless had to pay the amount part stipulated on their part.

Further down along the scale, in the three groupings of so-called *"uppnámsmenn"* (that is: "men who shall collect payments from the slayer"), we observe that "father's brother" and "brother's son" are included in the first "uppnám", although they rank at the *third Roman degree* (2 steps up & 1 down) in the same way as cognates who follow in the next class. Instead of following a strict order according to computation of distance, they are here grouped in the first class, together with cognates being only *two steps away*. At the end of the list, two agnates being 5 steps way according to Roman computation ("father's brother's son" and the "son's son of father's brother") are in a similar way included in the group encompassing cognates only 4 steps away.

This seems to amount to a sort of *general principle*, which is also adopted in other sections of the Gulathing's Law, where the obligations of those relatives placed in the third canonical degree and onwards are expressed in more general terms. There, relatives of the male line at *one* particular step of distance are juxtaposed to relatives of the female line standing *one step closer* to the slayer/deceased.[27] All in all, these main regulations of the Gulathing's Law do seem to offer a sort of *balance between agnatic and cognatic kin*. The four categories of payment ("baugr" payments, plus 3 classes of 'uppnámsmenn') encompass 7(8) agnates and 10 cognates, of which one (FZS - 'father's sister's son') is a patrilateral relative.

The feature of *"reciprocal kinsmen"* does also stand out clearly, in the system of the Gulathing's Law. We notice that a series of relatives (10 out of 17 mentioned) are coupled and placed together, according to their reciprocal relationships around *Ego*. (That is to say: Person A relates to *Ego*, as *Ego* relates to person B.) This goes for the following pairs:

Father's brother (FB)	Brother's son (BS)
Mother's father (MF)	Daughter's son (DS)
Mother's brother (MB)	Sister's son (ZS)
Father's sister's son (FZS)	Mother's brother's son (MBS)
Mother's mother's brother (MMB)	Sister's daughter's son (ZDS)

It should however be noted, that payments are not at all confined to those contributions made by the slayer, to these categories of relatives, grouped in these three or four classes. Two other provisions of the Gulathing's Law stipulate payments stretching far beyond that. This is of particular interest

---

27. Cf. G 235, *NgL* I, p. 78, Robberstad 1969:214; see also the wergild regulative of Bjarni Márdarson, *NgL* I, pp. 104-110 and Robberstad 1969: 285ff.

for the discussion as to whether the compensatory obligations are assigned more narrowly to the slayer and his nearest kin, or if they draw upon a wider kindred.

In the first place, there are the so-called *"frendebøter"* or "fines of the relatives", which apparently come in addition to the contributions of the slayer (or his nearest kin). According to the regulations in chapters 225, 226 and 227 of the Gulathing's book[28], each and every of the 14-15 relatives mentioned in the three classes of 'uppnámsmenn', should receive payments from each and every one of the killer's 14-15 corresponding kinsmen. On top of it all, these 14-15 relatives of the deceased should also receive a payment from the *brother* of the killer. These provisions would produce a broad chart of payments extended between highly different categories of relatives, comprising in all a minimum of $14^2 + 14 = 210$ transactions.[29] One thing is certain, however: the implementation of such an encompassing system of payments has never been reported in any source that presumably reflects social practice – such as the sagas for instance – nor indeed anything like it. One is therefore led to believe that these regulations represent a construct, a subtlety of legalistic hair-splitting with the aim of drawing up a system that *should involve the largest number of people, in order to promote social peace*.

Furthermore, it should be noted that the Gulathing's Law also contains another provision, according to which the constructions are carried even further, to an extent beyond all practicality. It is chapter 235, which stipulates the obligations of relatives more distant than the ones incorporated in the three classes of "uppnámsmenn". Here the relatives are classified according to the principle of distance in general terms, something which in itself would indicate that it has been added at a later point of time. It starts with "the nearest patrilateral relative after the last 'uppnám'", and follows up with "second man", "third man" and so on – up to the extension of the *"thirteenth* man" – who by canonical standards is related to the deceased in the 8th (!) degree. Thus this extension of the scale surpasses even the most far-reaching computation of kinship according to canonical terms, something which clearly brings out its character as a construct. However, the amount of the fines to be paid shows a sharp break in value calculation when moving *from the sixth to seventh canonical degree*.[30] This would also suggest that the theoretical scheme originally had been limited to the actual extension of the *canonical marriage prohibition* – as

---

28. *NgL* I, pp. 76-77; Robberstad 1969: 209-211.
29. Or a maximum of $152 + 15 = 240$ transactions.
30. See G 235, Robberstad 1969:214, with further explanation p. 381. Up to and including the 6th canonical degree, 1 "ertog" (1/3 of a *mark*) is held equivalent with 10 "penninger" ("pence"); for the 7th and 8th degrees it is equal to 20 "penninger".

implemented in the Norwegian archdiocese[31] – and that a further construction had been appended at a later time.

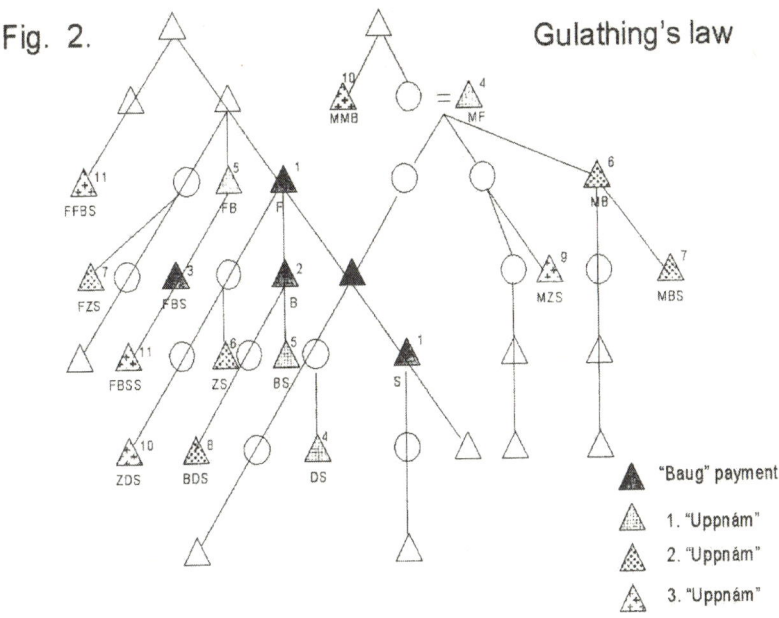

Fig. 2. Gulathing's law

The Frostathing's Law Book

Turning now to the Frostathing's Law,[32] we observe *a very clear-cut distinction between the members of the patriline, and the cognatic relatives*. In fact, all the agnatic relatives belonging to the patrilineal core, the "minimal ætt" in Vestergaard's terminology (– with one possible

---

31. At the inauguration of the Nidaros archdiocese in 1152/53, the papal legate *Nicholas Brekespear* (later pope Hadrian IV) had granted the Norwegian church province the privilege of practicing the marriage impediments up to and including the 6th canonical degree, and not the 7th as canon law prescribed at that time. Cf. responsum from pope Celestine III to Nikolas Arneson, bishop elect to Oslo, DN XVII, nr. 8; see also Robberstad, Knut: "Hadrians-løyvet i ekteskapsretten", in: [Norwegian] *Historisk Tidsskrift*, vol. 41, 1962-4, pp. 341 - 344.
32. The wergild scale of Frostathing's Law makes up Section VI of the edition that has been preserved as a paper copy of *Codex Resenianus*, lost in the fire of Copenhagen 1728. It is printed in *Norges gamle Love, vol. 1*, pp. 184 - 197, and in translation into modern Norwegian by Hagland & Sandnes 1994:98 - 119. However, a fragment of a presumably older wergild scale has also been preserved (NRA 1 C IV) and is printed in *NgL* II, pp. 520 - 521.

exception[33] –) have here been grouped together in the first class of payers, contributing to the *"baugr"* payment. They are called "vissingar", that is: "certain ones" – a designation which alludes to their compulsory obligation to take part in the payments made by the slayer, if they are alive. This class stands in opposition to the two following, comprising the so-called *"nevgilde"* payers, that is: those who pay individually, *per capita*. Both the *Great* and the *Little "nevgilde"* are exclusively made up by cognatic kinsmen. Thus, we observe a more consequent priority given to the patrilineal kinsmen than in the Gulathing's Law, where they were scattered over all the three "uppnám" classes, even if that law book also gave agnates priority before cognatic kinsmen in the same numerical distance from Ego (the slayer/deceased).

In this way the Frostathing's Law shows very few features of *bilaterality*. In fact, when scrutinizing the scale made up by all three classes, we notice a very consistent principle of ordering the relatives, which firstly distinguishes among patrilineal and cognatic relatives, and secondly combine the Roman and the Canonical way of computing genealogical distance. At the same time, each class is made to comprise exactly 7 persons. All the nearest patrilineal kinsmen are selected in the first class, and then the cognates are left to the first and second group of "nevgilde"-payers. The further division is then dictated by following a) the degrees of distance according to canonical rules, and b) by Roman or single-step computation (see table below). In this way, all the cognatic relatives selected for the "Great nevgilde" are 2 canonical degrees away from the slayer/deceased, and those paying the "Little nevgilde" are 3 degrees away. Within each class, however, they are specified according to single steps or Roman computation. This gives a neat ordering of the 3 x 7 kinsmen when looking at the distribution of wergild payers according to the Frostathing's Law (chapter VII):

		Order:	
		Canon. comp.:	*Roman comp.:*
1) 'Baug'-payers, "vissingar":	7 *agnatic* kinsmen	1	1-2
		2	3
		2-3	4-5
2) Great 'nevgilde'	7 *cognatic* kinsmen	2	2
		2	3
		2	4
3) Little 'nevgilde':	7 *cognatic* kinsmen	3	3
		3	4
		3	5

---

33. FFBS.

Regarding *reciprocity*, it should be observed that we meet exactly the same grouping of the cognatic relatives in *reciprocal pairs*, as we have encountered in the Gulathing's Law, though with one pair left out:

Father's brother (FB)	Brother's son (BS)
Mother's father (MF)	Daughter's son (DS)
Mother's brother (MB)	Sister's son (ZS)
Father's sister's son (FZS)	Mother's brother's son (MBS)

In the "little nevgilde" we also meet a few cognatic relatives which are not mentioned specifically in the Gulathing's Law:

Son's daughter's son (SDS)
Daughter's daughter's son (DDS)
Father's sister's daughter's son (FZDS)
Mother's brother's daughter's son (MBDS)
Mother's sister's daughter's son (MZDS)

The principle of *bilaterality* may thus be expressed to a limited degree within the group of the "little nevgilde" payers, but this aspect does not stand out with any regulating force for the list in its entirety. However, due to the selection of only cognatic relatives in the "nevgilde" categories, the net outcome is that 7 agnates and 14 cognates are implied in the specified payments, It should also be noted than *none of the cognatic relatives who should pay fines according to the "little nevgilde" are included in the group of enumerated inheritors*. Since the obligation to share in the ordinary payments is more extensively defined than the group of heirs given priority, one may well interpret this as a consciously applied device with the aim of *involving as many persons attached to other patrilines as possible*.[34]

However, we do not find such a comprehensive system of transactions between each and every member of the cognatic groups, as stipulated by the Gulathing's Law. Each cognatic relative of the slayer mentioned should pay his "nevgilde" fine individually to the corresponding cognate of the slain, and is not responsible for the other payments within the class of "nevgilde". Compared to Gulathing the system of the Frostathing's Law may be conceived as a restriction or confinement of a system that has been regarded as too comprehensive and complex. The introductory remark to the whole chapter dealing with wergild payments also points out that "*The Frostating book* (apparently a preceding, earlier version) *stipulates legal payment for each and everyone according to birth and rank, and not payments of the*

---

34. Gaunt, David: *Familjeliv i Norden*, Stockholm 1983, pp. 203 - 207; Sørensen 2000, pp. 71 - 72.

kind that are raised or pressed down, due to people who sit in the courts and make settlements." Nevertheless, the Frostathing regulations to include in the "nevgilde" scale of payments relatives whose participation must be considered quite unrealistic and therefore indicating a kind of theoretical construction. For instance, it is hard to imagine how "son's daughter's son" and "daughter's daughter's son" would be able to fulfil their obligations, even though they are included among the last payers of the "little nevgilde".

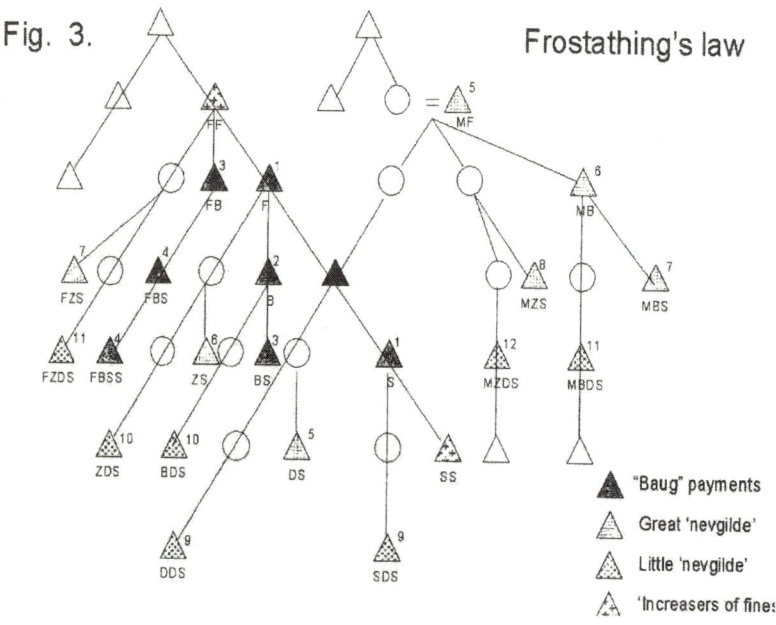

In the Frostathing's Law too, we encounter a kind of *"frendebøter"* or *"relatives' fines"* which involves more remote kinsmen than the "nevgilde"-men, stretching from 4th to 6th canonical degrees away from the deceased. The kinsmen within these degrees receive payments from both the "bauggildes"-men and the "nevgildes"-men. However, the system of "relatives' payments" is much more limited and does not encompass such comprehensive payments between all the members of the specified classes, as is seen in the Gulathing's Law. In general, the total amount of the payments also diminishes rapidly, when one moves out from the most central categories, as may be seen from the figure (histogram). The *"relatives' fines"* of the Frostathing's Law are of a considerably less amount than the ones paid in "baugr" or "nevgilde". The principle adopted for these payments is that a fixed, lesser amount at the outset (in all 5 1/3 øyre) is consequently partitioned in 3 and 2 fifths, giving the first three fifths to the men at one level and leaving the remaining two fifths to the next degree, whereupon the same kind of division is repeated. It is also worth noting that these *"relatives' fines"* do not extend farther than the 6th canonical degree, which is explicitly motivated with a reference to the canonical marriage prohibition: "Further out in the kin we do not give fines, due to the reason that at this point marriage is allowed and kinship is out. Considerate must the relationship be, between wergild and kinship." (Ftl. VII, 11.)

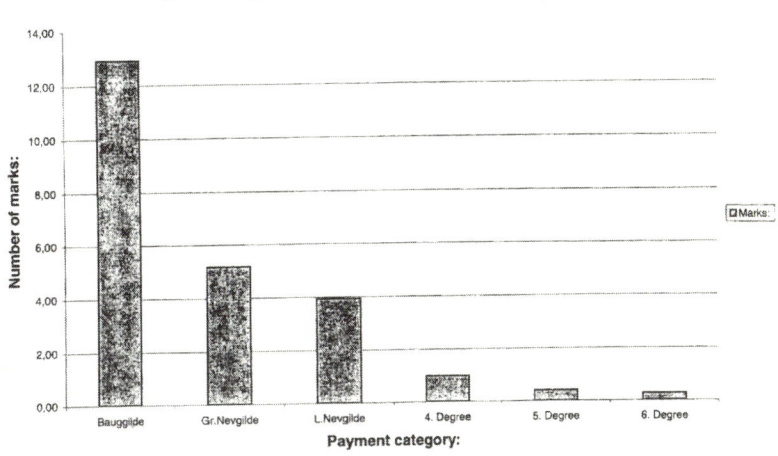

Fig. 4. Wergild payments according to Frostathing's law:

The "Baugatal" of the Icelandic Law-Book *Grágás*

In the *"Baugatal"*[35] section preserved in the Konungsbók manuscript of the Icelandic law-book *Grágás*, we are presented with a wergild scale where the principle of *reciprocity* is very pronounced. Here the coupling of reciprocal

---

35. Literally "baugatal" means "counting of the rings", i.e. rings of gold used for payment. The Icelandic law book Grágás contains two sections dealing with compensations and fines for manslaughter, *"Baugatal"* and *"Vígslóði"*. Their mutual relationship is unclear and debatable. Some scholars hold "Baugatal" to be the oldest one and reflecting the oldest provisions, while others see it as a later construction. Yet others maintain that it probably served as an appendix to Vígslóði. See Philpotts, Bertha S.: *Kindred and Clan in the Middle Ages and After. A Study in the Sociology of the Teutonic Races*, (Cambridge Archaeological and Ethnological Series), Cambridge 1913; Lárusson, Magnús Már: "Mansbot" (Island), in: *Kulturhistorisk leksikon for nordisk middelalder*, vol. 11, 1966, cols. 335 - 337; Ingvarsson, Lúðvik: "Straff" (Island), in: *Kulturhistorisk leksikon for nordisk middelalder*, vol.17, 1972, sp. 267-275; cf. Arnórsdóttir 1990, pp. 49-50.

male relatives on either side has been most consistently and systematically implemented, forming a system which is *fundamentally bilateral* in character.[36] In contrast with both the Norwegian provincial laws, even the "father's father" (FF) of Ego, and his reciprocal patrilineal kinsman, Ego's "son's son", have been included, and in a prominent place. Similar to the scales of the Gulathing and the Frostathing, the "Baugatal" also specifies as most prominent the paying of '*baugr*', but this payment is broken down into four sub-classes, each portioned out on two patrilateral and two matrilateral kinsmen, who are mutually defined by reciprocal relationships. After the first 'baugr', which is reserved for the nearest agnatic males (father, son and brother), the system moves upwards one step, and includes *the grandfathers on both sides*, as well as their reciprocal male relatives, that is "son's son" (SS) and "daughter's son" (DS). Then the system moves out laterally one step (– or two steps up and one step down, according to Roman computation –) and incorporates *both parents' brothers* on an equal footing, alongside with their reciprocally defined kinsmen, namely Ego's "brother's son" (BS) and "sister's son" (ZS). Finally, at the fourth and last of the specified "baugar", the system incorporate *all first cousins*, irrespective of whether they are parallel cousins ('broeðrungar', 'systrungar') or cross cousins ('systkinasynir'), and whether they are patrilineal or matrilineal.

Having finished with the 'baugar', the system goes on to define wider sets of male relatives on both sides, using a fine graduation based on counting steps upwards and downwards, similar to the Roman computation. All along the way, the classes of "cousins once removed" to a certain level are given priority before the next (even) level. These principles are then pursued on through to the *fourth cousins* or 'Þriðjubroeðrar', who are related to Ego (the slayer/the slain) in 5th canonical degree.

This seems to coincide with *the particular Icelandic adaptation of the canonical marriage prohibitions, as they were implemented before 1217*. With regard to the rules concerning consanguinity, the marriage sections of Grágás distinguished between various grades of incest, depending on the closeness measured in canonical degrees, and opening up for dispensations in some cases. Incest within the first three canonical degrees was regarded as a "great offence" ("frændsemisspell it meira") and was punished with the harshest form of outlawry ('skoggangr'). Incestuous relationships between the 3rd and 5th canonical degrees, called "frændsemisspell it minna" were punished with forced exile ('fjörbaugsgarð') – unless it could be proved that

---

36. This bilateral aspect has recently been analyzed by Nashat, Yasmin: *Slektskapsideologi i lov og saga - en analyse av slektskap og ideologi i Baugatal, Gudmund dyres saga og Tord kakales saga* (Mastergradsavhandling i nordisk vikingtids- og middelalderkultur), Universitetet i Oslo 2002, see especially pp. 17 - 21 and 79 - 82.

the relationship had been started unknowingly about the consanguineal connection.[37] Between the 5th and 7th canonical degrees, however, *marriages could under certain conditions be tolerated, and get dispensation.* In such cases the couple had to pay fines both to the church and the council of legislation ('logretta') at the Althing. For partners related in the 5th degree, the payments amounted to the so-called "capital tithe" ('hovudtiend') to the church, as well as a part thereof to the secular authorities.[38] This particular interpretation of the impediments following from consanguinity is usually held to be an arrangement from the days of Iceland's second bishop, *Gissur Ísleifsson* (1082-1118), residing at Skálholt. While relatively many cases of spouses related to each other in the 4th and 5th degrees are known from the 9th and 10th centuries, the majority of spouses having consanguineal connections after 1080 were supposedly related in the 5th and 6th degrees, and therefore covered by the option of dispensation.[39] By an amendment to Grágás, in the Icelandic annals dated to the time of Skálholt bishop *Magnús Gissurarson* (1216-1237), the forbidden consanguineal degrees were adapted to those promulgated by the

---

37. *Grágás, Islændernes lovbog i fristatens tid (I)*, udgivet efter det kongelige Bibliotheks Haandskrift og oversat af Vilhjálmur Finsen, for det nordiske Literatur-Samfund. *Konungsbók*, I a, Første Del, København 1852; I b, Anden Del, København 1852, Ib 30-31, 59-60, 236-237, II 181-182, 190, III 457; cf. *Grágás* 1997:111, 127 - 128, 134. - In a similar way relationships between people already bound together by affinal ties were considered incestuous (and a "great offence") if the ties were within two degrees (cousins). Breaks against affinity from the second and through to the fourth and fifth degrees (third cousins once removed) were defined as "minor offences".
38. *Grágás, Konungsbók*, I b, p. 30 - 31, as well as p. 60-61: "Ef frændsemi er með monnom byGiande *oc* nanare eN at siavnda m*a*nne, þa scal af þes þei*r*ra fe b*e*ra iii. m*e*rc*r* ilögretto er þat vill *e*igi fyrir raðom lata standa. Ef frændsemi er þar at .vi.ta m*a*nne oc at vii.da þa scal b*e*ra .iii. m*e*rc*r* ilögretto, eN þar m*e*rc*r* vi. *er* at vi.ta m*a*nne er hvartveGgia. EN ef frænds*e*mi er at .v.ta m*a*nne *oc* at .vi.ta þa scolo þav þa þó raða rað*om* sin*om* ef þar vilia. eN þav scolo g*e*ra tiund af fe si*n*o ena meire. enda s*c*al b*e*ra vi. m*e*rc*r* af því tiundar feno ilögrétto ef sva viNZ til. EN þoat tiund se miNe oc s*c*al þo b*e*ra vi. m*e*rc*r* ilögrétto *oc* s*c*al gialda .c. alna vaðmala fyrir þær .vi. m*e*rc*r* eN b*y*scop s*c*al raða fyrir þei*r*re tiund *er* v*m* er fra*m*. oc ef h*ann* gorir *e*igi tiund ena meire. þa varðar fiorbavgs Garð oc scal queðia til ix. bva aþi*n*gi a hue*r*r söc er vill." (Cf. Lárusson, Magnús Már: "Incest" (Island), in: *Kulturhistorisk leksikon for nordisk middelalder*, vol. 7, 1962, cols. 374 - 376 1962; Maurer, Konrad: Über Altnordische Kirchenverfassung und Eherecht, *Vorlesungen über Altnordische Rechtsgeschichte*, bd. II, Leipzig 1908, pp. 553ff.")
39. Hugason, Hjalti: Frumkristni og upphaf kirkju, *Kristni á Íslandi*, vol. I., Reykjavík 2000, p. 367.

Fourth Lateran Council in 1215.[40] The obligation of payments to the secular authorities was, however, to remain in force.[41]

In this way, Icelandic medieval law until 1217 operated with a *relative marriage prohibition defined at certain canonical degrees, which is unknown elsewhere in Nordic medieval law*. Provided that certain fines were paid, marriages were accepted from the 5th (parallel) canonical degree and onwards. This coincides neatly with the wergild scale of "Baugatal" which extends kinship until the very same degree. Thus, we can conclude that it is the Icelandic "Baugatal" which – among all the West-Nordic wergild systems – *most systematically brings forth the bilateral kinship system*. To be sure, a slight preference to the patrilineal kin can be observed, in that the paying and receiving of "baugar" were distributed with three fifths on the patrilineal kinsmen, and two fifths on the cognatic ones.[42] But in all, the wergild scale is structured by systematically shifting between the patrilateral and the matrilateral kinsmen. In this respect, the contrast is most striking with the Frostathing wergild scale, with its strict priority of the relevant agnatic kinsmen in the category of 'vissingar'. Thus, "Baugatal" and the wergild system of the Frostating's Law stand out as almost *diametrically defined opposites* at each end of a continuum, with the scale of the Gulathing placed somewhere in between, but pointing more in the direction of the Frostathing scale than to "Baugatal". It should be mentioned, though, that the "Baugatal" scale is not known to have been in practical use. In the Icelandic family sagas, for instance, no cases are documented as being solved in the ways "Baugatal" prescribes.[43]

---

40. See the amendment ('nymæli') to the "Betrothals Section", *Staðarhólsbók*, II, p. 157, *Grágás (II), efter det Arnamagnæanske Haandskrift Nr. 334 fol.*, *Staðarhólsbók*, København 1879 and *Grágás* 1997:110-11, as well as the amendment to the "Christianity section" of *Grágás, Konungsbók*, I a, p. 36 - 37; cf. *Grágás* 1997:34: "Það var nýmæli gert þá er Magnús Gissurarson var biskup orðinn að nú er lögskylt að fasta nætur þær átta er áður voru eigi lögskyldar. ... Það var annað nýmæli að jafna ætt skal byggja sifjar og frændsemi, að fimmta manni hvorttveggja þar sem hjúskaparráðum skal ráða, og skal þar er frændsemi er að fimmta manni gjalda hina meiri tiund. En þar er frændsemi er að fimmta manni og sétta skal gjalda hundrað álna. En þar er að sétta manni er hvorttveggja skal gjalda tiu aura, þá liggur ekki fégjald á þaðan frá þótt hjúskaparráðum sé ráðið". Cf. also the observations in *Annales regii* and *Skálholt annals* for the year 1217: "Færð frændsemi ok omegð i lavgum", Storm 1888: 125, 184. Moreover: Maurer II, 1908:552pp.; Hjalti Hugason 2000:130.
41. Maurer II, 1908:554; Robberstad 1962:343.
42. The share of the fines paid/received by patrilineal kin was called 'bauggildi', and the share paid/received by cognatic kin 'nefgildi'. Magnús Már Lárusson ("Mannsbot", 1966) has interpreted this as a relic of a presumably older arrangement, whereby only patrilineal kinsmen took part in the compensation payments.
43. Philpotts 1913, pp. 22, 37.

In general, this seems to agree well with the picture drawn up by *Vestergaard* and other scholars who have studied the western Nordic kinship systems (Hastrup, Arnórsdóttir), whereby it is ascertained that it is the Norwegian provincial laws that define the core of the "ætt" most sharply, by delineating a 3-generational agnatic group, structured in relation to Ego's "father's father". Even though the fundamentally bilateral order is highly recognizable in the kinship systems of both Norway and Iceland, the bilateral features appear most outspoken and consequently implemented in the latter case. One may conjecture that this characteristic has something to do with the nature of the settlement process – where old kinship ties to Norway were severed, and where a new settler situation may have accentuated the need for forming alliances in several directions, making use of both agnatic and cognatic ties, as tactical and strategic purposes brought them forward.[44]

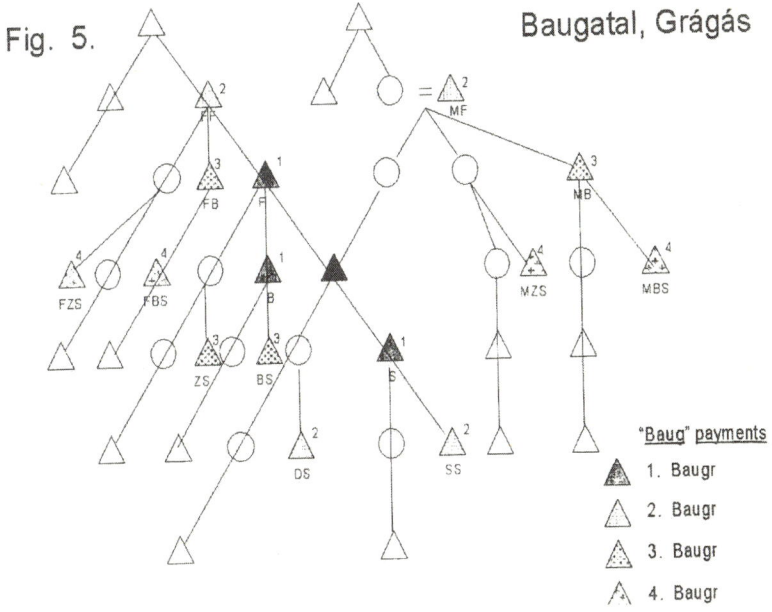

Fig. 5. Baugatal, Grágás

That is not to deny that a strengthening of the patrilineal ties could not take place in Iceland too, in certain periods: as for instance during the sharpened conflicts between the greater families of the late 12th and early 13th

---

44. Philpotts 1913, p. 35; similar viewpoints in Byock, Jesse L.: *Medieval Iceland: Society, Sagas, and Power*, Berkeley 1988, pp. 127 - 128, although he considers "Baugatal" as having a "distinct patrilineal emphasis".

centuries, which are depicted i.e. in the Sturlunga saga. This goes also – and not least – for ideological expressions ascribing great status to the patriline.

Bjarni Márdarson's Wergild Scale for the Gulathing

Turning lastly to the wergild scale attributed to *the "lagmann"* (royal judge) *Bjarni Márdarson* and appended at the end of the Gulathing's Law book, we cannot observe any strict structuring principle similar to the ones dominating the other scales. Rather, the scale may be conceived as a compromise between various contending principles. It contains some of the features we observed in the main wergild regulation of the Gulathing's Law, as well as some similar to the Frostathing scale. Until the third canonical degree, the priority of the relatives does not follow any strict order of genealogical distance either. However, a certain priority given to agnatic kinsmen can be observed, similar to the other Norwegian laws.

The scale can best be analyzed as being structured in three groups, although it does not in itself contain any classes or sub-categories as "baug"-payers, "uppnáms"-men or "nevgildes"-men. Among the first 4-5 payers we find the nearest agnatic kin, within two degrees from Ego. This group is defined more widely than the "baugr" payers in the Gulathing's Law's main scale, but more restricted than the group of "vissingar" in Frostathing's Law. The second group, comprising the next 6 categories of payers, contains both cognatic and agnatic kinsmen until three degrees from Ego, and partly organized in *reciprocal pairs*. A peculiar feature of this group is that the "son's son of father's brother" (FBSS) and "brother's son of father's father" (FFBS) – those marginal, overlapping members of the "minimal ætt" according to Vestergaard – appear in between two sets of cognatic relatives. This may seem like an innovative compromise, as these two agnatic relatives are given low priority and included only in the "third uppnám" in the main scale of Gulathing, while one of them (FBSS) is among the highest ranking in Frostathing's Law. At the time, the inclusion of these two represents a preference of agnatic kin before cognatic, since they – being 5 degrees away from Ego according to Roman computation – precede cognatic kinsmen who are 4 degrees distant.

This preference of the agnatic kin is also manifest in the regulations of the last group of payers, who take up a position somewhat similar to the "relatives' fines" ("frendebøter") of the Gulathing and the Frostathing. This class encompasses both agnatic and cognatic kinsmen from the third canonical degree and onwards, but agnatic relatives of one definite degree are always juxtapositioned with cognatic relatives of one lesser degree. However, there are no traces of the comprehensive transaction system between cognatic kinsmen that characterized the main wergild scale of the Gulathing's Law.

All in all, the wergild scale attributed to Bjarni Márdarson may be conceived as a combination and adaptation of certain features from both the Frostathing and former Gulathing systems. In particular in relation to the main Gulathing scale, it must be viewed as a necessary simplification and limitation. It is worth noting, though, that the obligations for paying extend just as far out as in these two other scales, viz. to the 6th canonical degree. No trace of the revision of the consanguinal marriage prohibition that was promulgated by the Fourth Lateran Council can be seen here either. As Bjarni Márdarson is mentioned both in connection with the opposition to King Sverrir in 1198/99 and as participant in a national assembly meeting in 1223, his term of office must have covered the time when the new, revised canonical regulations were announced. One obvious conclusion is therefore that he must have edited it before 1215, possibly with the regulation of the Frostathing's Law as a model in some respects. The relative dating of the two is however subject to disagreement. P.A. Munch maintained that Bjarni Márdarson's scale was the younger of the two, while Konrad Maurer held it was the older one, and A. Taranger that they dated from the same time.[45]

Conclusions

1) All the four scales of penalties show a clear affinity to the extension of consanguineal kinship as defined by canon law through the marriage prohibition regulations – *as they were before the Fourth Lateran Council of 1215*. The wergild lists of both the Frostathing and the Gulathing's Law books, as well as the regulation ascribed to Bjarni Márdarson, relate in one way or another to *a distinction by the 6th canonical degree*, which was the delimitation for Norway, according to the particular privilege granted in connection with the establishment of the Norwegian archdiocese in 1152/53. Some parts of the payment scale in the Gulathing's Law relate to this indirectly, and the gradation of Bjarni Márdarson simply stops at the 6th degree. The Frostathing's Law refers explicitly to the end of kinship, and the possibility of marriage at this degree of kinship.

The wergild scale of "Baugatal", for its part, relates to the particular adaptation of the marriage impediments in Iceland prior to 1217. Although the general canonical impediments until the 7th degree were upheld, marriages within the 5th - 7th canonical degrees could get dispensation and become accepted on the condition that fines were paid to the church and the secular legislative council at the Althing.

---

45. Robberstad 1969:401-402.

The particular formulation of the Norwegian wergild regulations - in their preserved shape – must therefore have taken place sometime between the establishment of the Norwegian church province in 1152/53 and the revision of the incest prohibitions for marriage following the Fourth Lateran Council. Correspondingly, the framework of the wergild scale in "Baugatal" must have been laid down before 1217, when the revision was promulgated in Iceland – possibly in the time of the bishop Gissur Ísleifsson, as some scholars argue. In both cases, the understanding of how far kinship solidarity extends – or should extend – seems to be heavily influenced by the ecclesiastical concept.

2) All the scales of payments show traits of *construction*, in that they present a rather theoretical, extensive framework of fines, of which some parts seem rather unrealistic. In particular this goes for the "payments between relatives" ("frendebøter") according to the main scale of the Gulathing's Law book, where the objective clearly is to involve the greatest possible number of people. The use of more general, abstract terms in describing kinship more distant than three degrees also seems to indicate the influence of learned or ecclesiastical circles. This is also true for the Icelandic "Baugatal". The Frostathing's Law, for its part, offers a more restricted, confined definition of the sum of payments that the relatives should be involved in, but even these regulations contain some rather unrealistic features – in particular when dealing with the cognatic relatives involved in the "little nevgilde".

3) All four scales also demonstrate *a deliberate linking of the cognatic relatives in reciprocal pairs, around 'Ego'*. This is a striking feature, not reflected in any of the other Nordic laws as far as I am aware. It may seem difficult to draw any specific conclusions about the background or reasons for this practice. One guess might be that it plainly served as *a mnemotechnical device*; when one kinsman was enumerated in the scale of payments, it followed automatically that his reciprocal relative was remembered as well. However, it seems to be attached to *the gradual system* of calculating kinship distance as such, as this was the underlying principle of both inheritance laws and wergild scales in the western Nordic laws. And it appears as a strict way of defining *a "cognatic descent group"*,[46] breaking fundamentally with the parentela principle. If one were to seek out elements of the Nordic kinship concept that might be characterized as domestic or autochthonous, one might venture this peculiar feature as an option.

4) Though all four scales of payments encompass a combination of agnatic and cognatic male relatives, it is the Icelandic "Baugatal" which shows the most consequential and systematic application of *bilaterality*. In the Norwegian laws, preference is generally given to the patrilineal

---

46. Hastrup 1985, p. 101; cf. Hamre: "Ætt", 1976.

kinsmen, and this is most strikingly and consistently carried out in the Frostathing's Law, where the agnatic, three-generational group has been completely separated from the cognatic kinsmen. Thus, in this respect "Baugatal" and the wergild system of Frostathing make up opposites, each representing an extreme end of a continuum, with the scales of the Gulathing and Bjarni Márdarson's amendment placed somewhere in between.

It is generally held that the Norwegian provincial laws underwent great revisions during the latter half of the 12th century, in particular concerning the so-called "Christianity sections" of the law books. New provisions about matrimonial practice and sexual offences were introduced, inspired by canon law regulations of the time, but new measures concerning legal proceedings may also have been introduced.[47] The so-called "*Magnus text*"of the Gulathing's Law book – provisions attributed to the reign of *Magnus Erlingsson* (r. 1161-1184) – is one example. But the Frostathing's Law book too may have received important modifications and amendments due to such a revision inspired by Archbishop *Eysteinn Erlendsson* (1161-1188), even though he is supposed to have edited a separate version of the "Christianity law", called "*Gullfjær*" ("Golden feather").[48] Concluding from the evidence presented in this article, one may well surmise that these revisions also had a great impact on *the concept of kinship* as it was defined in *the wergild sections* of the laws.

In the shape it has been handed down, the Frostathing's Law book is a product of King *Hákon Hákonarson*'s efforts to modernize legislation, explicitly dated to 1260. But it is also generally considered to reflect earlier revisions, by some scholars dated to the 1240s,[49] and by others to the first two decades of the century.[50] While we have seen that the wergild scale of the Frostathing's Law does not reflect the revised version of the marriage prohibitions from 1215, other parts of the law book do, as for instance the sections dealing with "odal right". One therefore supposes that the law book has undergone successive revisions and modifications over a longer period. At the same time, a fragment of a presumably older wergild scale is preserved in a separate manuscript.[51] A probable hypothesis might therefore be that the fully preserved wergild scale of the Frostathing's Law represents a revision carried out during the first decades of the 13th century, with a view to constricting the extension of the relevant kin group and to reducing

---

47. Gunnes, Erik: "Erkebiskop Øystein og Frostatingsloven", in: [Norwegian] *Historisk Tidsskrift*, vol. 53, 1974 - 2, pp. 109 - 121; cf. Taranger 1928.
48. Gunnes 1974; Norseng 1987, p. 52; Hagland and Sandnes 1994:X.
49. Hagland & Sandnes 1994:XXX.
50. Knudsen: *Frostatingsloven*, 1959.
51. NRA 1 C IV, printed in *NgL* II: 520 - 521.

their obligations somewhat, compared to an older, more comprehensive gradation. If this was the case, the wergild scale of the Frostathing will stand out as a parallel to Bjarni Márdarson's regulation for the Gulathing, brought about by the same motives.

The Concept of Kinship

Appendices

Table 1. The Gulathing law book:

	Patrilineal rel.:		Cognatic rel.:		Genealogical distance from Ego: Roman comput.: Canonical comput.:	
Main 'baug':	S (1d)	F (1u)			1	1
Brother's 'baug':	B (1u1d)				2	1
Father's brother's son's 'baug':	FBS (2u2d)				4	2
1. 'uppnám':			MF (2u)	DS (2d)	2	2
	FB (2u1d)	BS (1u2d)			3	2
2. 'uppnám':			MB (2u1d)	ZS (1u2d)	3	2
	FBS (2u2d)		FZS (2u2d)	MBS (2u2d)	4	2
			BDS (1u3d)		4	3
3. 'uppnám':			MZS (2u2d)		4	2
			MMB (3u1d)	ZDS (1u3d)	4	3
	FFBS (3u2d)	FBSS (2u3d)			5	3

Table 2. The Frostathing law book:

	Patrilineal rel.:		Cognatic rel.:		Genealogical distance from Ego: Roman comput.: Canonical comput.:	
'Bauggilde':	F (1u)	S (1d)			1	1
	B (1u1n)				2	1
	FB (2u1d)	BS (1u2d)			3	2
	FBS (2u2d)	FBSS (2u3d)			4-5	2-3
The Great 'Nevgilde':			MF (2u)	DS (2d)	2	2
			MB (2u1d)	ZS (1u2d)	3	2
			FZS (2u2d)	MBS (2u2d)	4	2
			MZS (2u2d)		4	2
The Little 'Nevgilde':			SDS (3d)	DDS (3d)	3	3
			BDS (1u3d)	ZDS (1u3d)	4	3
			FZDS (2u3d)	MBDS (2u3d)	5	3
			MZDS (2u3d)		5	3

Table 3. 'Baugatal', Grágás:

	Patrilateral rel.:			Matrilateral rel.:		Genealogical distance from Ego: Roman comput.: Canonical comput.:	
'Bauggilde':							
1. baug:	F (1u)	S (1d)	B (1u1d)			1-2	1
2. baug:	FF (2u)	SS (2d)		MF (2u)	DS (2d)	2	2
3. baug:	FB (2u1d)	BS (1u2d)		MB (2u1d)	ZS (1u2d)	3	2
4. baug:	FBS (2u2d)	FZS (2u2d)		MZS (2u2d)	MBS (2u2d)	4	2

Payments following the 'baugar':

1. Male relatives (both patrilineal and cognatic, more distant than cousins (father's brother's sons); related by 2. and 3 degree (2u3d)
Ex.: FBSS, FBDS, FZDS, FZSS, MBSS, MBDS, MZSS, MZDS — 5 — 3

2. Second cousins ('Næstabroeðrar') (3u3d) — 6 — 3

3. Second cousins once removed (3u4d) — 7 — 4

4. Third cousins ('Annarabroeðrar') (4u4d) — 8 — 4

5. Third cousins once removed (4u5d) — 9 — 5

6. Fourth cousins ('ridjubroeðrar') (5u5d) — 10 — 5

Table 4. Bjarni Márdarson's wergild regulative:

Patrilineal rel.:		Cognatic rel.:		Genealog. dist.from Ego: Roman comput.: Canonical comp.	
S (1d)				1	1
B (1u1d)				2	1
FB (2u1d)				3	2
F (1u)				1	1
		MF (2u)	DS (2d)	2	2
		MB (2u1d)	ZS (1u2d)	3	2
FBSS (2u3d)	FFBS (3u2d)			5	3
		FZS (2u2d)	MBS (2u2d)	4	2
		BDS (1u3d)		4	3
FBSS ?					
		FBDS (2u3d) FZDS (2u3d) MBDS (2n3d)		5	3
"4th man in the male line" (4u4d)		"3rd man in the female line" (3u3d)		6-8	3-4
"5th man in the male line" (5u5d)		"4th man in the female line" (4u4d)		8-10	4-5
"6th man in the male line" (6u6d)		"5th man in the female line" (5u5d)		10-12	5-6
		"6th man in the female line" (6u6d)		12	6

ON ECCLESIASTICAL JURISDICTION AND THE RECEPTION OF CANON LAW IN THE SWEDISH PROVINCIAL LAWS

Mia Korpiola

Introduction

When discussing the dimensions of ecclesiastical jurisdiction and canon law in medieval Sweden, we are undoubtedly dealing with the most international (perhaps even supranational) field of law. Therefore, the preliminary assumption must be that canon law was implemented as such, with few regional variations. Still, considering that the Catholic church had been established effectively in Sweden only from about 1100,[1] Christianity was in the country – and especially in its eastern part, Finland – a fairly "new plantation" (*nouella plantacio*).[2] The archiepiscopal see of Uppsala was founded in 1164. The council of Skänninge of 1248, attended by the papal legate William of Sabina, arranged the Church in Sweden in accordance with the requirements of canon law. This council has been

---

1. The Christianization of Sweden has been divided into three chronological periods: first, the infiltration period since the Great Migrations, second, the missionary period from 829–830 or Ansgar's first visit to Birka, a trading centre on an island in the lake Mälaren, not very far from modern Stockholm. Thirdly, the establishing period from about 1100 depending on the region in question. The archbishopric of Lund was established in the Danish province of Scania (Skåne) in 1104 as the centre of the new faith in Scandinavia. The Christianization process was concluded in Sweden around 1200, Anne-Sofie Gräslund: "Religionsskiftet i Norden, Kyrka – samhälle – stat. Från kristnande till etablerad kyrka", ed. Göran Dahlbäck. *Historiallinen Arkisto* 110:3 (1997), Helsinki, pp. 11–13.
2. *Registrum Ecclesiae Aboensis eller Åbo Domkyrkas Svartbok*. National Archives of Finland. Jyväskylä 1996, hereafter REA, docs. 7 and 9, pp. 4–6.

interpreted as a sign that Sweden had truly become a part of Catholic Europe.[3]

Yet, we are reminded that the medieval Church was neither a single, uniform, or monolithic institution, nor was canon law completely homogeneous. There was also space for regional variation. For example, regarding canon law of marriage, it has been assessed that "[w]here no dogmatic issue was involved, the church's law of marriage could be flexible and sensitive to differences in custom."[4] Canon law acknowledged custom (*consuetudo*) as a legal source on certain conditions. The legal custom could not be inconsistent with the Christian faith, natural law, truth or reason. Furthermore, for custom to attain this position as a legal source, it had to remain unchallenged, recognized and tolerated by those who had the authority to abrogate it. Moreover, it had to be generally accepted in the region.[5] Thus, some heterogeneity and variation between universal canon law and local law or custom was tolerated.[6] The question of regional variation regarding Sweden has hitherto been raised in some studies. This article aims at contributing to this discussion by raising some comparative points regarding the ecclesiastical jurisdiction in medieval Sweden.

For this essay I have gone through most of the provincial laws of medieval Sweden in their translation into present-day Swedish.[7] My aim is to assess, on one hand, how the jurisdiction of the church was generally defined and what the scope of ecclesiastical jurisdiction was. I will focus more closely on some aspects in which the sources reveal interaction between Church and society. On the other hand, I will also raise some issues

---

3. Ljungfors, Åke 1950: "Mötet i Skänninge 1248", *Kyrkohistorisk Årsskrift* 50 (1950), p. 5; Gräslund 1997, pp. 12–13; Skovgaard-Petersen, Inge: "Kirkens etablering", Kyrka - samhälle - stat. Från kristnande till etablerad kyrka, ed. Göran Dahlbäck. *Historiallinen Arkisto* 110:3 (1997), pp. 62–63; Inger, Göran 1961: *Das kirchliche Visitationsinstitut im mittelalterlichen Schweden*. Bibliotheca theologiae practicae, 11. CWK Gleerup, Lund, pp. 244–251.
4. Brundage, James A. 1995: *Medieval Canon Law*. Longman, London – New York, p. 86; D'Avray, David 1998: "Marriage ceremonies and the church in Italy after 1215", *Marriage in Italy, 1300-1650*, eds. Trevor Dean and K.J. P. Lowe. Cambridge University Press, Cambridge, p. 115.
5. Brundage 1995, pp. 158–159.
6. Helmholz, R. H. 1994: *Roman canon law in Reformation England*. Cambridge University Press, Cambridge, pp. 11–12.
7. For this essay, I have used the provincial laws of Eastern and Western Gothia, Södermanland, Uppland, Västmannaland, Dalarna and Hälsingland and the chapter on the church of the law of Småland – all in the versions edited by Holmbäck and Wessén (*Svenska landskapslagar I–V*, hereafter SLL. Eds. and trans. Åke Holmbäck and Elias Wessén, 1933–1946. Hugo Gebers förlag, Uppsala). However, I have omitted the provincial law of Gotland and the Bjärköa law for the town of Stockholm.

in the provincial laws relating to the influence of canon law and its reception in Swedish medieval society. My intention is also to shed some light on the theory proposed by the Swedish Elsa Sjöholm that the provincial laws were produced by a legislative policy. According to Sjöholm, the provincial laws were not a result of independent development towards greater uniformity, but rather a product of conscious and deliberate reception lead by the archbishop of Lund as the primate of Sweden. Sjöholm's theory does allow for some variation in the contents of the law, which can be explained with the diverging position of the bishops in their dioceses *vis-à-vis* the other political players: king, magnates and people.[8] The question of ecclesiastical jurisdiction would seem an excellent means of testing the theory. If there was such a predetermined legislative policy lead by the Church, one would suppose that the ecclesiastical jurisdictional boundaries would have been drawn quite uniformly. But, before going into the contents of the various Swedish provincial laws, first a few words on the laws themselves.

The Swedish Provincial Laws

The provincial laws represent the oldest layer of laws in Sweden. As their names indicate, each of them was in force in a province of its own. Two nationwide laws were compiled in the mid-fourteenth century in the reign of King Magnus Eriksson (r. 1319–1364), one for towns (King Magnus Eriksson's Town Law) and another for the countryside (King Magnus Eriksson's Law of the Realm), the latter being updated in 1442 (King Christopher's Law of the Realm). Despite this, the provincial laws remained at least nominally valid legal sources until the Swedish Code of 1734.

The exact dating of each surviving manuscript is a somewhat disputed matter between philologists and palaeographers. For my purposes, however, it suffices to state that their oldest existing versions date mainly from around 1280 up to the 1350s.[9] Most of these existing laws are known in their entirety. Still, the law of Småland (known also as the law of Tiohärad), mentioned in a mid-fourteenth-century list of books owned by King Magnus

---

8. Sjöholm, Elsa 1988: *Sveriges medeltidslagar. Europeisk rättstradition i politisk omvandling*. Rättshistoriskt bibliotek, 41. Skrifter utgivna av Institutet för rättshistorisk forskning grundat av Gustav och Carin Olin, Lund, esp. pp. 15–16, 50–51, 236–237, 250–251.
9. For a thorough discussion of the trends of dating and interpreting the older Nordic medieval laws, see Per Norseng, "Law Codes as a Source for Nordic History in the Early Middle Ages", *Scandinavian Journal of History* 16:3 (1991), for the dating of the Swedish provincial laws, see esp. pp. 146–147.

Eriksson, is only known through its chapter on the church (*kyrkobalk*).[10] The character of these provincial laws is generally thought to vary: some of them, like the laws of Uppland and Södermanland, were apparently compiled by a special commission of local judges. The former compilation was approved by King Birger Magnusson (r. 1290–1318) in 1296, the latter by King Magnus Eriksson in 1327. Certain other law books were apparently of a private nature, belonging to individual judges. A distinction is usually made between the provincial laws of Southern Sweden, the Göta laws, and those of Central Sweden, the Svea laws.[11]

The *communis opinio* considers the Swedish provincial laws a compromise between several interested parties: the king, the secular and ecclesiastical magnates, and the people.[12] In the same way, bishops and the people of their dioceses could reach an agreement regarding various financial concerns related to the bishop, parish priests and parishioners. An example of this is the settlement between the bishop of Strängnäs and the people of the diocese made on 26th October 1325 and incorporated in the revised provincial law.[13] These agreements were evidently perceived as reciprocal and binding for both parties.[14] Each of these laws is divided into chapters (*balkar*) according to their topic. The extent of ecclesiastical jurisdiction was regulated mainly in the chapter on the church. Yet in a broader perspective the chapters on homicide, matrimony, procedure, inheritance, and heinous crime also deal with many matters pertaining to ecclesiastical jurisdiction and norms and they have to be culled from all over the text.

The contents of Swedish provincial laws are clearly a mixture of older elements and new legislation. To accept this, one needs not take literally, for example, the claim of the foreword (*praefatio*) of the law of Uppland that parts of the law date from an unspecified pagan past and the lawgiver Viger the Wise. Moreover, it is also evident that Christian elements –

---

10. The law of Småland had, therefore, been written down before 1340, when the king was said to own a "*legisterium smalenzt*", *Diplomatarium Suecanum* (hereafter DS) IV, doc. 3484, p. 710.
11. Norseng 1991, p. 150.
12. Sjöholm 1988, pp. 21–24, 244–249. See also Gabriela Bjarne Larsson, *Stadgelagstiftning i senmedeltidens Sverige*. Rättshistoriskt bibliotek, 51. Skrifter utgivna av Institutet för rättshistorisk forskning grundat av Gustav och Karin Olin, Lund, 1994, pp. 9–12.
13. Inledning, SLL III, pp. xv–xvii; Åqvist, Gösta 1989: *Kungen och rätten. Studien till uppkomsten och den tidigare utvecklingen av kungens lagstiftningsmakt och domrätt under medeltiden*. Rättshistoriskt bibliotek, Vol. 43. Skrifter utgivna av Institutet för rättshistorisk forskning grundat av Gustav och Karin Olin, Lund, p. 120.
14. For the perception of reciprocity see also Inledning, SLL IV, pp. xxxix–xxxx.

kristnu ræt ok kirkiu laghum – had been added to the beginning of the law, its chapter on the church. To me, there would seem no reason to doubt the allegation of the foreword that the law commission included old elements in the revised law, but excluded parts considered unnecessary or unfair.[15] The provincial laws combine old and new elements, secular and ecclesiastical interests, and are thus a synthesis of these aspects.[16]

Even after King Magnus Eriksson's Law of the Realm had started to be applied in various regions, especially the chapters on the church of the provincial laws continued to be in daily use. Namely, the Church did not see eye to eye with the law commission comprising of royal judges (*legiferis*). In 1347, several canons as representatives of almost all of the Swedish dioceses, having orally remonstrated a couple of weeks earlier, signed a common protest against the "bettering and ameliorating" of the laws as far as they were against canon law or the liberties, statutes and privileges of the Church.[17] It has long been assumed, therefore, that the chapters on the church were omitted from national royal laws because the secular and ecclesiastical authorities did not manage to reach a compromise that would have satisfied both parties.[18] Because of this omission, the manuscript copies of the Law of the Realm and the Town Law came to include the chapter on the church of some of the provincial laws. The chapter on the church of the provincial law of Uppland came to be the most influential in the whole country: almost three of four copies of the medieval royal laws contain its chapter on the church. One of the reasons for this may be that *praepositus* Andreas Andreae And of Uppsala (d. 1317) was sitting in the commission compiling the law. Thereby it had received the indirect authorization of the archiepiscopal see.[19]

In comparison with Danish law, the laws of Scania (Skåne) and Jutland (Jylland) for example, it is obvious that the Danish and Swedish provincial laws were built on quite a different logic as far as ecclesiastical jurisdiction goes. The most notable difference between the two is the practically complete omission of references to ecclesiastical causes in Danish secular

---

15. UL, Förord, p. 7.
16. See also Norseng 1991, pp. 164–165.
17. *Diplomatarium Suecanum* (hereafter cited as DS). Different editors. Kungl. vitterhets historie och antikvitetsakademien och Riksarkivet, Stockholm, 1829–ongoing. DS V, doc. 4148, pp. 643–644.
18. Nataniel Beckman 1917: *Studier i outgivna fornsvenska handskrifter*. Samlingar af Svenska Fornskrift-sällskapet, 151. Stockholm, p. 13; Inger 1961, pp. 201–203.
19. UL, Konung Birger Magnussons stadfästelsebrev, pp. 5–6; Beckman 1917, pp. 14–15.

laws.[20] In contrast to the Danish silence, causes pertaining to ecclesiastical jurisdiction appeared in various parts of the Swedish provincial laws in addition to the chapters on the church. Yet, in Denmark, the relationship between Church and people was apparently regulated by the provincial Church laws. It has been assumed, for example, that the near-identical church laws of Scania and Seeland (Sjælland) were issued in 1171 through an agreement between Archbishop Eskil of Lund and Bishop Absalon. These Danish church laws are shorter and less detailed than the Swedish chapters on the church of the provincial laws.[21]

The laws of Jutland and Scania do not attempt to specify the ecclesiastical causes even to the extent that some of the Swedish provincial laws do. Yet, it has been assessed that episcopal jurisdiction in Sweden was more limited than in Norway and especially in Denmark, where the Law of Jutland gave the bishops extensive powers.[22] Let us turn our attention, therefore, to precisely this question, namely, the defining of ecclesiastical jurisdiction in Swedish provincial laws.

The Boundaries of Ecclesiastical Jurisdiction in Sweden at the Time of the Provincial Laws

The Catholic Church had very extensive jurisdictional claims based on various criteria. Some were based on the identity of the persons appearing in courts (*privilegium fori*): all clerics naturally belonged to this group, but crusaders, travellers, pilgrims, widows, orphans, and other *miserabiles personae* could equally claim the protection of the Church. More frequently, however, the jurisdictional claim depended on the subject of the case. The Church had labelled some causes as spiritual by nature (*causae spirituales*), for example, matrimony, ecclesiastical offices and benefices. Related to these were the *causae spirituales annexae*: namely, cases related to betrothal, affiliation, matrimonial property, patronage, tithes, wills, funerals, inheritances, oaths or vows. The Church also claimed that all sins fell under its jurisdiction precisely because of the sinfulness (*ratione peccati*), although this came very close to insisting that all crimes pertained to ecclesiastical courts. The Church conceded that some crimes were mixed (*delicta mixta*), belonging both to ecclesiastical and secular courts depending on where the case was first initiated, for example, blasphemy,

---

20. The law of Scania contains some references to ecclesiastical jurisdiction, see, e.g. SkL, Om jordatvister, 67, 69–70, 82, pp. 37, 42 and *e contrario*, SkL, Om dråp och sår, 102, 108, pp. 60–61.
21. Inledning, SLL IV, pp. xxxiv–xxxvi; Norseng 1991, p. 150
22. Sjöholm 1988, pp. 213–219.

forgery, homicide, theft, robbery and sodomy. It counted many other crimes, however, as ecclesiastical (*crimina ecclesiastica*): perjury and breach of an oath, apostasy, heresy, sacrilege, simony, adultery, incest, bigamy and fornication.[23]

It is well-know that the boundaries between ecclesiastical and secular jurisdictions were to some extent fluid during the Middle Ages: there was competition between the courts and variations both regarding both time and place even in the same region.[24] Moreover, the extent of the ecclesiastical *vis-à-vis* secular jurisdiction was never quite clearly or uniformly defined in medieval Sweden. It has been estimated that the Church countered much less opposition in its attempt to get new Church-related criminalization, like idolatry and heresy, certain sexual crimes and matrimonial cases, under its jurisdiction. This also applied to ecclesiastical discipline, while the transfer of "traditional" crimes to ecclesiastical jurisdiction was much harder.[25]

The oldest mention of ecclesiastical causes comes from King Erik Eriksson (r. 1222–1229, 1234–1250) who confirmed the late King Johan Sverkersson's (r. 1216–1222) privileges to the bishop of Skara that adultery, perjury and other causes that were against ecclesiastical law or religion pertained to the bishop by special liberty.[26] The 1279 privilege granted by the Swedish king Magnus Birgersson Ladulås (r. 1275–1290), who had come to the throne by toppling his brother and who thus rewarded the Church for having changed sides and supporting him, was more precise. The king conceded that the ecclesiastical jurisdiction included the crimes of incest, adultery, perjury, sorcery, disgraceful or infamous crimes against nature, non-observance of holy days, and fasting.[27] In comparison with the roughly contemporary (1273) Norwegian agreement between King Magnus Lagabøte of Norway (r. 1263–1280) and Archbishop Jon, according to which matrimonial cases, birth, patronage rights, vows, wills, church property, sacrilege, perjury, simony, heresy, adultery, incest and offences against pilgrims among others pertained to the ecclesiastical jurisdiction, this definition was restricted.[28] This discrepancy is probably partly due to

---

23. Inger 1961, pp. 41–44; Helmholz 1994, pp. 1–11.
24. Brundage 1995, pp. 70–72.
25. Hellström, Jan Arvid 1971: *Biskop och landskapssamhälle i tidig svensk medeltid.* Rättshistoriskt bibliotek, 16. Skrifter utgivna av Institutet för rättshistorisk forskning grundat av Gustav och Karin Olin, Lund, p. 344.
26. DS I, docs. 215–215a, pp. 226–227.
27. DS I, doc. 690, p. 557.
28. *Diplomatarium norvegicum* I, eds. Chr. C. A. Lange & Carl R. Unger. Christiania, 1849, doc. 64.a, p. 54: "*Omnes cause clericorum quum inter ser litigant vel a laicis impetuntur, matrimoniorum, natalium, iurispatronatus, decimarum, votorum, testamentorum, maxime cum agitur de legatis ecclesiis et piis locis et religiosis, tutio peregrinorum visitantium limina beati Olavi, vel aliorum sanctorum, et eorum*

the fact that some of the causes unmentioned by King Magnus Birgersson – such as matrimony – were already considered to belong to the Church.

With a few exceptions, most provincial laws do not contain lists of the ecclesiastical and mixed causes. Yet, the newer law of Western Gothia, for example, listed that the bishop was to judge the following cases: matters concerning clerics, litigation between two churches or between the priest and the parish church, disputes concerning debts or property of the church, excommunication, wills, and matrimony.[29] As this section mentions none of the offences defined as ecclesiastical causes in the privilege of 1279, the list was obviously perceived as supplementing it by listing only the crimes the bishop adjudicated. The chapter on the church of the law of Småland listed the following as episcopal causes: the defiling of the churchyard and church by violence, offences against penance prescribed by the bishop, excommunication, adultery, murdering an unbaptized child, intercourse with mother or daughter, sorcery, incest, and perjury.[30] The law of Eastern Gothia, on the other hand, considered that the following cases could be heard by the episcopal jury: cases pertaining to oaths of all kind, adultery, perjury, false witnesses, homicide if penance was not been performed, robbery from church, fighting on a holiday, and breaking the sabbath.[31] Even this list was probably not meant to be complete, as in matrimonial causes; for instance, the bishop would probably have adjudicated without a lay jury.

As to the Roman-canon influence in Swedish provincial laws, the chapters on the church of the provincial laws have been called the oldest and probably the most remarkable reception of foreign law in Swedish legal history.[32] Other scholars have gone even further. It has been claimed that all the essentials parts of Swedish medieval laws are products of reception partly from older Continental laws, the so-called *Leges barbarorum*, partly directly from Roman and Mosaic law.[33] Even though this opinion has not been generally accepted, no serious scholar would deny the influence of foreign – mainly canon – law in the provincial laws.

---

    cause. Item profanationum ecclesiarum, sacrilegii, periurii, usurarum, symonie, heresis, fornicationis, adulterii, et incestus, et omnes alie que ad forum ecclesiasticum possent de iure comuni quoquomodo spectare."

29. VgL II, Kk 59 and 61, pp. 216–217. The VgL IV (21:41) agreed: *"Item Episcopus debet iudicare de testamentis, matrimoniis, clericis cuiuscunque ordinis, excommunicatione, debitis ecclesiae, bonis ecclesiae, vel si litigauerint inter se due ecclesie, et super spiritualibus causis quibuscunque"*, VgL II, Kk 59, n. 95, p. 234.
30. SmåL, Kk 13, pp. 429–431.
31. ÖgL, Kk 13:3, p. 12.
32. Wilhelm Sjögren: "De fornsvenska kyrkobalkarna", *Tidsskrift for Retsvidenskap* (1904), p. 125.
33. Sjöholm 1988, pp. 15–16.

As scholars observed a century ago, canon law was not mentioned even as a subsidiary legal source in the provincial laws. This has been taken to signify that canon law still played an essential role in the argumentation, interpretation and treatment of the ecclesiastical causes, but that this concerned only the Church. In the ecclesiastical courts, canon law was used to a greater extent than the provincial laws alone suggest. The provincial laws were, after all, compromises or agreements between Church and laity, and lay society did not need to address internal issues of the Church.[34] Later in the Middle Ages, the Swedish church and its representatives cited the provisions of the ecclesiastical laws as binding for both the Church itself and secular officials.[35]

It has also been suggested that even though the contents of the chapters on the church largely corresponded with the canon law of the time, there seems to have been some discrepancy or regional variation in relation to the "common law" of the Church.[36] The Church had been forced to compromise on certain points: for instance, according to some provincial laws, the bishop was liable to a fine to the parishioners if he failed to consecrate their church on the agreed day. Similarly, the priest had to pay fines to his parishioners for failure to perform certain rites without legitimate cause – a practice that has been interpreted as uncanonical. The parishioners were also allowed greater power to choose the parish priest than canon law permitted: unanimous parishioners were allowed the right to name the candidate they wished. However, this may be due to the fact that the parishioners were considered the patrons of the church.[37] All in all, no Swedish law or document contains an exhaustive list of ecclesiastical – or mixed – causes.

---

34. Sjögren 1904, pp. 160, 174–175.
35. E. g. *Finlands medeltidsurkunder* V, ed. Reinhold Hausen. Helsingfors, 1928, doc. 4527, p. 432.
36. Sjögren 1904, pp. 125–126, Georg J. V. Ericsson: *Den kanoniska rätten och Äldre Västgötalagens kyrkobalk. En jämförande studie*. Rättshistoriskt bibliotek, vol. 12. Skrifter utgivna av Institutet för rättshistorisk forskning grundat av Gustav och Karin Olin. Lund, 1967, pp. 117, 120–121, 123.
37. Sjögren 1904, pp. 133, 150, 175; Ericsson 1967, pp. 96–99, 118–121, 125–126. The opinion of the wider rights of the Swedish community or parishioners as patrons has been endorsed by Sjöholm (1988, pp. 212–213), who adds that even on the local level the Swedish bishops had significantly less power than their Norwegian colleagues.

Matters Related to Clerics, Ecclesiastical Finances and Offences towards the Church or Its Peace

Ecclesiastical jurisdiction in medieval Sweden consisted of many elements. Even though clerical immunity was in practice a disputed matter in many countries,[38] the Church's aim to judge in criminal matters involving the clergy was largely accepted in the provincial laws. All the provincial laws were in accord that, as far as priests went, any criminal offences they committed or deeds they did (breach of duty, misconduct, damages) were to be tried in the ecclesiastical forum. In case the negligent clerics were sentenced to pay a fine – usually three marks[39] – it tended to be divided between the bishop and the injured party, i.e. a private individual, and/or the parish.[40] If the priest married a couple without the consent of the woman's legal guardian, for which offence he was condemned to pay – very uncanonically – a forty-mark fine, he had to be sued to appear in front of the bishop or the rural dean.[41]

The newer law of Western Gothia also mentions expressly that matters regarding clerics or the debts of the (parish) church belonged to the bishop. Likewise, the bishop passed judgment on causes involving the parish church disputing with a priest on property issues or litigation between churches.[42] Yet even the bishop could be sentenced to a forty-mark fine (going to the king, hundred and injured party) for refusing a year and a day to provide proper documentation to a penitent who had to perform a penitential pilgrimage, or to a six-mark fine for not visiting the parish on the prearranged day without a lawful excuse.[43] By contrast, actions regarding the deeds of priests' servants or animals were to be tried at the secular assizes along with litigation concerning sales or land in which a priest was involved.[44] Cases involving a priest's negligence in farming or village life belonged to the secular assizes even though the bishop could be awarded the

---

38. E. g. Campbell, Gerard J. 1964: "Clerical Immunities in France during the Reign of Philip III", *Speculum* 39. On the development of ecclesiastical immunities in Sweden see also Bååth, L. M. 1905: *Bidrag till den kanoniska rättens historia i Sverige*. Stockholm, pp. 203–229; Inger 1961, pp. 164–175; Andræ, Carl Göran 1960: *Kyrka och frälse i Sverige under äldre medeltid*. Studia historica upsaliensia, vol. 4. Scandinavian University Books, Uppsala, esp. pp. 132–172
39. 1 mark = 8 öre = 24 örtug.
40. ÖgL, Kk 5–7, pp. 8–9; UL, Kk 11–13, pp. 20–22; VgL I, Kk 5, 8, 14, pp. 4, 6; VgL II, Kk 12, 14, 28, pp. 206, 209; SmåL, Kk 11, p. 428; SdmL, Kk 9–10, pp. 18–19; HL, Kk 9–13, pp. 267–268; DL, Kk 4, p. 4; VmL, Kk 11–12, pp. 10–11.
41. ÖgL, G 6, p. 102.
42. VgL II, Kk 59, 61, pp. 216–217.
43. UL, Kk 15:8, p. 27; VgL II, Kk 3, p. 204.
44. SmåL, Kk 11, p. 428; UL, Kk 20, p. 30; HL, Kk 20, p. 271.

king's third in the possible fine.[45] Disputes concerning land or its unlawful use belonged to secular courts.[46]

Tithes provoked many disputes between laity and Church in medieval Sweden. It is not known exactly when tithes were introduced in Sweden, but in the late thirteenth century the tithing system was certainly well established in provincial laws. The same applied to other payments of the laity to the clergy: the episcopal fees of consecration and purification of the church, compulsory offerings and other payments for ecclesiastical rites, like solemnizing a marriage or purification after child-birth or wedding. Although the laws do not spell it out explicitly, tithes and other fees fell under ecclesiastical jurisdiction. Judging by the many disputes regarding tithes and ecclesiastic payments in the course of the fourteenth century, documented in the Black Book of the chapter of Turku, the system was established later in the Finnish half of the Swedish realm.

I cannot refrain from mentioning a documented incident from the late 1330s, because it sheds some light on the ecclesiastical jurisdiction in these matters. Not heeding their vicar Henricus Hartmanni's, admonitions and the subsequent interdict, twenty-five men of Sääksmäki in Tavastia (Tavastland) in present-day Finland had obstinately refused to pay their tithes. The conflict was prolonged by the Dominicans (*fratres predicatores*) of Turku, who offered their contending religious services to Henricus Hartmanni's parishioners on their portative altar and accepted offerings to the disadvantage of the local church and curate.[47]

The parishioners had not even been impressed by the hearing organised by Archbishop Petrus of Uppsala, conducted through his legate, canon Thomas Johanni of Uppsala, who had sentenced them to pay not only the tithe, but also the three-mark fine for each week of delay. The third of the fine was to go to the curate, a third to the building funds of the church and the remaining third to the bishop of Turku.[48] At the request of Henricus Hartmanni, Pope Benedict XII (1334–1342) confirmed the interdict of the people of Sääksmäki, and ordered the dean of Uppsala to put the decision

---

45. VgL II, Kk 63, p. 217.
46. E.g. UL, Kk 20, p. 30; SdmL, Kk 19, p. 24. Cf. VgL II, Kk 59, n. 95, p. 234, according to which cases concerning church property pertained to ecclesiastical courts.
47. 28.5.1340, REA, doc. 98, pp. 59–60. This kind of unfair competition pulled the rug from under the censure of the regular clergy, and therefore, the pope delegated the matter to the chapter of Uppsala to investigate and adjudicate.
48. See also the minute regulations concerning tithes in the law of Uppland about the division of the tithes, UL, Kk 7, p. 17. If the parishioner, who was obliged to pay a tithe, refused to perform, the priest could deny him the Holy Communion on Easter, UL, Kk 7:8, p. 18.

into force by using ecclesiastical penalties (*per censuram ecclesiasticam*).[49] At the same time the pope confirmed, at Henricus Hartmanni's request, that the people of Sääksmäki were to pay tithes on the yields of their lands instead of pleading to some false custom (*prauam consuetudinem*).[50] Later, in 1360, Archbishop Petrus Tyrgilli of Uppsala threatened the inhabitants of two Finnish provinces with excommunication and interdict if they refused to pay their tithes.[51]

Theft in a church, on the churchyard, or from a church were mentioned in most laws, usually distinguishing between burglary of the church and stealing from an individual attending church. In the latter case, as recognition of the breach of the peace of the church, it was awarded its share in the fine, which also went to the king and the hundred. Burglary was commonly considered a more serious crime and thus punished with higher fines, even occasionally with the death penalty. In such a case the church was considered the injured party and again awarded a corresponding third of the fine.[52] The interest of the Church was also acknowledged in homicides or acts of violence against clerics or during ecclesiastical feasts – most notably Christmas and Easter – and certain particular feasts in each diocese. In such cases, the bishop was awarded a fine of several marks depending on the solemnity of the day and the nature of the act: homicide was usually fined more highly than mere injuring.[53] The law of Eastern Gothia seems to have followed the canon *Si quis suadente* of the Second Lateran Council in 1139 in insisting that violence towards clerics had to be redeemed by papal absolution in Rome.[54] The royal thirteenth-century peace legislation also

---

49. 16.6.1340, REA, doc. 99, pp. 60–62. See also the authorization of Bishop Hemming of Turku to canon Sigurd to force some inhabitants of Åland (Ahvenanmaa) to pay their seal tithes in full using ecclesiastical penalties, 30.5.1342, REA, doc. 103, p. 65.
50. 16.6.1340, REA, doc. 100, pp. 62–63.
51. 7.5.1360, REA, doc. 172, pp. 111–112.
52. ÖgL, Kk 13:3, p. 12; VgL I, Kk 7, p. 4 (burglary: 9 marks each to the church, hundred and king); VgL II, Kk 11, p. 206 (burglary: 9 marks each to the church, hundred and king/taken in the act or with stolen goods – execution); VgL III, Kk 93, p. 408 (larceny: excommunication and 9 marks each to the church, hundred and king), SdmL, Kk 14, pp. 21–22 (theft in church – normal fine + 3 marks to the church/on the churchyard – 3 marks of which one mark to the church, bishop and king each/ from the church – fine for excommunication + 20 marks to the church, 10 to the king and bishop each); HL, Kk 18, p. 270 (church/churchyard - normal fine + 3 marks to the bishop).
53. VgL II, Kk 50–52, pp. 208–209; ÖgL Kk 13:3, 22–23, pp. 12, 16–17; UL, Kk 17, M 12:2, pp. 28, 94; SdmL, Kk 18, 21, pp. 24–25; VmL, Kk 24:2, 26, pp. 17, 19–20; HL, Kk 17, pp. 269–270; DL, Kk 13, M 15, pp. 9, 33.
54. ÖgL Kk 30, p. 19.

protected people from violence on their way to or from church as well as in the church itself (peace of the church).[55]

Similarly, if the assault took place either in the church or the churchyard, the episcopal fine was graded according to the location of the violent deed and its consequences: wounding or death.[56] If blood or semen had been shed, this necessitated the reconsecration or purification of the church, for which the culprit was fined. He also had to pay for the expenses of the purification, meaning the upkeep of the bishop and his entourage, which could involve a retinue of dozens of persons, for the ceremony.[57] Breaches of sanctuary were also condemned in certain laws: to violently remove a person from a church or churchyard was punishable with a fine of eighteen marks.[58]

Violence within the family was treated differently. Most of the provincial laws decreed that if the husband killed his wife intentionally, he was executed, but if the wife's relatives accepted a high fine (of 100–140 marks going to the king and the injured party), he had to travel additionally to Rome in order to be absolved by the pope. This also applied to other inter-family manslaughter.[59] Lesser violence within the family was an offence for which the law of Dalarna awarded the bishop part of the fine, while the king, the hundred and the injured party were also secured their share. The law of Dalarna graded the fines from twelve marks plus three marks for the injury to three plus three marks according to the proximity of the kinship until the fifth degree.[60]

---

55. E.g. ÖgL, E 3:1–2, 4, pp. 35–36; UL, M 29, p. 103; Åqvist 1989, pp. 70–71 and Appendix. See also Korpiola, Mia 2001: "'The People of Sweden Shall Have Peace': Peace Legislation and Royal Power in Later Medieval Sweden", *Expectation of the Law in the Middle Ages*, ed. Anthony Musson, pp. 35–51. The Boydell Press, Bury St Edmunds.
56. E.g. VgL I, Kk 3, 12, pp. 3, 5; VgL II, Kk 22, 25, pp. 208–209; SmL, Kk 13:2, p. 429; Åqvist 1989, pp. 70–71 and Appendix.
57. E.g. VgL II, Kk 22, p. 208; ÖgL, Kk 24:1, 25, p. 17; UL, Kk 15:7, p. 27.
58. E.g. HL, Kk 21:3, p. 272: half of the fine was to go to the king, half to the church. Unregenerate excommunicates or criminals, who were guilty of a crime against the very church where they claimed sanctuary, could be extracted even forcefully from the church, see also HL, Kk 18:1, p. 270.
59. UL, Kk 17: 3, M 13, pp. 28, 96. See also VgL I, G 8:1, p. 99; VgL II, U 2 and G 15, pp. 248, 285–286; SdmL, M 28, p. 178; VmL, M 12, p. 71; HL, M 22, p. 332; DL, M 2, p. 30.
60. DL, M 2, p. 30.

Perjury, Usury, Heresy, Sorcery and Excommunication in the Swedish Provincial Laws

Oaths and especially perjury were mentioned as ecclesiastical or mixed causes in all the provincial laws except the older law of Western Gothia. Those found guilty of perjury were sentenced to a three-mark fine to the bishop (occasionally also to the king) and/or penance.[61] Only the law of Uppland mentions usury, punished with a six-mark fine, as a crime pertaining to ecclesiastical jurisdiction.[62] This is surprising because the crime came to be frequently mentioned in Swedish late-medieval synodal statutes.[63] It is illustrative, nonetheless, that the law did not define the crime in any way – possibly a sign that it was perceived to be of little practical value at the time. Indeed, it has been assumed that this issue became more topical in late fourteenth and early fifteenth-century Sweden as a result of an increasing influence of the Continental monetary economy in the country.[64]

None of the laws mention heresy or blasphemy. This is not surprising as far as heresy went, as it was a *crimen mere ecclesiasticum* pertaining exclusively to the competence of the ecclesiastical courts. It is more difficult to fathom, however, why blasphemy was excluded altogether. It belonged typically to the crimes of mixed jurisdiction (*crimen mixti fori*) that were criminalized in both ecclesiastical and secular laws.[65] We do know of the existence of medieval Swedish cases involving blasphemy, most notably the famous heresy case of the peasant Botolf of Gottröra in 1311.[66] As for heresy, canon law pure and simple was surely used for the cases, but blasphemy was probably of marginal interest to the secular society – and the Swedish church at this time. Moreover, unless the blasphemous words were heretical or had created public outcry, the Church tended to consider them

---

61. HL, Kk 19, pp. 270–271; ÖgL, Kk 13:3, 16–19, R 2, 5, 16, pp. 12–15, 175, 177–178, 184; VgL II, Kk 52, Add. 13, pp. 215, 393–394; UL, R 5:7–6, pp. 198–199; SdmL, Kk 15:3, 16, R 9, pp. 22–23, 223–224; VmL, Kk 24:5–11, R 13, pp. 17–18, 170; DL, R 14, p. 106. See also SmL, Kk 13:8, p. 430 (penance only, no fine).
62. UL, Kk 15:4, p. 26.
63. E.g. 20, provincial statutes of Arboga from 1396, *Synodalstatuter och andra kyrkorättsliga aktstycken från den svenska medeltidskyrkan*. Ed. Jaakko Gummerus, 1902. Wretmans tryckeri, Upsala, p. 29; Provincial statute on usury from 1412, *Statuta synodalia veteris ecclesiæ sveogothicæ*, ed. H. Reuterdahl, 1841. Lund, pp. 109–110.
64. Brilioth, Yngve 1925: *Svensk kyrka, kungadöme och påvemakt 1363-1414*. Uppsala universitets årsskrift 1925, teologi 1, Uppsala, p. 319, note 2.
65. Helmholz 1996, pp. 272–274.
66. For the case of Botolf, see DS III, doc. 1789, pp. 13–15; Lesch, Bruno 1927: "En svensk kätteriprocess i början av 1300-talet", *Historisk tidskrift för Finland* 11 (1926); Inger 1961, pp. 484–485.

as having been spoken privately, hence belonging to the spiritual forum and the confessional like other private or occult crimes.[67]

Sorcery was mentioned in some of the provincial laws. Here again the Church was usually considered as one of the interested parties along with the king and the hundred, between which the fine was divided. The newer law of Western Gothia, however, made a distinction between "superstition" (*widskiplum*) – probably lesser spells or magic – and killing a domestic animal or person through witchcraft (*maleficium*), the latter of which was punishable with death if the culprit was caught in the act. The fine for the former was sixteen örtugs for the bishop, hundred and king each. If the sorcerer was not taken in the act of witchcraft, s/he had to pay nine marks to the injured party, hundred and king each, but three marks of the king's lot would go to the bishop.[68] By contrast, the chapter on the church of Småland considered sorcery a case pertaining to the Church, but apart from the small six-öre fine to the peasant in whose house the magic charms were found, the guilty person was to perform penance.[69]

Most provincial laws mention breaking the sabbath – by hard work on a feast day, non-attendance of divine service or non-observance of the fast – as an ecclesiastical offence punishable with a fine ranging from six öres to three marks.[70] The boundaries of ecclesiastical jurisdiction and ecclesiastical spiritual powers, the *cura animarum*, were not so clearly demarcated in the provincial laws that occasionally mention either supplementary or alternative penance to be performed for several crimes. Some laws also mention that the bishop had a right to all cases involving excommunication: for revoking the ban, he received three marks.[71] The laws of Gothia also know an offence called *skriftabrott*, which meant relapse into serious crime for which one had previously performed public penance (such

---

67. Helmholz 1996, p. 274.
68. VgL II, R 10–11, p. 294. According to DL (Kk 11, p. 8) the forty-mark fine was divided between the king, church and hundred. In addition, the convicted witch had to pay nine marks for the upheaval of the excommunication. In case of non-payment the witch was to be executed. Cf. Åqvist 1989, pp. 73–74 and Appendix.
69. SmL, Kk 13:7, p. 430. According to the law of Dalarna, penance was additional to the fines, DL, Kk 11, p. 8.
70. ÖgL 13:3, 20, pp. 12, 15 (3 marks or 6 öres depending on the importance of the feast); VgLII, Kk 52, 56, pp. 215–216 (8 öres – working/half mark – non-observance of fast); UL, Kk 14:9, 16, pp. 24, 27–28 (3 marks); SdmL, Kk 17:1, pp. 23–24 (3 marks/6 öres/3 öres depending on the time and on the importance of the feast); HL, Kk 16, p. 269 (3 marks); DL, Kk 13:1, p. 9 (3 marks); VmL Kk 12:1 (3 marks), p. 11.
71. E.g. VgL II, Kk 52, p. 215; SmåL, Kk 13:4, p. 430.

as homicide, perjury, incest, adultery).[72] Similarly, if a man had publicly abjured his concubine before Easter, but relapsed into fornication with her after Easter, he was fined three marks.[73] In addition, several laws imposed a three-mark fine for minor offences relating to excommunication or contumacy: e.g. for eating meat during penance, for associating with an excommunicate or for a penitent to attend mass during penance.[74]

The argument between the curate of Sääksmäki and his parishioners regarding tithes demonstrated that the Church could have problems with obdurate sinners. Its spiritual sword was simply not sharp enough against the unregenerate excommunicates. Heresy was probably the first crime in which canon law came to rely heavily on the temporal sword and the cooperation was confirmed in the decretal *Ad abolendum* of Pope Lucius III (1181–1185). According to the decretal, all obdurate or relapsed heretics were to be handed over to the secular authority for execution of the ecclesiastical judgment by imposing punishment on them – burning at the stake. In fact, secular officials refusing assistance were *ipso facto* excommunicated and their lands put under interdict.[75] In Sweden, the above-mentioned heresy case of the peasant Botolf was an example is this: Botolf had relapsed in his heretical views and therefore the secular officials were to impose punishment on him.[76]

In some countries, like England, legal mechanisms, for example special writs, of evoking the help of the secular arm in capturing heretics and excommunicates had been developed.[77] In Sweden the cooperation of

---

72. Esp. ÖgL 15:1, p. 13, but see also VgL I, G 8:2, p. 99; VgL II, Kk 52 and 57, pp. 215–216. The Norwegian church law knew a similar offence, the *skriptrof*, Sjöholm 1988, p. 216.
73. E.g. VgL II, Kk 57, p. 216.
74. VgL II, Kk 56, p. 216; SmåL, Kk 13:3, p. 429; UL, Kk 16:1, 21:1, pp. 28, 31; SdmL, Kk 20:1, p. 25; VmL, Kk 24:1, pp. 16–17; HL, Kk 16, 21:1, pp. 269, 271; DL, Kk 13:1, p. 9.
75. Helmholz, R. H. 1996: *The Spirit of Classical Canon Law*. The University of Georgia Press, Athens – London, pp. 360–363.
76. DS III, doc. 1789, p. 15.
77. In England the procedure had its origins in the late eleventh century, and more than a century later the common law courts had developed particular writs for dealing with obdurate excommunicates. The close cooperation between the royal and ecclesiastical courts in medieval England is demonstrated by the approximately 7600 surviving requests from the pre-Reformation period of the capture of excommunicates. The assistance of the secular arm against obdurate excommunicates gave the ecclesiastical ban more importance, even if it meant that the Church became dependent on the crown. The Church returned the favour by using excommunication against ordinary criminals and political enemies of the crown, Logan, F. Donald 1968: *Excommunication and the Secular Arm in Mediaeval England. A Study in Legal Procedure from the Thirteenth to the*

the Church and the secular arm concerning excommunicates authorized the king to have unrepentant excommunicates executed after they had been under the greater ban for a year and a day. The body of this unregenerate criminal was not buried in consecrated ground.[78]

This norm was mentioned in nearly all of the provincial laws in a way that to me would suggest that a royal statute from the late thirteenth century might be behind it. The contents of this disappeared statute would then have been incorporated into the provincial laws. There are even other cases of such similarities, for example, with regard to treason legislation and lesemajesty in the provincial laws. Researchers have assumed that a since disappeared common source may have been behind them.[79] Thus, it would resemble the royal peace statutes sanctioning any breach of the peace of the home, assizes or church, which were all incorporated in the provincial laws. Even though the laws differ in discussing whether the king was to have the confiscated chattels of the executed recalcitrant excommunicate or whether all his property was to go to his heirs,[80] this may have been a matter left unregulated by the statute. This procedure had probably been adopted in Sweden from Germany where, by the end of the thirteenth century, the period after which an excommunicate fell under the imperial ban had become a year and a day. Somewhat similar practices, however, existed also in Aragon, Italy and France.[81]

Sixteenth Century. Studies and Texts, 15. Pontifical Institute of Mediaeval Studies, Toronto, pp. 17–24, 66–68, 72–74; Wright, J. Robert 1980: *The Church and the English Crown 1305–1334. A Study based on the Register of Archbishop Walter Reynolds*. Studies and texts, 48. Pontifical Institute of Mediaeval Studies, Toronto, pp. xv, 195, 199–200, 210.

78. ÖgL, Kk 25:1, p. 17; VgL III 93, p. 408; SmåL, Kk 13:4, pp. 429–430; UL, Kk 13:2, p. 22; DL, Kk 15, p. 10; VmL, Kk 12:2, p. 12; SdmL, Kk 10:2, p. 20; HL, Kk 21:3, p. 272.
79. Fritz, Birgitta 1987: "Spår av en förlorad stadga från 1200-talet?", *Arkivvetenskapliga studier* 6, esp. p. 96; Hjärne, Erland 1951: *Fornsvenska lagstadganden I–III*. Almqvist & Wiksells Boktryckeri AB, Uppsala, pp. 43–44, 78–81, 88, 158, 176; Åqvist 1989, p. 69.
80. E.g. according to the law of Uppland, his heirs were to inherit his property, UL, Kk 13:2, p. 22. Cf. ÖgL, Kk 25, p. 17: the heirs received his land and the king his chattels.
81. Vodola, Elisabet 1986: *Excommunication in the Middle Ages*. University of California Press, USA, pp. 165–177; Logan 1968, pp. 16–17; Lea, Henry Charles 1896: *A History of Auricular Confession and Indulgences in the Latin Church*, I. Swan Sonnenschein & Co, London, pp. 250–251.

Sexual Crimes and Ecclesiastical Jurisdiction

Sexual crimes are traditionally the bread and butter of ecclesiastical courts – and were so also in medieval Sweden. The provincial laws were quite in accord that adultery and incest were ecclesiastical causes. The majority of the laws considered adultery to belong to the ecclesiastical forum. Where they differ is in the punishment. Some laws doubled the fine for single adultery in cases of double adultery.[82] Other laws considered only the male partner liable to a fine in addition to the penance, while the female partner only had to perform penance.[83] The majority, like the law of Södermanland, fined both parties equally.[84]

Yet adultery seems to some extent have been, or developed into, a mixed cause. In nearly all provincial laws the husband was awarded the right to kill his adulterous wife and her lover on the spot if he caught them in the act.[85] Moreover, the law of Hälsingland also awarded the injured party, the king and the hundred two marks each for adultery, while the bishop got three or six marks.[86] The so-called excerpts of Lydekinus from the early 1300s, additions to the newer law of Western Gothia, represent an even more advanced stage. They clearly show that the royal judicial powers were also extended to adultery: the text grants both the king and the bishop twelve öres each for single adultery, while the fine for double adultery was three times nine marks paid to the king, the injured party and the hundred – like any other crime, that is. However, the ecclesiastical interest was acknowledged by awarding the bishop a three-mark portion from the nine marks going to the king.[87]

In nearly all laws, incest was considered an ecclesiastical cause, for which a fine had to pay to the bishop.[88] This fine was usually graded according to the degree of kinship between the culprits.[89] In addition, some

---

82. HL, Kk 15, p. 268 (3 marks – 6 marks); VgL II, Kk 52, p. 215 (12 öres – 3 marks).
83. HL 15, p. 268; ÖgL, Kk 15, p. 13 (man fined 3 marks – penance not mentioned).
84. SdmL, Kk 15, p. 22; DL, Kk 9:3, p. 7 (3 marks); VmL, Kk 21, p. 15 (3 marks); UL, Kk 15:3, p. 26 (3 marks); SmåL, Kk 13:5, p. 430.
85. VgL I, Om mandråp 11, p. 26; VgL II, D 22, pp. 259–260; ÖgL, E 26, pp. 42–43; DL, Kk 9:4, pp. 7–8; SdmL, G 4:1, p. 66; HL, Ä 6, p. 304; UL, Ä 6, p. 66; VmL, Ä 6:2, p. 46.
86. HL, Kk 15, pp. 268–269. Cf. DL, Kk 9:3, p. 7 (the 3-mark fine is divided between king, bishop and hundred).
87. VgL III, 121, p. 411.
88. E.g. UL, Kk 15, p. 25 (6 marks irrespective of proximity or type of kinship); ÖgL, Kk 15, p. 13 (man, who as impregnated the woman pays 3 marks); HL, Kk 15, p. 269 (man pays evidently 6 marks, both perform penance).
89. SdmL, Kk 15, p. 22 (3 marks until and inclusive the third degree, 6 öres in the fourth degree); VmL, Kk 24:12 (3 marks within the third degree, and both perform penance, in the fourth degree 12 öres), 24:14 (spiritual affinity – 3 marks and

laws mention that public penance had to be performed. The newer law of Western Gothia insisted that for incest in the first or second degrees the penitent had to be absolved by the pope in Rome.[90] Even here there is considerable difference. The law of Småland considered incest only to belong to the *forum internum*, necessitating penance, but no fine.[91] By contrast, the newer law of Western Gothia and the law of Dalarna considered incest a normal crime: apart from the bishop, the king and the hundred – in the former even the injured party – were allotted their share of the fine.[92]

Swedish late-medieval ecclesiastical councils repeated the international statutes that it was heresy to claim that fornication was not a capital sin.[93] As for the provincial laws, however, they mainly treated fornication as a secular offence, which the injured party – usually the woman's marriage guardian (*giftoman*) – initiated at the secular assizes and received a smallish fine.[94] The provincial laws contain no mention that fornication pertained to ecclesiastical jurisdiction or that the Church had a right to fine the culprit. The law of Eastern Gothia expressly stated that fornicators only had to perform penance – even if they lapsed into the same sin again. Indeed, if the priest denied them Communion at Easter, he was liable to a three-mark fine.[95] Yet in the course of the later Middle Ages, the Church seems to managed to transfer fornication into the group of mixed crimes so that fornicators were also tried at ecclesiastical courts and fined three marks.[96]

While the newer law of Western Gothia insisted that for bestiality the culprit had to be absolved by the pope in Rome, it also imposed on him a high fine that was to be divided between the king, bishop, hundred, and the

---

penance), pp. 18–19; DL, Kk 9, p. 7 (father&daughter/mother&son/in the third degree 9 marks, brother&sister/niece 6 marks, in the fourth degree/spiritual affinity 3 marks); VgL II, Kk 52, U 3, pp. 215, 248 (incest in the first and second degrees of consanguinity and affinity 27 marks, 12 öres within the third or fourth degrees), VgL III 103, p. 409 (spiritual affinity – 3 marks).

90. VgL II, Kk 52 and U 3, pp. 215 and 248. See also HL, Kk 15, p. 269 (both perform penance); VmL, Kk 24:12 and 24:14, pp. 18–19 (for spiritual affinity and consanguinity within the three first degrees both perform penance).
91. SmåL, Kk 13:8, p. 430.
92. VgL II, U 3, p. 248; DL, Kk 9, p. 7.
93. E.g. statutes of the provincial council of Uppsala 1368, DS IX: 1–2, doc. 7777, p. 454.
94. E.g. SdmL, Ä 3:1, p. 74 (12-öre fine to the marriage guardian); HL, Ä 14, p. 308 (16 öres to her father, 8 to her brother and 4 öres to her sister's children).
95. ÖgL, Kk 15:1, p. 13.
96. E.g. 17, provincial statutes of Arboga from 1412, *Synodalstatuter och andra kyrkorättsliga aktstycken*, p. 30: "*Item fornicatores et fornicatrices inponitur pena pecuniaria Sz III marce. Et si non desistant eliminantur.*"

injured party – i.e. the owner of the animal.[97] Indeed, while the owner of the animal was still given some right to accuse the culprit and to decide whether he wanted to accept a fine or not, the trend in the provincial laws was to execute the guilty party, especially if he had been caught in the act. If there were no witnesses to the unnatural act or if the injured party was inclined to clemency, the culprit could escape with public penance and a fine, if he was unable to find oath-helpers. In such cases, the fine was divided between the king, bishop and injured party.[98] The other extreme was the law of Södermanland which always mercilessly condemned the culprits – man and beast – to burning or burying alive.[99]

Consequently, there are indications that the king was extending his interests into getting a share in the lucrative business of fining sexual offenders even at this stage. In 1281 the fines going to the bishop for sexual crime, listed in the statute issued by bishop Brynolf of Skara, were twelve öres for simple adultery and incest with a relative within the third or fourth degree. The fines for double adultery, sins against nature or incest within the first or second degrees, on the other hand, were higher: nine marks.[100] The section in the corresponding provincial law, the newer law of Western Gothia,[101] by contrast, listing "the rights of the bishop according to old law", had preserved the twelve-öre fines, but the nine-mark offences had been reduced to three-mark fines. The king was probably now awarded the nine marks that formerly exclusively went to the bishop, and of this sum he paid three marks to the bishop. For simple adultery the king received the same fine as the bishop.[102] Tentatively, this could be interpreted as an indication of the growing royal jurisdiction of sexual crime, visible in the fourteenth and fifteenth centuries. In assimilating unnatural sexual offences with heinous and unatonable crimes, the crown was also partly usurping the Church's jurisdiction. The trend is visible also in the royal late-medieval laws and statutes.[103]

---

97. VgL II, U 3, p. 248: 9 marks to the hundred and injured party, 6 marks to the king and 3 marks to the bishop.
98. UL, Kk 15:8, p. 27 (burial alive/6-mark fine divided between king, bishop and injured party); VmL, Kk 23, p. 16 (burial alive/6-mark fine divided between king, bishop and injured party); DL, Kk 10, p. 8 (burial alive/penance, 9 marks to the bishop for the excommunication, 12-mark fine divided between king, bishop and hundred);
99. SdmL, Kk 15:1, p. 22.
100. DS I, doc. 709, p. 576.
101. Manuscript from around 1350, Inledning, SLL V, p. xxxviii.
102. VgL II, Kk 52 and n. 73, U 3, pp. 215, 231, 248. See also VgL III, 121, p. 411.
103. Korpiola, Mia 2001: "Fördelningen av domsmakten mellan kyrkan och staten avseende äktenskapsrätt och sexualbrott i Sverige cirka 1200–1620: observationer och hypoteser", *Rättslig integration och pluralism. Nordisk rättskultur i omvandling*. Rättshistoriska skrifter, III. Institutet för rättshistorisk forskning

Family and Matrimony: Reception of Canonical Norms

Some sections of law demonstrate a particular debt to canon law. I will leave out questions regarding the building and furnishing a church, the administration of the parish church's property, ecclesiastical fees and so on. Rather, I will discuss some aspects of canonical family law, namely wills, the status of children and matrimonial law. While many of the provincial laws more or less directly indicate that matrimonial and affiliation causes pertained to the ecclesiastical courts, it is quite clear that secular norms also regulated marriage formation.

Only the newer law of Western Gothia mentioned the Church's jurisdiction of wills.[104] Researchers believe that testamentary cases were not part of the episcopal jurisdiction, only the execution of wills, and especially those of clerics. At first sight it would seem, therefore, that this was not a generally accepted part of ecclesiastical jurisdiction in Sweden, unlike, for example, England where it was an ecclesiastical cause by virtue of local custom.[105] This notion had been accepted by others: "[i]n civil cases, such as land disputes and wills, the Church encountered so much hostility that is can safely be said that it never managed to get them under its jurisdiction".[106] Yet, the Church was responsible for introducing the custom of wills, gifts for one's soul, and donations *mortis causa* in Sweden in the first place. There are also some indications that matters regarding estates of the deceased did belong to the Church through custom, rather than through law.[107]

The Swedish bishops had the recognized powers to make or break (*lösa eller binda*) the bond of marriage.[108] In fact the law of Uppland, for example, specifies that no other person than the bishop or his representative had the right to prosecute in cases of matrimony and incest. He had the right to investigate if an impediment existed between the nupturients and dissolve the union if necessary.[109] The same applied to engagements or betrothals: according to almost all provincial laws, the party that caused the break had

---

grundat av Gustav och Karin Olin, Stockholm, esp. pp. 89–93; Korpiola, Mia forthcoming, "Rethinking Incest and Heinous Sexual Crime: The Changing Boundaries of Secular and Ecclesiastical Jurisdiction in Late Medieval Sweden", *Mapping the Law*, ed. Anthony Musson. Ashgate; Inger 1961, pp. 211–215.

104. VgL II, Kk 59, p. 216.
105. Bååth 1905, pp. 176, 179, 188–189. Cf. Westman 1915, p. 230. For England, see Helmholz 1996, p. 117.
106. Hellström 1971, p. 344. On the problems between Church and secular society caused by wills see also Bååth 1905, pp. 123–190.
107. DS V, doc. 3877, p. 394.
108. ÖgL, Kk 18, p. 19.
109. UL, Kk 15, p. 25; ÖgL, Kk 18, p. 19.

to pay a three- or six-mark fine to the bishop.[110] Even most of the provincial laws mention the solemnization of marriage *in facie ecclesiae* including the reading of the banns.[111]

The provincial laws show that the ecclesiastical claim on defining the status of children had largely been successful. Some laws expressly indicate that affiliation causes – establishing of paternity and legitimacy – belonged to the ecclesiastical forum, which naturally corresponds with the Church's claims of jurisdiction. In this field, however, even a wider influence is visible. The laws accept the canonical rule of paternity of children of married women (*pater est quem nuptiae demonstrant*).[112] Many provincial laws made baptism a precondition of inheritance rights in the abstract,[113] which has even been considered uncanonical and against natural law.[114]

The weakening position of illegitimate children demonstrates that the canonical dogma had made inroads in Sweden. While the inheritance rights of natural children (*naturales*) were severely curtailed – even in default of other offspring – adulterine and incestuous children (*spurii*) were separated from all inheritance rights.[115] In addition, the canonical institution of legitimation by subsequent matrimony (*legitimatio per subsequens matrimonium*) was accepted in the Swedish provincial laws in the course of the thirteenth century.[116] But there are two exceptions to the canonical doctrine of legitimacy even though their practical relevance may have been slight. A child conceived through rape was able to inherit his father and thus treated as legitimate,[117] while a child born to lawfully married parents, while his father was outlawed, was unable to inherit and was thus treated as illegitimate.[118] Thus, the notions of legitimacy do not correspond exactly to

---

110. ÖgL, Kk 28, p. 19; VgL I, G 2:1, p. 97; VgL II, Kk 52, p. 215; UL, Kk 15:1, p. 25; SdmL, Kk 15:2, p. 22; VmL, Kk 20, pp. 14–15; HL, Kk 15:1, p. 269.
111. UL, Kk 15:2, pp. 25–26; SdmL, Kk 13, p. 21; HL, Kk 15:1, p. 269; DL, Kk 7, p. 6; VmL, Kk 8 and 20:1, pp. 9, 15; VgL II, Kk 69, p. 218. See also ÖgL, Kk 31, G 6–7, pp. 30, 102–103.
112. E.g. VgL I, Ä 8:1, p. 77; VgL II, Add. 12, p. 391; VmL, Ä 7:2, p. 46; DL, G 8, p. 80.
113. E.g. HL, Ä 13:7, p. 308; ÖgL, Ä 7, pp. 126–127; VgL I, Kk 1, p. 3; VgL II, Kk 1, p. 203.
114. Ericsson 1967, pp. 54–55.
115. ÖgL, Ä 4 and 13, pp. 125, 130; HL, Ä 10:1, p. 306; VmL, Ä 18:3, pp. 53–54; SdmL, Ä 3:3, p. 74; UL, Ä 24:1, p. 76; VgL I, Ä 8, p. 77; VgL II, Ä 10–12, p. 271.
116. E.g. SdmL, Ä 3:1, p. 74; HL, Ä 13:1, 13:6, p. 307; VgL II, Ä 12, p. 271. England was the most notable example of regions where the doctrine was rejected by the secular nobility, Sheehan, Michael M. 1996: *Marriage, Family and Law in Medieval Europe: Collected Studies.* Ed. James K. Farge. University of Toronto Press, Toronto – Buffalo, p. 257.
117. E.g. ÖgL, Ä 8:1, p. 127.
118. E.g. UL, Ä 21, p. 74.

the canonical ones nor did they become identical in the course of the Middle Ages.

Restricting the Inquisitorial Procedure of the Church

Another matter worth stressing, especially regarding sexual crimes, is the fact that nearly all the Swedish provincial laws curtailed to some extent the ecclesiastical accusers' right to prosecute laymen at church courts. This was hardly in harmony with canon law and must be regarded as a restriction – at least in principle – of the functioning of ecclesiastical courts in Sweden. The older canonical norms had preserved many elements of the accusatory procedure, which presupposed that a person accused another of a crime. The court then investigated the truth of the claim and adjudicated upon the matter. Since the twelfth century, however, a new innovation, the inquisitorial procedure, had been replacing the accusatory system in ecclesiastical courts. The inquisitorial procedure signified that the court could initiate criminal investigations *ex officio*, of its own accord, based solely on suspicion, rumour or common fame (*fama publica*). In practice, a public prosecutor would then initiate the criminal procedure.[119]

Even though the inquisitorial procedure had become part and parcel of the Church's *ius commune* all over Europe, Swedish society had obviously taken a dislike to the Church's unrestricted power to investigate and inquire.[120] This may be attributed to the strong position of the injured party as a private accuser in pressing charges and initiating the criminal procedure at the assizes. (This, by the way, has been one of the most enduring features of Swedish and Finnish law of procedure up to the twentieth century.) Most provincial laws contain such restrictions commonly in cases of adultery and/or incest. The Episcopal prosecutor (*biskopens länsman*), which has normally been interpreted to mean the rural dean (*prost*), could only initiate

---

119. E.g. van Caenegem, R. C. 1976: "Public Prosecution of Crime in Twelfth-Century England", *Church and Government in the Middle Ages. Essays Presented to C. R. Cheney on his 70th Birthday*. Eds. C. N. L. Brooke et al. Cambridge University Press, Cambridge, esp. pp. 61–72; van Caenegem, R. C. 1965: "The Law of Evidence in the Twelfth Century: European Perspective and Intellectual Background", *Proceedings of the Second International Congress of Medieval Canon Law*. Eds. Stephan Kuttner and J. Joseph Ryan. Monumenta Iuris Canonici, series C: subsidia, vol. 1. Città del Vaticano, pp. 299–300; Brundage 1995, pp. 144–150.
120. For similar criticism in England, see van Caenegem 1976, pp. 65–70.

the criminal procedure if one of these criteria was met.[121] The couple had been caught in the act,[122] there were two witnesses to the crime,[123] the woman had become pregnant,[124] the wife had eloped with her lover,[125] the husband had taken his mistress into his home and bed[126] or one spouse publicly (in the church, at the assizes, at a meeting or feast) accused the other of adulterous intercourse and did not recant the allegation.[127]

As can be seen, the preconditions varied depending on the law. The wish to restrict the initiating of a case in the ecclesiastical courts is also more generally visible in the law of Eastern Gothia, which decreed that all lawfully summoned cases could be brought to the Episcopal jury, "but not cases grounded on suspicions alone".[128] The cases had to be notorious (*uppenbara*) and lawfully initiated.[129] According to the law of Dalarna, the Episcopal prosecutor was under the same restrictions as his secular colleague: both could only initiate one case each at certain assizes (*tingsstämma*) against the same person unless a private accuser existed.[130] The law of Hälsingland insisted that the Episcopal prosecutor needed either to have the injured party or two witnesses with him in order to initiate the case ("to have the right to an oath or a fine"). Incidentally, these witnesses did not need to swear any oath, so if the accused managed to purge himself free of the charge, the witnesses did not have to pay a fine for perjury.[131]

If the Episcopal prosecutor did not have the necessary witnesses or justification to accuse an unmarried woman for incest or adultery, he was, according to the law of Eastern Gothia, sentenced to pay three marks – divided equally between the king, the injured party and the hundred – for each assizes to which he summoned the accused without necessary evidence. However, if the accused woman was married and her husband had not first accused her of the crime, the Episcopal prosecutor was fined forty

---

121. Some laws, like the law of Eastern Gothia, restricted even prosecution for fornication by a private accuser to cases in which the woman had become pregnant or the couple had been caught in the act, ÖgL, Ä 16, p. 131.
122. ÖgL, Kk 27:2, pp. 18–19; VgL II, Kk 58, p. 216; SmåL, Kk 13:5, p. 430 (in the act and two witnesses); DL, Kk 9:3, p. 7; VmL, Kk 21, p. 15; SdmL, Kk 15:3, p. 22; UL, Kk 15:3, p. 26.
123. VmL, Kk 21, p. 15; SdmL, Kk 15:3, p. 22; UL, Kk 15:3, p. s26.
124. ÖgL, Kk 15 and 27:2, pp. 13, 18–19; SmåL, Kk 13:5, p. 430.
125. SmåL, Kk 13:5, p. 430.
126. VgL II, Kk 58, p. 216.
127. ÖgL, Kk 27, p. 18; SmåL, Kk 13:5, p. 430; DL, Kk 9:5, p. 8; VmL, Kk 21, p. 15 (no place was mentioned, accusing the other of adultery sufficed); SdmL, Kk 15:3, p. 22; UL, Kk 15:3, p. 26.
128. ÖgL, Kk 13:3, p. 12.
129. ÖgL, Kk 26:1, p. 18.
130. DL, Kk 4, p. 102.
131. HL, Kk 15:2, p. 269.

marks.[132] Even if there were two witnesses, "who had seen the couple come and leave", the couple could purge themselves free of the allegation by oath-helpers according to some laws.[133] Thus, the canonical theory of proof (full proof, *plena probatio*) was not applied in its true nature, as the witnesses are mainly used as an initiating element for the prosecution against the wishes of the injured party.[134]

For all practical purposes, the ecclesiastical procedure of the provincial laws does not differ from that of the secular assizes. Like secular courts, local ecclesiastical courts were actually also called assizes, "the episcopal assizes", which contained "the episcopal jury" (*Biscops næmpd*).[135] The bishop's role in the court is rather unclear.[136] Naturally, the bishop, either alone or at least later with his chapter, could also adjudicate matters like matrimonial causes, but in criminal cases at the parish level, local structures were used. The law of Småland explains that the priest was to nominate twelve men from the parish to act as jurors for the bishop and the parish to accept. The function of these men was partly to investigate the case, partly to evaluate the evidence and based on it either free or convict the accused.[137]

Conclusion

As demonstrated in this essay, according to the provincial laws, the scope of ecclesiastical jurisdiction as a whole was fairly wide in medieval Sweden. But as this paper only focuses on law texts, at least three reservations must be made. First, some types of causes, such as jurisdiction over wills, sorcery and usury, were only mentioned in some isolated provincial laws, while heresy was not mentioned at all. Therefore, variation between the laws forms an element of uncertainty that cannot be remedied entirely. Later evidence suggests that heresy and usury were indeed part of the ecclesiastical jurisdiction. Moreover, the lack of sufficient contemporary sources, including ecclesiastical court records, prevents us from knowing whether, for example, the criminalization of usury was universally applied all over Sweden at the time despite the silence of the provincial laws.

---

132. ÖgL, Kk 27 and 27:2, pp. 18–19.
133. E.g. UL, Kk 15:3, 15:6, pp. 26–27.
134. See also Bååth 1905, pp. 66–68.
135. ÖgL, Kk, 13:3, p. 12; SmåL, Kk 13 and 13:6, pp. 429–430.
136. Inger 1961, pp. 197–198.
137. SmåL, Kk 13, p. 429. See also ÖgL, Kk 13:2, p. 12; Bååth 1905, p. 73. The defiling of the churchyard and church by violence, offences against penance prescibed by the bishop, excommunication and adultery were to be tried by the episcopal jury, which then either freed or sentenced, SmåL, Kk 13:2–6, pp. 429–430.

"A complete description of the ecclesiastical jurisdiction cannot be attempted without constantly considering canon law and Swedish ecclesiastical statutes", was the observation of Wilhelm Sjöholm in his article a century ago.[138] This remark is highly relevant even today, but a thorough study would necessarily have to include the larger corpus of medieval documents and sources. Even in such a case the picture would be riddled with uncertainties because, linked to the lack of sources, we do not know to what extent the jurisdictional powers were exercised, whether they underwent changes in the course of the later Middle Ages and what their practical relevance was. Some causes or crimes were surely more common than others. In addition, the political instability of later medieval Sweden may have undermined the normal functioning of ecclesiastical jurisdiction in some areas and periods. These are questions that will and can never be satisfactorily answered.

As seen above, the authority of the Church did not always suffice to settle disputes concerning the implementation of ecclesiastical norms of jurisdiction. On some occasions, the Church had to appeal to the help of the king. Thus, in 1345 King Magnus Eriksson had to interfere in a dispute between Archbishop Hemming of Uppsala and the burghers of Stockholm concerning the extent of the jurisdictional powers of the town and the Church. Apparently, the secular officials had not shown sufficient respect to the ecclesiastical jurisdiction much to the dissatisfaction of the archbishop and the king was then called upon to decide the case. Magnus Eriksson confirmed that the crime of adultery pertained to the mixed cases, wherefore parts of the fine were to go to the king, the town and the Church. The town officials were to collect the ecclesiastical fine, but immediately render it up to the Church, while the archbishop or his representative (*vice gerente*) was allowed to impose a penance on the culprit. If the offenders were too poor to pay the whole fine, surely a very common occurrence, the shares of all the recipients were to diminish in equal proportion. The town was not allowed to deal with cases related to matrimony, betrothals or with estates of the deceased (*reliquis*), which belonged by virtue of the law (*de iure*) or custom (*de consuetudine*) to the ecclesiastical courts (*ad forum ecclesiasticum*).[139]

King Magnus Eriksson settled differences between the Church and the people even later. During his visit to Finland in 1347 he issued many letters relating to tithes and the financial rights of the bishop of Turku.[140] He also

---

138. Sjögren 1904, p. 126. However, not quite consistently, perhaps Sjögren regarded the Swedish synodal statutes of lesser legal historical interest as he mainly considered that they dealt with liturgical matters and ecclesiastical discipline, which he though should be left to the discipline of ecclesiastical history, ibid. p. 127.
139. DS V, doc. 3877, pp. 393–394.
140. See, e.g. docs 118–120, 125, REA, pp. 76–77, 80.

decreed that should a cleric suspect his parishioner of not paying the tithe correctly, the parishioner was to produce two witnesses, who would swear that they were present and had seen him pay the tithe correctly and lawfully (*recte et legittime decimauit*).[141] Some fifteenth-century lawsuits also suggest that cases that had validly been resolved by the papal curia and the Swedish bishops several times had to have royal authority behind them in order to be respected and obeyed by the powerful and litigious parties.[142] Such cases are revealing in exposing the risks of a purely normative study. Still, I will venture further in my conclusions.

Considered as a whole, the provincial laws are by no means coherent as far as ecclesiastical influence and jurisdiction are concerned. The laws convey the strong impression that they are compiled mainly independently and at various times. I have not found any concrete support to the theory that Swedish provincial laws would have been a product of a deliberate legislative policy lead by the archbishop of Lund.[143] Admittedly, certain sections of the provincial laws of southern Sweden bear a resemblance to those of Scania. For example, the restrictions concerning the property a person was allowed to will to the Church were based on the same logic in the southern Swedish provincial laws as in the Danish provincial law of Scania. Similarly, the notion that baptism was necessary for the capacity to inherit is also the same in all Scandinavian countries, including Sweden.[144] But had either the archbishop of Uppsala or Lund, pursuing a conscious

---

141. 4.9.1347, REA, doc. 123, p. 79.
142. Korpiola, Mia forthcoming: "The Two Husbands of Helleka Horn: Interpreting the Canon Law of Marriage in Late Medieval Sweden", *Studies in Honor of Manlio Bellomo*; Nordmark, Marie-Louise 1942: "Nanne Kärling, munk och frälseman. Studier kring en medeltida arvsprocess", *Kyrkohistorisk Årsskrift* 42 (1942), esp. pp. 137–151; Salonen, Kirsi 2001: *The Penitentiary as a Well of Grace: The Example of the Province of Uppsala 1448–1527*. Annales academiæ scientiarum fennicæ, 313. Academia Scientiarum Fennica, Saarijärvi, pp. 402–405; Hockman, Tuula et al. 2002: "Karanneen munkin tarina", *Agricolan tietosanomat* 2/2002, http://www.utu.fi/agricola/tietosanomat/numero2-02/, cited on 5 January 2004.
143. Naturally, there are also other weaknesses to Sjöholm's theory. For example, the practical importance of the politically explosive nominal primacy of Lund over Uppsala in the late thirteenth and early fourteenth century when the provincial laws were being written down is highly questionable. In fact the Swedish clergy was keen to emphasize its independence of Lund – and Denmark, see Inger 1961, pp. 306–338. For criticism against Sjöholm and her method see also Norseng 1991, pp. 154, 156–157, 164.
144. The Law of Scania allows a healthy person to give or will one son's share to the cloister, but only a half if he was ill, SkL, Om arv, 38, 40 and note 84, pp. 10 and 30. See also ÖgL, Kk 24, p. 17; VgL II Kk 60, pp. 216–217. As to baptism and inheritance rights in the Law of Scania, see SkL, Om arv, 3–4, pp. 3–4; Skovgaard-Petersen 1997, p. 72.

policy, been the prime mover behind the compilation of these laws, one would assume that the privileges and jurisdictional powers of the Church would be relatively uniform. In this case – even allowing for some differences in the local power factors – each chapter on the church is a sufficiently individual entity to suggest that many issues regulated in them were the result of customs and compromises within the province or diocese. This would correspond to the later medieval evidence of the relative independence of the actions of bishops even in matters belonging to other spheres.[145]

Yet there is no doubt that many of the Swedish provincial laws had an effect on each other: regional variations over provincial and ecclesiastical boundaries or more direct imitation.[146] The laws were certainly influenced by the same sources – universal canon law, royal and ecclesiastical statutes, papal letters – and sharing the same secular and ecclesiastical traditions. This probably accounts for many of the similarities in the laws. For example, the norms of nearly all the provincial laws regulating the reading of banns before the solemnization of marriage in church are directly based on canon 51 (*Cum inhibitio*) of the Fourth Lateran council of 1215 and the subsequent papal letter (1216) to the archbishop of Uppsala and his suffragans on matrimony *in facie ecclesiae*.[147]

The mixture of domestic and international, ecclesiastical and secular shows that medieval Sweden was firmly anchored in the medieval Catholic Church and the larger legal community. Yet, the reception of foreign was by no means automatic, entirely passive or complete. The local environment, conditions and preconditions were also taken into account. In the later Middle Ages, the Swedish Church had, moreover, to reckon with greater political instability and factionalism in addition to the growing judicial and jurisdictional powers of the royal courts. Indeed, the provincial laws represent a stage of the evolution of the Church's jurisdiction and the reception of canon law in medieval Sweden. The greater story of the reception of canon law in medieval Sweden is still to be written and this is a challenge for the future.[148]

Aknowledgement: I am grateful to prof. Richard Holt, University of Tromsø, for having commented on the language of my paper.

---

145. Salonen 2001, p. 256.
146. Sjögren 1904, p. 175.
147. DS I, doc. 156, pp. 182–183.
148. This is a project that I hope I will be able to embark on in a few years' time.

NORDIC MEDIEVAL LAWS REVISITED

Kjell Å. Modéer

I can't find any better time and any better place for us legal historians to meet and discuss the identity of our Nordic heritage, than now in the flourishing month of May and here in Copenhagen with the convention located at the Carlsberg Academy. Here we are upholding two of our most magnificent Nordic myths, firstly: the fascinating Nordic Light and the secondly: Carlsberg as *the* Nordic Beer. The Nordic Summer nights and frothing Danish Beer, however, are two important parts of our identity.
Ingmar Bergman has given us the legitimating of the Nordic summer in his classical movie *Wild Strawberries*. It is actually a road movie from the 1950's, before the road movies even were invented. I'm sure you remember the story. *Wild Strawberries* is about a senior doctor in Stockholm, Ivar Borg. In the marvellous month of May he makes the drive down to Lund to participate in the doctoral promotion. With 50 years of his life in retrospect he makes as well a physical as a mental journey back to Lund University, where he shall receive his jubilee doctorate in the Lund cathedral – the cathedral and archbishopric which has played such an important role in our convention here these days. As most of you know this is a movie about relations between generations, the generation to go and the generation to come.

Bergman's movies give me the preamble to open up my speech here tonight. Yes, I consciously say movies in plural, for I also want you to consider another of Bergman's classical movies from the late 1950's, *The Seventh Seal*. This movie also tells us a story from Southern Scandinavia, but not from contemporary times but from the Middle Ages. It's about the threat of the Black Death in the Mid-14th Century – an epidemic very close in style to those of Aids and Sars in our times, two epidemic disasters, however, unknown for Bergman and his generations when he produced the movie. The crusader Antonius Block is returning home with his esquire John/Jöns from the crusade to the Holy Land after ten years abroad. Jöns tells us about all their experiences: We let "snakes snap us, winged insects sting us, beasts bite us, heathens slaughter us, wine poison us, women infest us with lice, lice consume us and fevers moulder us – all for the love of God!"[1] And Antonius' wife Karin, who had waited for him through all these years, puts the unforgettable questions: "– My dear, was it a good and funny crusade? Could you kill many heathens, ride hard and break many swords and lances? Could you pray many prayers at the Holy Sepulchre and rape many women..." in the name of God?[2]

The movie is about the role of Christian culture in the periphery of Europe at the time of the Black Death, at the time of the peak of the development of the Nordic laws, and for the adoption of the unified Swedish law about 1350. It's tempting for me to bring in a *Law and literature*-perspective to the theme of our convention. But I will resist that temptation, and stop by giving you this little appetizer.

On the other hand I will use some of the keywords I already have mentioned and elaborate on them. First I would like to comment on myths in legal history. Michael H. Gelting yesterday in a comment to his brilliant talk bluntly stated that the originalities, the characteristics of the Nordic laws as specific Nordic is just a myth, a construct of the National romanticism of the 19th century. I'm sure he is right! It's the same comment e.g. Dick Helmholz has made about the English common law, as a unique English system in his splendid work on *The Spirit of Classical Canon Law*.[3] And it is the same type of construct, for our times totally obsolete, we meet in the universalistic systematisation of the comparative law into *legal families* made by the German comparativists Konrad Zweigert and Hein Kötz in their big work *Introduction to Comparative Law* from the late 1960's.[4]

---

1. The origin of *The Seventh Seal* is a chamber play *Trämålning [Wooden painting]*, is a one-act-play written for the School of theatre at the municipal theatre in Malmö, where Bergman worked as a producer in the 1950s. Ingmar Bergman, *Trämålning, Moralitet av Ingmar Bergman* (Stockholm 1956), 4.
2. Ingmar Bergman, *Trämålning*, 16.
3. Richard H. Helmholz, *The Spirit of Classical Canon Law* (Athens & London 1996).
4. Konrad Zweigert & Hein Kötz, *An Introduction to Comparative Law*, [transl. by Tony Weir], 3 ed., (Oxford 1998), cf. Hein Kötz, "Abschied von der Rechtskreislehre?" *Zeitschrift zür europäisches Zivilrecht* 3:1998, 492ff.; Mathias Reimann, "Rechtsvergleichung und Rechtsgeschichte im Dialog", *Zeitschrift für europäisches Zivilrecht* 3:1999, 496ff.

They are all constructs, today we use comparative law not only to compare norms but also to find the methods to observe and compare the norms in their cultural contexts.[5]

As a legal historian you can be pejorative to much of all theories and methods being told by the post modernists, but one dimension of their theories has been very valuable for the hypothesis in our legal historical research, and it's their views on deconstruction, the deconstruction of old static, unusable or obsolete constructs. It has given us the methodological instruments to break through the old myths, to give new angels to our perspectives, and of course, to make it possible for us to produce new constructs in our contemporary, late modern time.

Another key word is about generations to go and generations to come. These days we made commentaries on the texts and of the language of the Nordic medieval laws. In Sweden we owe a lot of thanks to Carl Johan Schlyter [1795–1888], not only a great legal historian, but also a great philologist and for more than half a century the editor of The Medieval Laws of Sweden. For 55 years he analysed about 800 kept legal manuscripts and edited them in their original medieval language in 13 volumes of the Old Laws of Sweden.[6] In the style of Savigny he produced this work for the use of the legislator. Of course! Only with help of the legal roots you had the possibility to make an organic development of the law, he stated. But when he had concluded his work after 55 years, new trends in legal science and different views on legislation "outsourced" (to use a modern term) the *Historical School*. Schlyter's heritage was a huge material left over to the legal historians. The late professor of legal history at Uppsala University, Gösta Hasselberg, addressed in his inaugural lecture in Uppsala in the late 1960s the younger generation of legal historians: "Schlyter constructed the foundation, now it's up to you to build the house. You have to begin to write the history of the Swedish law."[7] Hasselberg and his senior generation at that time told my generation to do so. Hasselberg and his contemporaries were the first post-war generation of European legal historians. It included also the Swedish legal historian Sten Gagnér, for decades the Nordic Ambassador to the University of Munich. They all had read Paul

---

5. Kjell Å Modéer, "Der Verlierer als Sieger? Rechtsgeschichte und Rechtsvergleichung – ein neuer Schulstreit", Kjell Å. Modéer (ed.), *Europäische Rechtsgeschichte und europäische Integration, Rättshistoriska skrifter, Vol. 4* (Stockholm 2002), 93ff.
6. Kjell Å Modéer, "Schlyter, Carl Johan", Michael Stolleis (ed.), *Juristen: Ein biographisches Lexikon. Von der Antike bis zum 20. Jahrhundert* (München 2001), 561.
7. Gösta Hasselberg, *Rättshistoriens dilemma Rättshistoriska studier, Vol. 3* (Lund 1969), 300.

Koschaker's *Europa und das römische Recht* as a programmatic platform,[8] and they were filled up with the concept of *ius commune* as a common legal heritage in a transparent European legal culture.

Today, 35 years after Hasselberg's lecture, we have to accept that we, Nordic legal historians of today, to a great extent have failed to fulfil the mission of our close ancestors. We have given priority to other green and interesting fields of legal history. But it's not to late, we're still around, and especially today there are quite better conditions to make that research. I will comment on that later.

But let us turn back to Lund. One month ago, at Easter Sunday, there was a great celebration in the Cathedral in Lund. It was the 900 Anniversary of the metropolitan Archbishop site in Lund of the Nordic Church province. Michael H. Gelting mentioned this event by saying it occurred in 1103 or 1104. The sources can be interpreted differently, so even if there was a great celebration some weeks ago there is a good reason to arrange a new celebration next year again.

The colourful painting Peter Landau gave us yesterday, demonstrates that either Lund nor Dalby or Trondheim/Nidaros belonged to the periphery of Europe of the 12th century. Not only were *Ivo's Decretum* from the late 11th century and *Gratian's* from the mid 12th century, very early introduced to the Scandinavian intellectual clergymen. Also the high percentages of the papal decretals to Scandinavian receivers were adopted in the cognitive structure of the common canon law and refer to legal problems within the Nordic church province. I think what we especially have learnt these days so far is how we increasingly have to shift our focus from observing the Nordic Laws as secular legal documents within a European "law books"-concept. Instead we have to focus on their role as documents belonging to a common European canon law culture, within the legal, political and religious culture of the time. We also have to shift the chronological focus of our interest to the 12th century and to the introduction of the Christian legal culture to the Nordic region.

And in making our constructs of this time we perhaps we shouldn't focus directly on the social context but more on the cognitive structures of the intelligentsia of the times between the introduction of the Nordic church province 900 years ago and the time of the Black Death, 250 years later.
At last, let me reflect on the fascinating fact, that we all together are sharing a memorable experience in the constructed environment of the mansion of the brewer Jacobsen, constructed on the profits and virtues of Nordic beer. We have all accepted the invitation to come here to discuss the importance of remembering our legal heritage. To remember, to keep in mind, to bear in mind, are words we use to explain our needs to uphold our traditions, our

---

8. Paul Koschaker, *Europa und das römische Recht*, 4 ed., (München 1966).

history and culture. In our post-modern fragmentised society we have a very short memory. It was also emphasized in the modern society of the 20th century where the critics of traditions and history have been very loud-voiced especially in the law faculties. It's one reason why medieval legal history became of lower priority for the legal historians. However, today we focus on the importance of time to reflect and remember, to focus on the theme in the Danish pilgrim's hymn: "Ages will come, ages will disappear, one generation will follow the other".[9] It gives me a good conclusion for my speech. On one hand we have found the character of a *longue durée* in the mentalities and attitudes concerning Nordic legal culture. The role of reconciliation and compromises within this culture follows us as a red thread from the 12th century up to today. Let us keep this in mind each time we are mixing in a glass of Orvieto Classico into our beer-drinking! On the other hand we can notify that a new generation of legal historians again are eager in giving focus to the medieval legal culture. I'm sure not only Ivar Borg in *Wild Strawberries*, but also late legal historians from Gösta Hasselberg to Ole Fenger are sending us a smile of satisfaction tonight. Also we "still-arounders" are congratulating the organizers of this convention to a break-through for new, reconsidered research regarding the Nordic Medieval Laws.

---

9. B.S. Ingemann (1850), "Tider skal komme, Tider skal henrulle, Slægt skal følge Slægters Gang" Hymn 111, v. 2. In: *Den Danske Salmebog* [The Danish Hymnbook] (København 1998).

CONTRIBUTORS

PER ANDERSEN is Associate Professor at the Department of Jurisprudence at the Law School, Aarhus University. His main research interests are legal change in Denmark and Europe in the twelfth and thirteenth century, especially concerning legal procedure, and the interaction between learned law and local lawmaking.

MARIO ASCHERI is Full Professor of Legal History at the School of Law, University of Roma Tree. His research concentrates on the history of Italian courts during the Middle Ages and Renaissance, as well as on the institutions of a typical commune with a republican tradition: Siena. His collected essays are published in *Giuristi e istituzioni dal Medioevo all'Et moderna (secc. XI-XVIII)* (Keip Verlag, Stockstadt: 2009).

LARS BJÖRNE is Professor of Legal History and Roman Law at the Faculty of Law, University of Turku. His main research interest is Nordic legal history. He has written a comprehensive four volume discourse (1995-2007) on Nordic legal science from the 16th to the middle of the 20th century.

MICHAEL H. GELTING is senior research archivist at the Danish National Archives (Rigsarkivet) and chaired professor of Early Scandinavian Studies at the University of Aberdeen. His main research topics are legal and social change in Denmark in the twelfth and thirteenth centuries, and the effects of the Black Death on fourteenth-century society, in Europe in general and more particularly in Maurienne (Savoy).

LARS IVAR HANSEN is dr. philos. and professor of medieval and early modern history at the University of Tromsø. His main fields of research are economic and social history, where he has been focusing on resource rights, the role of social networks of alliance and inheritance practices, as well as the inter-ethnic relations between the peoples of northern Fennoscandia.

DIRK HEIRBAUT is head of the department of Legal Theory and Legal History at Ghent University. The themes of his research are: feudal and customary law in the medieval Low Countries, the history of private law in

Belgium since 1795 and codification. He is a member of the board of editors of the Legal History Review.

TORE IVERSEN is Professor emeritus at the Department of History and Classical studies at the Norwegian University of Science and Technology in Trondheim. His main interests are the history of bondage in Europe during the middle Ages and reception of Roman law in the Middle Ages, especially concerning the law of land property and land lease. He is now completing a project comparing peasants control over land and resources in Norway, Scandinavia and the East-Alpine region (1000-1750).

MIA KORPIOLA is Adjunct Professor (Docent) in Legal History and currently working as a research fellow at the Collegium for Advanced Studies (University of Helsinki). Her main research interests are the history of family and criminal law, the reception of foreign law in Sweden and the history of law studies in Finland.

PETER LANDAU is Prof. Dr.Dr.h.c. mult. emeritus of Canon Law, Legal History, Legal Philosophy and Civil Law and President of the Stephan-Kuttner-Institute of Medieval Canon Law at the University of Munich. His main research interests are the history of medieval Canon law (especially the sources, institutions and principles), the history of the Protestant Church and the history of legal philosophy.

KJELL Å. MODÉER is Senior Professor in legal history at the Faculty of Law, Lund University, Sweden. His current research is within comparative legal cultures and traditions. His latest book *The Lawyers' near Past* (*Juristernas nära förflutna*, 2009) is a comparative analysis of the legal cultures in Sweden, Germany and the U.S.A. in the twentieth century.

DITLEV TAMM is Professor in Legal History at the Faculty of Law, University of Copenhagen. He has written several articles and books on Danish and European legal history. He is a member of the Royal Danish Academy of Science.

HELLE VOGT is Associate Professor in Legal History at the Faculty of Law, University of Copenhagen. Her main research topics are Nordic legal history and the interaction between local law and learned Christian legal ideology.